OKANAGAN UNIV/COLLEGE LIBRARY

03134129

P9-CKR-988

RC 564 .S585 2003
Springer, David W.
Substance abuse treatment fo
criminal offenders : an
evidence-based guide for

DATE DUE

BRODART   Cat. No. 23-221

Substance Abuse Treatment
for Criminal Offenders

Substance Abuse Treatment for Criminal Offenders

AN EVIDENCE-BASED GUIDE FOR PRACTITIONERS

DAVID W. SPRINGER

C. AARON MCNEECE

ELIZABETH MAYFIELD ARNOLD

AMERICAN PSYCHOLOGICAL ASSOCIATION
WASHINGTON, DC ·

Copyright © 2003 by the American Psychological Association. All rights reserved. Except as permitted under the United States Copyright Act of 1976, no part of this publication may be reproduced or distributed in any form or by any means, or stored in a database or retrieval system, without the prior written permission of the publisher.

Published by
American Psychological Association
750 First Street, NE
Washington, DC 20002
www.apa.org

To order
APA Order Department
P.O. Box 92984
Washington, DC 20090-2984
Tel: (800) 374-2721, Direct: (202) 336-5510
Fax: (202) 336-5502, TDD/TTY: (202) 336-6123
Online: www.apa.org/books/
E-mail: order@apa.org

In the U.K., Europe, Africa, and the Middle East, copies may be ordered from
American Psychological Association
3 Henrietta Street
Covent Garden, London
WC2E 8LU England

Typeset in Goudy by AlphaWebTech, Mechanicsville, MD
Printer: Sheridan Books, Fredericksburg, VA
Cover Designer: Berg Design, Albany, NY
Technical/Production Editor: Rosemary Moulton

The opinions and statements published are the responsibility of the authors, and such opinions and statements do not necessarily represent the policies of the American Psychological Association.

Library of Congress Cataloging-in-Publication Data

Springer, David W.
   Substance abuse treatment for criminal offenders : an evidence-based guide for practitioners / David W. Springer, C. Aaron McNeece, Elizabeth Mayfield Arnold.
      p. cm.
   Includes bibliographical references and index.
   ISBN 1-55798-990-7
   1. Substance abuse—Treatment. 2. Criminals—Drug use. 3. Dual diagnosis.
I. McNeece, Carl Aaron. II. Arnold, Elizabeth Mayfield. III. Title.

   RC564.S585 2003
   616.86'06'086927—dc21   2003001420

British Library Cataloguing-in-Publication Data
A CIP record is available from the British Library.

Printed in the United States of America
First Edition

In honor of my mother and memory of my father,
Elizabeth Springer and Paul David Springer.
David W. Springer

To Elmore Hudgens, 1916–2000, who took seriously the
injunction, "Remember those in prison as if you were their
fellow prisoners, and those who are mistreated as if you
yourselves were suffering." (Hebrews 13:3)
C. Aaron McNeece

This book is dedicated to my children, Will and Cameron,
and to the memory of my grandmother,
Irene Locke Mayfield.
Elizabeth Mayfield Arnold

CONTENTS

FOREWORD TO THE SERIES

When the American Psychological Association (APA) launched its *Law and Mental Health Professionals* book series in 1993, it broke new publishing ground by offering clinicians comprehensive reviews of the law that affects them in each jurisdiction. This review of the relevant law is essential for practitioners so that they can understand how that law controls their professional practice; specifies situations in which the legal system needs their assessment, therapeutic, and administrative services; and affects clinical services when patients become involved in legal entanglements.

What is not covered in that series is the clinical information that will help mental health professionals practice ethically and competently in forensic situations. The APA *Law and Public Policy: Psychology and the Social Sciences* book series partially addresses this need by publishing volumes that consider the science underlying law-related mental health practice. *Violent Offenders: Appraising and Managing Risk* by Vernon L. Quinsey, Grant T. Harris, Marnie E. Rice, and Catherine A. Cormier (1998) and *Treating Adult and Juvenile Offenders With Special Needs* edited by José B. Ashford, Bruce D. Sales, and William H. Reid (2000) are excellent examples of this type of book. Although the information contained in these volumes is critical for mental health professionals to understand if they plan to provide, or are providing, forensic services, the volumes tend to be lengthier because of this series' concern with scholarly and scientific comprehensiveness.

Experience teaches that clinicians also need guidebooks that will accurately convey, with brevity and clarity, how to participate in the myriad forensic practice areas. That is the purpose of the *Forensic Practice Guidebooks* series. Over time, volumes in this series will cover all topics for which clinicians may be asked to provide services to clients enmeshed in the law or to provide services to a legal system (e.g., the courts, social services, and corrections) to aid in the administration of the law. The overarching goal of the *Forensic Practice Guidebooks* series is to help clinicians engage in forensic practice ethically and competently in today's changing professional environment.

Bruce D. Sales, PhD, JD
Series Editor

PREFACE

This book emerged out of a book chapter that we initially wrote for *Treating Adult and Juvenile Offenders With Special Needs*, edited by José B. Ashford, Bruce D. Sales, and William H. Reid. When APA series editor Bruce Sales contacted us about the possibility of developing our chapter into a book, we accepted with the intent of writing an evidence-based book that could guide practitioners' work with adult or juvenile substance-abusing offenders. This entire book rests on the assumption that treatment is an effective approach to helping substance-abusing offenders.

There is a growing body of literature indicating that substance abuse treatment can be effective, and more treatment options are available today than ever before. The National Institute on Drug Abuse has recently launched a clinical trials network, and within the next few years the number of randomized clinical trials of substance abuse treatment models will increase exponentially. Advances are being made daily regarding the relationship between brain chemistry and addictions.

At the same time, it has become clear to us and to many others that we are not winning the "War on Drugs," and we probably never will. People have used and abused psychoactive substances for most of recorded history, and they are not likely to stop now. One of the most logical alternatives to the drug war is to provide treatment to any substance abuser who seeks it, while providing prevention programs that target those who are most vulnerable.

It is our hope that this book, a compendium of knowledge about substance abuse treatment, will assist treatment professionals everywhere in making informed decisions about how to help juvenile and adult offenders who abuse psychoactive drugs. If just one substance-abusing offender is better off because of this book, it will have been worth the effort.

ACKNOWLEDGMENTS

It is only through the collective labor of many hands that a book can be realized. Much thanks and appreciation goes to the team at APA, beginning with series editor Bruce Sales and acquisitions editor Susan Reynolds. Our development editor Linda McCarter provided timely encouragement throughout the process of writing and rewriting just when it was most needed. Special thanks also goes to our production editor Rosemary Moulton for guiding us through the home stretch. We are indebted to the reviewers who took time out of their busy schedules to wade through earlier drafts of this manuscript—their thoughtful comments and suggestions had a significant impact on the finished product. Special thanks goes to Dr. William R. Kelly, of the University of Texas at Austin (UT-Austin), for sharing his expertise with us on mental health courts.

David W. Springer would like to thank his dean, Barbara W. White, for providing a climate in which he is able to balance his administrative responsibilities with his scholarly pursuits, and who was kind enough to award him with a Dean's Fellowship so that he could immerse himself in writing this book. He is grateful to his faculty mentor and friend, Allen Rubin, for his sage advice and guidance, and to all his colleagues at the UT-Austin School of Social Work who, on a daily basis, create an enriching work environment. He would like to extend a special thanks to his administrative associate Hollee Ganner who was instrumental in helping him protect his writing days and keep track of copyright permissions, and to the many graduate students who conducted endless literature searches. Finally, he is indebted to his wife and soul mate, Sarah, for her steadfast support, nurturance, and encouragement of his professional development and personal growth.

C. Aaron McNeece would like to acknowledge his wife Sherri for her strong support of his scholarly efforts for the past 36 years.

Elizabeth Mayfield Arnold would like to thank her husband David for his ongoing support and encouragement of her work.

Substance Abuse Treatment
for Criminal Offenders

1

INTRODUCTION

Treatment is an effective approach to helping substance-abusing offenders.[1] Over the past few decades, treatment has been used increasingly as a way of helping this population. Accordingly, this book, written for practitioners working with adult or juvenile substance-abusing offenders, emphasizes the available best practices by describing the most effective and commonly used interventions and summarizing the corresponding evidence-based literature. Given the extent of the drug problem and the growing number of adult and juvenile offenders with substance abuse problems, it is critical that practitioners, administrators, and policymakers avail themselves of the most effective interventions available to treat this population.

According to the White House's Office of National Drug Control Policy (ONDCP, 2000), overall national crime rates continue to decline while arrests for drug law violations continue to climb, and the rate of incarceration for drug offenses has reached an all-time high. Almost 1.6 million Americans were arrested for drug crimes in 1998, and 60% of all prisoners in the federal prison system were sentenced for drug offenses (Mumola, 1998). Drug

---

[1]Throughout this book, we interchangeably use the term *offender* with the more generic term *client* to refer to substance-abusing adults and juveniles receiving a variety of services across the justice system spectrum.

offenders also accounted for the largest amount of growth in state prison populations between 1990 and 1998 (Beck & Mumola, 1999).

The extent of the drug problem is far worse than these statistics suggest. Anyone who is familiar with how the U.S. criminal justice system operates knows that the crime for which an offender is sentenced does not tell the full story. Plea bargaining results in many less serious drug charges simply being dropped. Many offenders are sentenced for a non-drug offense who also have a substance abuse problem, which may not appear in the official records. The National Institute of Justice's (NIJ) Arrestee Drug Abuse Monitoring System discovered that in 24 sites in 1998, between 59% and 79% (in Houston and Philadelphia, respectively) of adult arrestees tested positive for at least one illicit drug, with marijuana being the most common drug detected (NIJ, 1999). From January to September 2000, between 51% and 79% (in Des Moines and New York, respectively) of adult male arrestees in 27 sites tested positive for any "NIDA-5" drug (those illegal drugs offenders most commonly use according to the National Institute on Drug Abuse[2]) (NIJ, 2001).

Two things have become increasingly clear in recent years. First, that from just about any perspective—law enforcement, health care, or general social functioning—substance abuse is a massive problem confronting America in the 21st century (cf. NIDA, 1998; RAND Corporation, 1994; Zimmer & Morgan, 1997). Second, the War on Drugs has done little to resolve this problem since President Nixon introduced it in 1971. (It has actually made the problem worse: It is the largest factor in the growth of the inmate population, and it has disproportionately criminalized and stigmatized large numbers of minorities.)

FAILURE OF THE WAR ON DRUGS

It has become quite clear in recent years that the War on Drugs has not been successful (McNeece, Bullington, Arnold, & Springer, 2002; Rasmussen & Benson, 1994). We know that (a) incarceration alone does little to break the cycle of illegal drug use and crime, (b) offenders sentenced to incarceration for substance-related offenses exhibit a high rate of recidivism once they are released (Drug Court Clearinghouse and Technical Assistance Project, 1997, p. 8), and (c) drug abuse treatment has been shown to be demonstrably effective in reducing both drug abuse and drug-related crime (NIDA, 1999c, pp. 18–19).

Treatment for substance dependence is seen as a key component in preventing re-offenses. Recent estimates from the National Household Survey on Drug Abuse and the Uniform Facility Data Set indicate that approximately 5 million drug users needed immediate treatment in 1998, but only

---

[2]Marijuana, cocaine, methamphetamine, opiates, and phencyclidine (PCP).

2.1 million received it (Office of National Drug Control Policy, 2000, p. 54). Even the most conservative estimates indicate that, if we took half of the present drug intervention–related law enforcement expenditures and redirected them to drug treatment, and even if the number of substance abusers doubled, we would still be better off from a cost-effectiveness perspective (McNeece & DiNitto, 1998).

Some states are beginning to realize this. As of this writing, eight states—Alaska, California, Colorado, Hawaii, Maine, Nevada, Oregon, and Washington—have already taken some step toward permitting medicinal marijuana use. The Massachusetts legislature is considering restructuring the state's drug law to reduce harsh mandatory minimum punishments for first-time drug offenders, and New York Governor George Pataki has announced plans to reduce prison terms and provide treatment for nonviolent drug offenders. Officials in Michigan have already replaced mandatory life sentences with parole-eligible prison terms for first-time heroin and cocaine offenders, and nonviolent drug offenders in both Arizona and California receive drug treatment in lieu of jail time.

EXTENT OF THE DRUG PROBLEM IN THE JUSTICE SYSTEM

Drug arrests will continue to guarantee the growth of our rapidly expanding correctional system well into the 21st century. During the past few decades, a record number of people have been brought under some form of correctional control in the United States. The number of adult men and women under the supervision of federal, state, and local correctional authorities rose to a record 6.3 million in 1999, according to the U.S. Department of Justice's Bureau of Justice Statistics (BJS; Bonczar & Glaze, 2000). This number, which represents 3.1% of all adult residents in the United States, or one in every 32 adults, includes people incarcerated in jails and prisons and those supervised in the community under probation or parole.[3]

During the early 1990s, the United States easily surpassed the Soviet Union and South Africa in incarceration rates, making it the leader among industrialized nations in the imprisonment of its citizens. At mid-year 2001, 1,965,495 persons were incarcerated in the nation's prisons and jails (BJS, 2002), and 1 out of every 113 American men were in a state or federal prison, more than were serving in the armed forces. In 1999, the highest rate of incarceration was in Louisiana (1,025 per 100,000 residents) and the lowest in Vermont (203 per 100,000; Beck, 2000, p. 1). Furthermore, despite the continuing increase of substance abusers in the nation's prisons, only 10,186 federal inmates received substance abuse treatment in 1998, from a population of 123,041 inmates (Mumola, 1998).

---

[3]Jails contain people convicted of minor crimes; prisons house those convicted of serious crimes.

The results of the growth in incarceration rates were often not what law enforcement agencies, the courts, and the legislative bodies who mandated harsher sentences for drug offenders had anticipated. For example, in Florida various new penal provisions for drug offenders that were passed in the 1980s resulted in serious criminal offenders actually serving *less* time than they had before, and many violent offenders were released prematurely to increase the availability of prison beds for nonviolent drug offenders incarcerated under mandatory sentencing provisions (Rasmussen & Benson, 1994). Although these trends were halted in the 1990s, they had a marked effect on prison and nonprison correctional populations at the time and will continue to influence the correctional system for some time to come.

The drug problem has had an even greater impact on systems for supervising nonincarcerated offenders. Currently, about 20% of sentenced persons are actually serving time in prisons or jails; the remaining 80% are involved in some alternative sanction provided under both federal and state justice systems (Clear, 1995). This increase impacted the total correctional populations (not just prisons). While the total estimated correctional population rose 179% from 1.8 million in 1980 to 5.1 million in 1994, the increase in the parole population was 213%, and for adult probationers the increase was an astounding 1,565% (BJS, 1995)! Probation and parole caseloads have continued to increase since 1995, with nearly 4.5 million adult men and women on probation or parole at the end of 1999, an increase of about 119,000 during the year. As of December 31, 1999, approximately 3,773,600 adults were under federal, state, or local jurisdiction on probation, and nearly 713,000 were on parole (Bonczar & Glaze, 2000). Drug- and alcohol-related offenses accounted for more than one fourth of the offenses charged against adult probationers. Drug possession (9.8%) and drug trafficking (9.7%) accounted for a large proportion of probationers' offenses. The most common offense for probationers was driving while intoxicated (16.7%). Among probationers 45 years old and older, driving while intoxicated accounted for 27.7% of *all* offenses (BJS, 1997).

Juvenile Offenders

A similar trend is noted in juvenile offenses. In 1995, juvenile courts in the United States handled an estimated 159,100 delinquency cases involving drug law violations. Drug offenses accounted for 9% of all delinquency cases in 1995, compared with 5% in 1991. Drug offenses include possession or sale of marijuana, cocaine, and other illegal drugs (Stahl, 1998). These figures include only cases in which a drug offense was the most serious charge, not cases involving juveniles charged with drug offenses in addition to more serious offenses. As is the case with the adult statistics, we can assume that many more juveniles who were not charged with drug offenses did, indeed, have a substance abuse problem.

The number of juvenile drug offense cases processed by the courts during 1995 was 28% greater than in 1994 and 145% more than in 1991. Juvenile courts experienced a decline in their drug offense caseloads from 1988 to 1991 but then saw a sharp increase from 1991 to 1995. The number of juvenile arrests involving drug offenses followed a similar pattern as juvenile court dispositions (Stahl, 1998). Between 1991 and 1999, juvenile drug arrests increased 132%, while violent crime and property offenses by juveniles decreased substantially (H. Snyder, 2000). The total number of substance abuse arrests for juveniles in 1999 was substantial (385,8000); of those, 198,400 were for drug abuse, 165,700 for liquor law violations, and 21,700 for drunkenness (H. Snyder, 2000).

The number of juveniles placed on probation grew by 48% between 1988 and 1997. In 1997, 55% of total juvenile cases were placed on probation; 56% of adjudicated juvenile drug offenders were placed on probation (Scahill, 2000). There is no reliable estimate regarding the proportion of these juveniles (either incarcerated or on probation) who were referred to treatment or who actually received treatment.

Female Offenders

The number of women incarcerated in the United States tripled in the 1980s alone. In the 15 years from 1980 to mid-1995, the number of women incarcerated in U.S. prisons rose by 460%! The same pattern is evident with the jail population: More than three times as many women were in jail in mid-1997 as in mid-1985, according to 1998 BJS data (as cited in Kassebaum, 1999). Most of the women entering our criminal justice system are younger than 40 years old, and 8 of every 10 are mothers (Kassebaum, 1999). In 1997, about three quarters (74%) of women in federal and 35% in state prisons had been sentenced to prison for a drug crime (Mumola, 2000). Women's involvement in drug crime is typically low-level dealing or delivery activity, although 10% of federal and 15% of state female inmates have been incarcerated for possession (Mumola, 2000). Low socioeconomic status partly explains why some non-using women sell drugs (Radosh, 2002). Greenfield and Snell (1999) reported that, of those women incarcerated during the 1990s, only 40% indicated that they had been employed during the months prior to their arrest, and 30% had been receiving welfare benefits (as cited in Radosh, 2002).

EFFECTIVE SUBSTANCE ABUSE TREATMENT AND RESEARCH

Our position throughout this book is that treatment is more effective than any other approach that we can take with both juvenile and adult substance-abusing offenders. One of the main issues of contention among practitioners and researchers who work with substance abusers has been an operational definition of the term *effective treatment*.

The Treatment Outcome Working Group, a panel of treatment and evaluation experts sponsored by the ONDCP, established the following results and outcomes that define effective treatment:

1. reduced use of the primary drug
2. improved functioning of drug users in terms of employment
3. improved educational status
4. improved interpersonal relationships
5. improved medical status and general improvement in health
6. improved legal status
7. improved mental health status
8. improved noncriminal public safety factors such as reduction in diseases (ONDCP, 1996).

Furthermore, reviews of the literature and of substance abuse treatment programs within the criminal justice system indicate key principles that are associated with successful treatment of offenders (cf. Andrews & Kiesling, 1980; Bush, Hecht, LaBarbera, & Peters, in press; Falkin, Wexler, & Lipton, 1990; Gendreau & Ross, 1984; Leukefeld & Tims, 1992; Wexler, Falkin, Lipton, Rosenblum, & Goodloe, 1988, as cited in Kassebaum, 1999). These principles, drawn from experiences in implementing both jail and prison treatment programs, are outlined in Exhibit 1.1.

NIDA (1999c) has asserted that "effective treatment attends to multiple needs of the individual, not just his or her drug use" (p. i). In short, effective treatment must address the user's medical, psychological, social, vocational, and legal problems. Others have argued that treatment could be improved by diverting the resources we now allocate to arresting substance-abusing offenders to treatment (McNeece et al., 2002). We are certainly not the first to engage in this debate!

In 1966, the New York State Governor's Special Committee on Criminal Offenders charged Robert Martinson and colleagues to examine "what works" in rehabilitating criminal offenders. The committee was formed on the premise that prisons could rehabilitate, that New York's prisons were not making serious efforts at rehabilitation, and that the prisons' function should be transformed from a custodial to a rehabilitative one (Martinson, 1974).

In their six-month search of reviews of all rehabilitation studies published in English from 1945 to 1967, Martinson and colleagues found 231 studies that met the following operationalization of *rehabilitation:* the extent to which a prisoner adjusted to prison life, experienced vocational and educational achievements, underwent personality and attitudinal changes, made a general adjustment to society, and returned to crime (recidivism). To be included, the study had to have a control or comparison group.

Martinson's (1974) first published account synthesizing the 1,400-page report addressed only "the effects of rehabilitative treatment on recidivism, the phenomenon which reflects most directly how well our present treat-

1. **Develop commitment from jail administrators** to support the substance abuse treatment program and to provide adequate staff and technical resources.
2. **Use a coordinated approach in the design and implementation** of the in-custody substance abuse program, involving both substance abuse and custody staff.
3. **Conduct cross-training** for substance abuse treatment staff, custody staff, and key administrators to review the program philosophy, inmate management techniques, policies and procedures, and other common areas of interest.
4. **Provide a treatment unit that is isolated from general population inmates.** This strategy tends to remove participants from the corrosive influences of the jail/prison subculture and encourages development of prosocial behaviors and group cohesion.
5. **Provide incentives and sanctions** to encourage inmates to enter and complete in-custody treatment programs.
6. **Develop a sequence of in-custody treatment services** that is consistent with the expected length of incarceration.
7. **Provide comprehensive assessment** examining an inmate's treatment needs, risks presented to the institution (e.g., suicidal or aggressive behavior), and level of supervision required. Match inmates to treatment services according to the results of this assessment.
8. **Develop a structured treatment environment.** An intensive array of in-custody program services tends to encourage self-discipline and commitment to treatment, and is necessary to address the many skills deficits and areas of psychosocial dysfunction among this population.
9. **Provide clear consequences for inmate behavior within the institutional treatment program.** Positive and negative consequences for inmate behaviors should be clearly indicated. Program rules and guidelines are reinforced through a system of formal and informal sanctions.
10. **Encourage sustained participation in substance abuse treatment.** Institutional programs of less than 3 months duration should develop procedures to ensure that inmates are placed in supervised aftercare treatment within the community.
11. **Provide multimodal treatment services.** Treatment activities should address the range of psychosocial problems and areas of skills deficits that may inhibit successful recovery from drug and alcohol dependence.
12. **Encourage identification and modification of criminal thinking patterns, values, and behaviors.** Program counselors systematically model and reinforce prosocial behaviors within the treatment unit. Clearly defined sanctions are provided for antisocial behaviors.
13. **Use cognitive–behavioral treatment techniques.** Self-management strategies such as cognitive restructuring and self-monitoring should be addressed in treatment programs. Opportunity should be provided for modeling, rehearsal, and overlearning (repeated practice) of these techniques.
14. **Involve inmates in skills-based interventions.** Programs should encourage the acquisition and rehearsal of drug-free and prosocial skills to deal with interpersonal problems, stress, anger, and other personal, parental, and professional challenges faced during recovery.
15. **Provide training in relapse prevention techniques**. Exercises should promote awareness of individual relapse patterns, including warning signs, high-risk situations, and covert setups. A range of coping skills should be provided to anticipate the high rate of relapse among drug-involved offenders. Opportunities should

(continues)

EXHIBIT 1.1
(Continued)

be provided to rehearse these skills in the institutional treatment program and during aftercare.

16. **Involve inmates in "core" group treatment experiences**. Involvement in a primary treatment or therapy group provides a catalyst for behavior change. This behavioral change is achieved through reinforcement of the client's progress toward recovery and the confrontation of his or her denial and resistance. Group treatment also provides a cost-effective vehicle for educational and skills-based interventions.

17. **Provide prerelease planning and assist program participants in the transition to aftercare services.** Successful in-custody substance abuse treatment programs help to coordinate placement in follow-up treatment services. Most program participants are in need of at least 1 year of follow-up treatment and regular drug testing that is provided within the context of probation and parole supervision. Treatment Alternatives to Street Crime-like agencies have proven to be particularly useful in linking offenders to community treatment and in monitoring compliance with aftercare treatment.

18. **Develop measures to ensure accountability to short- and long-term program objectives.** Evaluation strategies are implemented in the early stages of program development. Evaluation should include process, impact, and outcome measures.

Note. From "Drug Treatment in Jails and Detention Settings," by R. H. Peters. In *Drug Treatment and Criminal Justice* (pp. 44–80), J. A. Inciardi, Ed., 1993, Thousand Oaks, CA: Sage. Copyright 1993 by Sage Publications. Excerpted and adapted with permission.

ment programs are performing the task of rehabilitation" (p. 24). However, Martinson noted that even this one measure brings with it several methodological limitations, such as the challenge of determining whether what works for one offender also works for another given the disparate groups being studied and the wide range of definitions ascribed to "recidivism rate" across studies. Nevertheless, in response to seven questions he explored, Martinson (1974) provided the following "bald summary" of the findings: "With few and isolated exceptions, the rehabilitative efforts that have been reported so far have had no appreciable effect on recidivism" (p. 25).

In response to Martinson's (1974) seminal work, others have conducted systematic and sophisticated analyses to determine what treatment strategies are effective with different populations. This has been done, in part, using a methodology referred to as meta-analysis, a statistical procedure that allows data to be summarized across many studies. Because such reviews for juvenile and female offenders have historically been given scant attention, below we attempt to synthesize some of the existing meta-analyses of treatment efforts with these two populations.

Meta-Analyses on Treatment With Juvenile Offenders

Although Martinson (1974) and colleagues (cf. Lipton, Martinson, & Wilks, 1975) declared that "nothing works," recent research has been more encouraging.

Several recent meta-analyses suggest that the most effective treatment approaches for juveniles are those with a cognitive–behavioral component combined with close supervision and advocacy, and there is evidence that more positive treatment effects are obtained in community settings than in institutionalized settings (Deschenes & Greenwood, 1994).

Garrett (1985) conducted a meta-analysis of 111 studies. The treatment effect obtained was .37, which means that treated juvenile offenders function at the 64th percentile and untreated offenders function at the 50th percentile. There was evidence to support the effectiveness of behavioral treatment, cognitive–behavioral therapy, and guided group interaction. Psychodynamic therapy and interventions based on the medical model were found to be the least effective (Ferrara, 1992).

In a review of literature and meta-analyses that focused on both institutional- and community-based programs for juvenile offenders, Palmer (1992) concluded that interventions produced "moderate reductions" in recidivism rates. Palmer used the following thresholds to determine the degree of change in recidivism rates: A large reduction in recidivism was considered to be 25% or higher, a moderate reduction was 24–10%, and a small reduction was less than 10%.

Most recently, Lipsey and Wilson (1998) conducted a meta-analysis of experimental or quasi-experimental studies of interventions for serious and violent juvenile delinquents. They reviewed 200 programs, which were further divided into programs for institutionalized juveniles ($n = 83$) and noninstitutionalized juveniles ($n = 117$). McBride, VanderWaal, Terry, and VanBuren (1999, p. 58) synthesized the findings of Lipsey and Wilson's meta-analysis.

Noninstitutionalized programs that demonstrate good evidence of effectiveness include behavioral therapies (family and contingency contracting), intensive case management (including system collaboration and continuing care), multisystemic therapy (MST), restitution programs (parole and probation based), and skills training. Program options that require more research to document their effectiveness include 12-step programs (Alcoholics Anonymous [AA], Narcotics Anonymous [NA]), adult mentoring (with behaviorally contingent reinforcement), afterschool recreation programs, conflict resolution/violence prevention, Intensive Probation Services (IPS), juvenile versions of Treatment Alternatives to Street Crime (TASC), peer mediation, and traditional inpatient/outpatient programs. Program options that show no evidence of effectiveness include deterrence programs, vocational training or career counseling, and wilderness challenge programs.

Institutionalized programs that demonstrate good effectiveness include behavioral programs (cognitive mediation and stress inoculation training), longer term community residential programs (therapeutic communities with cognitive–behavioral approaches), multiple services within residential communities (case management approach), and skills training (aggression replacement training and cognitive restructuring). More research is needed to determine the effectiveness of day treatment centers, as there were too few studies to review. Juvenile boot camps, short-term residential facilities, and state training schools have been shown to be ineffective.

Based on conclusions of recent reviews, such as those presented above, Henggeler (1997, p. 255) synthesized the most consistent correlates of adolescent drug use and abuse (see Exhibit 1.2).

Meta-Analyses on Treatment With Female Offenders

Research on female offenders has been sparse (Morash, Bynum, & Koons, 1995). However, Dowden and Andrews (1999) conducted a meta-analysis on what works for female offenders. They reviewed 45 effect sizes from 26 studies that examined the effectiveness of correctional treatment programs for female offenders, addressing various principles (risk, need, and responsivity) as they relate to effective treatment with this population.

According to Dowden and Andrews (1999), the risk principle is "concerned with identifying those clients who should receive the most intensive allocation of correctional treatment resources and those who require less attention," whereas the need principle is "concerned with the targets for change identified within the treatment program" (p. 439). Finally, the responsivity principle is "concerned with the characteristics of program service delivery, and it states that the styles and modes of service used within a treatment program should be matched to the learning styles of offenders" (p. 440).

Under the need principle, Dowden and Andrews explored criminogenic versus noncrimogenic needs of offenders. Criminogenic needs are met when specific risk factors have been modified, and lower recidivism rates result (Andrews & Bonta, 1998). Accordingly, a major premise of the need principle is that, for treatment efforts to reduce recidivism, the criminogenic needs (e.g., antisocial cognition) of offenders must be targeted rather than the noncriminogenic needs (Dowden & Andrews, 1999).

Dowden and Andrews found strong support for each of these three principles in the meta-analysis. They found stronger treatment effects in programs that "targeted higher versus lower risk cases (η = .31), predominantly focused on criminogenic versus noncriminogenic needs (η = .49), and used behavioral–social learning versus nonbehavioral treatment strategies (η = .38)" (Dowden & Andrews, 1999, p. 445). It is interesting to note that substance abuse, as a primary target for intervention, was not found as an important predictor of treatment success. In fact, substance abuse had a slightly negative correlation (–.01) with reduced reoffending. The strongest predictors of treatment success with female offenders were family process variables. Additionally, there is evidence that programs that target past victimization and self-esteem issues may help female offenders (Koons, Burrow, Morash, & Bynum, 1997).

EXHIBIT 1.2
Consistent Correlates of Adolescent Drug Use and Abuse

- *Individual:* other antisocial behaviors, low self-esteem, low social conformity, psychiatric symptomatology, positive expectancies for drug effects, genetic loadings
- *Family:* ineffective management and discipline, low warmth and high conflict, parental drug abuse
- *Peer:* association with drug-abusing peers, low association with prosocial peers
- *School:* low intelligence, achievement, and commitment to achievement
- *Neighborhood:* disorganization, high crime

Note. From "The Development of Effective Drug-Abuse Services for Youth," by S. W. Henggeler. In *Treating Drug Abusers Effectively* (pp. 253–279), J. A. Egertson, D. M. Fox, and A. I. Leshner, Eds., 1997, New York: Blackwell. Copyright 1997 by Blackwell Publishers. Reprinted with permission.

In 1997 the Center for Substance Abuse Treatment (CSAT) conducted its first large-scale national study of clients in publicly funded substance abuse treatment programs, the National Treatment Improvement Evaluation Study, which showed that substance abuse treatment reduces subsequent criminal activity (as cited in Kassebaum, 1999). Among 1,374 women clients in this study, preliminary results demonstrated large decreases in the client's involvement in violent crime, illicit drug distribution, and prostitution after both residential and outpatient treatment. The percentage of clients involved in prostitution was reduced from 28% before treatment to 7% 12 months following treatment. The final National Treatment Improvement Evaluation Study report reveals that before treatment, more than 50% of women clients reported having been involved in some form of illegal activity. After treatment, arrests dropped by 67%; the number of women selling drugs decreased 82%; shoplifting decreased 88%; and reports of the women "beating someone up" decreased 89% (CSAT, 1997).

WHO IS THIS BOOK FOR?

This book is written for a wide range of professionals, including forensic practitioners, psychologists, social workers, chemical dependency counselors, mental health counselors and therapists, judges, criminologists, corrections officers, and policymakers who are planning or implementing interventions for substance-abusing offenders. In each chapter, we attempt to answer questions commonly asked across these groups of professionals, such as

- How do I conduct an assessment with a dually diagnosed offender (an offender with both substance abuse and mental health disorders)? What are the best scales to use?
- How can I tailor existing treatment approaches to deliver effective services for female or juvenile substance-abusing offenders?

- What are the most effective methods for treating substance-abusing offenders? What about dually diagnosed offenders?
- What are some of the more innovative approaches being used to treat substance-abusing offenders? How effective are these approaches (e.g., drug courts, boot camps)?
- Should the offender's family be involved in treatment? Once the family shows up, what do I do with them?
- How should I structure a therapy group for aggressive, substance-abusing juvenile offenders?
- Are electronic monitoring and intensive supervision probation cost-effective?
- How do I match treatment interventions to the offender's needs and readiness for change?

These are just a few of the questions we address throughout this book. We attempt to distinguish treatment modalities from treatment settings. Whereas the former are characterized by a particular theoretical model of treatment, the latter are mostly a combination of the physical setting in which treatment takes place and the program structure. In some cases, such as therapeutic communities, treatment models and treatment settings are difficult to separate. Where the information is available, we summarize the outcome literature on the effectiveness of different interventions.

Given the recent and important emphasis on the gender-specific treatment needs of women involved in the justice system, we integrate information about interventions designed specifically for women throughout the text, as well as variations in the application of specific interventions to make them more sensitive to the needs of female offenders. Additionally, where outcome data exist, we provide findings from the research about the effectiveness of certain forms of treatment for women. Unfortunately, even with the recent high priority given to women's treatment needs, most of the existing literature and research is focused on male offenders (Doweiko, 2002). In the remaining chapters of this book, we are concerned primarily with describing the current state of the art in intervention with substance-abusing adult and juvenile offenders and with providing a guide to assessment and diagnosis (chapter 2), individual treatment (chapter 3), family-based treatment (chapter 4), and group intervention (chapter 5) with this population. Traditional and innovative treatment settings and approaches will be reviewed in chapters 6 and 7, respectively. Due to the increasing prevalence of offenders with both substance abuse and mental health disorders, we devote an entire chapter to treating dually diagnosed offenders (chapter 8). Finally, we address monitoring substance-abusing offenders (chapter 9) and provide suggestions for the future direction of treatment and research with this population (chapter 10).

The field has come a long way since Martinson (1974) concluded that "nothing works" three decades ago. We now have more refined assessment and treatment tools to meet the multiple needs of the offending population faced with substance abuse (and mental health) problems (cf. McNeece, in press; NIDA, 1999c). In each chapter we attempt to synthesize the vast knowledge base and, where possible, direct readers down the path of using evidence-based practice.

2

ASSESSMENT AND DIAGNOSIS

ASSESSMENT

Although this book is primarily about interventions for substance-abusing offenders, a chapter on assessment and diagnosis is essential because *assessment is the first active phase of treatment*. A thorough assessment is the cornerstone of a solid treatment plan.

"Assessment is the act of determining the nature and causes of a client's problem" (Lewis, Dana, & Blevins, 1994, p. 71). There are various ways to go about conducting a thorough substance abuse assessment. These include, but are not limited to, face-to-face interviews, psychological testing, self-observation, observation by others, individualized rating scales, rapid assessment instruments (RAIs), and standardized assessment protocols. We encourage practitioners to use a combination of these methods to conduct a complete assessment of an offender. It is imperative that the practitioner attempt to understand the offender's substance abuse problems from his or her perspective, taking into account the offender's cultural background while being aware of the worker's own biases.

Information is typically gathered through some sort of intake interview such as a psychosocial history or by administering appropriate measurement

17

tools to the offender. The practitioner–client interaction that takes place while conducting a substance use history contextualizes information that is lost through self-report, pencil-and-paper methods. However, what is gained by administering pencil-and-paper assessment tools, such as the widely used Michigan Alcoholism Screening Test (MAST), is an account of the problem in a standardized manner with a reliable and valid tool.

It is important to keep in mind the differences among screening, diagnosis, and assessment. *Screening* is defined as "the use of brief instruments or other tools to determine the likelihood that an individual has a chemical abuse or chemical dependency problem" (McNeece & DiNitto, 1998, p. 69). Screenings can be conducted informally (e.g., reviewing an offender's "rap sheet") or using standardized screening tools. Examples of screening tools reviewed in this chapter include the CAGE Questionnaire, MAST, and the Index of Drug Involvement (IDI).

Diagnosis is the "confirmation of a chemical abuse or dependency problem, often using more than one source of information" (McNeece & DiNitto, 1998, p. 69). Results obtained from a standardized tool and an in-depth psychosocial interview might help a practitioner reach a diagnostic impression using the *Diagnostic and Statistical Manual of Mental Disorders* (DSM–IV–TR; American Psychiatric Association, 2000). Previous medical, psychological or psychiatric, criminal, educational, employment, and other records may also be used (McNeece & DiNitto, 1998).

Assessment is "an in-depth consideration of the client's chemical abuse or dependency problems as they have affected his or her psychological well-being, social circumstances (including interpersonal relationships), financial status, employment or education, health, and so forth" (McNeece & DiNitto, 1998, pp. 69–70). The assessment is more comprehensive than a diagnosis. A thorough assessment will inform treatment planning. Assessment can be informed using a face-to-face psychosocial history, as well as standardized instruments such as the Addiction Severity Index (ASI) or the Child and Adolescent Functional Assessment Scale (CAFAS) (both reviewed below).

The following discussion on conducting assessments with substance-abusing juvenile and adult offenders rests on the assumptions about assessment presented by Springer (in press-a): "(1) assessment is empirically based, (2) assessment must be made from a systems perspective, (3) measurement is essential, (4) ethical practitioners evaluate their clinical work, and (5) well-qualified practitioners are knowledgeable about numerous assessment methods in developing assessments" (p. 3). These assumptions should serve as a guide for practitioners when determining what type of assessment protocol to implement with their client.

This chapter reviews assessment methods commonly used with juvenile and adult offenders who have substance abuse problems. Methods of assessing the offender are presented, including the use of standardized instruments. Entire books have been written on using standardized assessment instruments with clients. Although we have attempted to select instruments that are widely used, it is beyond the scope of this chapter to comprehensively review available measurement instruments. Readers are referred to other excellent sources for a more thorough review (cf. Corcoran & Fischer, 2000; Hudson, 1982; Sederer & Dickey, 1996; Shaffer, Lucas, & Richters, 1999).

Interview and Psychosocial History

The initial interview with the offender serves several purposes. It allows an opportunity for the practitioner to establish rapport with the offender and for the offender to tell his or her story to an attentive listener. Involving the client's family for at least part of the interview should be strongly considered, particularly with juvenile offenders. Recall from above that one key assumption of conducting a good assessment is that one should operate from a systems perspective. Involving the family during part of the interview helps serve this purpose. Additionally, family members are almost always impacted by the client's substance use and need to be involved in the assessment and treatment process whenever feasible (see chapter 4).

We offer a template for conducting a psychosocial history with substance-abusing offenders in Exhibit 2.1. The interview should address various aspects of the client's life.

Ideally, the psychosocial history is conducted in a face-to-face interview with the client, but it can be conducted over the telephone if necessary. The Exhibit 2.1 template is intended to serve as a starting point; it is not intended to be an exhaustive list of all possible questions that a practitioner might ask.

Practitioners should modify the template to meet the needs of their particular agency and client population, and they should ask follow-up questions when more information is needed. For example, some agencies that serve substance-abusing offenders have adopted a strength-based perspective. A practitioner working in such a setting would want to expand on Section XIV of the Psychosocial History accordingly to more thoroughly tap what the client perceives to be his or her strengths. Cowger (1997, pp. 69–71) proposed exemplars for assessment of client strengths in five areas: cognition (e.g., Is open to different ways of thinking about things); emotion (e.g., Is positive about life); motivation (e.g., Wants to improve current and future situations); coping (e.g., Has dealt successfully with related problem in the past); and interpersonal (e.g., Makes sacrifices for friends, family members, and others).

For the complete listing of exemplars, readers are referred to Cowger (1997). The assessment of the client's strengths should be tailored to meet the specific needs of the population being served (e.g., juvenile offender from an abusive home, female trauma survivor). In any event, we assert that a

EXHIBIT 2.1
Psychosocial History for Substance-Abusing Offenders

I. Reason for Self- or Other-Referral/Presenting Problem
    1. Tell me in your own words what problem(s) you would like to work on.
    2. What has happened recently that might prompt you to seek help now (precipitating event)?
II. Family-of-Origin History
    1. Do/did your parents drink/use?
    2. Do/did others (siblings) in your family of origin drink/use?
    3. What are/were their drinking/using habits like?
    4. Is there anyone in your family who is an alcoholic/addict?
    5. What is your relationship like with the other members of your family of origin?
III. Current Family History (Partner[a]/Children)
    1. Are you in a committed relationship with someone? [Obtain relevant history.]
    2. Do you have any children? If yes, what is the custody status?[b]
    3. How does your drinking/using impact your relationship with your partner/children?
    4. Does your family avoid you when you drink/use?
    5. Do you avoid your family when you drink/use?
    6. Does your partner/children drink/use?
    7. Does your drinking/using cause any conflict between you and your partner/children?
IV. Relationships With Peers and Significant Others
    1. How does your drinking/using impact your relationships with your friends or significant others?
    2. Do most of your friends drink/use?
V. Abuse History [Prepare offender for sensitive nature of these questions]
    1. Were you ever physically, sexually, or emotionally abused during childhood? [If yes, ask for additional information.]
    2. Have you experienced physical, sexual, or emotional abuse as an adult? [If yes, ask for additional information. It is particularly important to assess female clients for domestic violence.]
VI. Education
    1. How far did you go in school?
    2. What was your favorite subject(s)?
    3. What training/degree have you received [when appropriate]?
    4. Would you like to receive/continue training/education? In what area(s)?
VII. Employment History [include military history when applicable]
    1. What is your current (or most recent) job? Is it full-time, part-time, or day labor?
    2. How long were you/have you been employed in that position?
    3. What is your favorite type of work?
    4. How does your drinking/using interfere with your ability to perform your job?
    5. Have you ever lost a job because of drinking/using?
    6. Are you having financial difficulties?
    7. What are your sources of income?
VIII. Alcohol Use History[c]
    1. What do you drink?
    2. When did you first start drinking?
    3. How often do you drink (daily, weekly)?
    4. When was the last time you had a drink?
    5. How much did you have?
    6. How much do you typically have?

(continues)

EXHIBIT 2.1
(Continued)

7. Do you ever drink more than you intended?
8. Do you ever drink more often than you intended?
9. Have you ever made and broken a promise to yourself about how frequently and how much you drink?
10. Have you ever tried to stop drinking? How?
11. Have you ever experienced withdrawal symptoms from alcohol?
12. Have you ever been hospitalized or treated for drinking?

IX. Drug Use History[c]
1. What drugs do you use?
2. What is your drug of choice?
   [All subsequent questions should be asked about each drug used.]
3. How often do you use (daily, weekly)?
4. When was the last time you used?
5. How much did you have?
6. How much do you typically have?
7. Do you ever use more than you intended?
8. Do you ever use more often than you intended?
9. Have you ever made and broken a promise to yourself about how frequently and how much you use?
10. Have you ever tried to stop using? How?
11. Have you ever experienced withdrawal symptoms from any drug?
12. Have you ever been hospitalized or treated for using?

X. Medical History
1. Do you have any current or past medical problems? If so, please describe.
2. Have you ever been tested for HIV? If so, what were the results? (Some agencies may have as a policy to ask about testing but not about results.) If no, are you interested in being tested?
3. Have you ever been hospitalized for a medical problem?
4. Are you currently taking any medications? If so, please provide the names of the medications and dosages.
5. Have you taken any medications in the past that you are currently not taking? If so, please provide the names of the medications and dosages.
6. Have you ever taken any medication for a purpose for which it was not intended?

XI. Psychological or Psychiatric History[d]
1. Do you ever feel depressed or anxious?
2. Have you ever been told that you have a mental health problem or disorder? If yes, ask for the name of the disorder, when the client was diagnosed, and who made the diagnosis.
3. Have you ever had counseling or been treated by a mental health professional (for depression, anxiety, etc.)?
4. Have you ever had a psychiatric hospitalization?
5. Have you ever thought about hurting or killing yourself?
6. Have you ever tried to kill yourself?

XII. Religious/Spiritual History
1. Do you practice a certain religion or spiritual faith? [Explore.]
2. How much of a role does religion/spirituality play in your life?

XIII. Legal History
1. Are you currently on probation or parole?
2. What charges have you had (legal history)?
3. Do you have any charges pending?
4. Have you ever been incarcerated? For what offense(s)?

(continues)

EXHIBIT 2.1
(Continued)

> 5. Have you ever been arrested for a drug-related offense?
> 6. Have you ever committed a violent crime?
>
> XIV. Assessment of Client Strengths and Weaknesses [This section may help with goal setting]
>
>   1. What do you consider to be your strengths? (Alternative phrasing: What do you like most about yourself?)
>   2. Tell me ways that you have dealt successfully with your problems in the past. How can we build on those successes?
>   3. If you could change anything about yourself or your life, what would it be?
>   4. What would your life look like if all of your problems were resolved?

[a] The more inclusive term *partner* is used here, but when appropriate, the terms *spouse/husband/wife* should be substituted.
[b] Inquiring about custody status is particularly important, as many offenders may have lost custody of children due to substance abusing and/or criminal behavior. For some, regaining custody may be a motivating factor for treatment (see chapter 3).
[c] Some practitioners may prefer to collapse sections VIII and IX or, for a more detailed history, leave them separate.
[d] If a client responds affirmatively to any question about self-harm (e.g., questions 5 and 6 in Section XI), the practitioner needs to get a complete history. Refer to the section "Mental Status Examination" for suicidal ideation.

thorough assessment includes a deliberate examination of the offender's unique strengths that, in turn, can be amplified over the course of treatment.

Mental Status Examination

"The Mental Status Examination (MSE) is an assessment of the patient's current state of mind" (Waldinger, 1990, p. 55). Most practitioners gather information with an MSE in various ways. There are times when those with advanced clinical training (i.e., psychiatrists, clinical psychologists, clinical social workers) may conduct a complete and formal mental status exam. However, the MSE can also be thought of as a way to organize and report information about a client. An outline of the components of a standard MSE is provided in Exhibit 2.2. While a discussion addressing each section of the MSE is beyond the scope of this chapter, below we explore the need to always assess for the presence of suicidal ideation when working with offenders. For a detailed exposition on the mental status exam, readers are referred to other sources (cf. Andreasen & Black, 1991; Waldinger, 1990).

Suicidal Ideation

The presence of *suicidal (or homicidal) ideation* should always be assessed as part of the MSE. Among incarcerated individuals, preincarceration and demographic characteristics can be used as a first step in assessing suicidal behavior (Ivanoff & Hayes, 2001). In their review of the literature, Ivanoff and Hayes (2001) found that most suicide victims in jail were young, white, male, single or divorced, intoxicated at arrest (M. S. Davis & Muscat, 1993;

EXHIBIT 2.2
Outline of Mental Status Examination

I   Appearance and Behavior
II.   Speech
III. Emotions
IV. Thought Process and Content
V.   Sensory Perceptions
VI. Intellectual Functioning and Mental Capacities
VII. Attitude Toward the Interviewer

Note. From *Psychiatry for Medical Students* (2nd ed., p. 56), by R. J. Waldinger, 1990, Washington, DC: American Psychiatric Press. Copyright 1990 by American Psychiatric Press. Reprinted with permission.

Hayes, 1983, 1989), had a history of psychiatric hospitalization or past suicidal behavior—including recent verbalizations or gestures (Farmer, Felthous, & Holtzer, 1996; Ivanoff, 1989; Marcus & Alcabes, 1993), and had experienced a recent negative life event (Ivanoff, 1989). In juveniles, suicidal attempts have been linked with the following characteristics: young age (younger than age 13), female, White or "other" race, history of injection or other drug use, history of sexual abuse, and history of sexually transmitted diseases (Morris et al., 1995, as cited in Ivanoff & Hayes, 2001). However, the rate of completed suicides is higher among male juveniles.

With new clients, particularly those that match part or all of the profile outlined above, the practitioner should ask the offender directly about suicidal or homicidal thoughts using unambiguous language (e.g., "Do you ever have any thoughts of hurting or killing yourself?"). However, Waldinger (1990) recommended that when assessing any thought content, the practitioner start out with a more general line of questioning (e.g., "Do you sometimes feel like giving up?") before moving to more direct, targeted questions.

There has been some debate surrounding how to deal with self-injurious behavior among incarcerated individuals. Some believe that it should be viewed (i.e., labeled) as manipulative or malingering, while others argue that all self-harm ideation or behavior should be taken seriously and treated accordingly (cf. Franklin, 1988; Haycock, 1992). Still others assert that self-harm behavior exhibited by inmates who are "truly suicidal" versus those who are "manipulative" warrants different interventions, although there is no evidence to support the impact of such a bifurcated approach on decreases in either suicide or nonfatal suicidal behavior (Ivanoff & Hayes, 2001). No staff in a correctional setting wants to be "manipulated" by an inmate, and there are instances when self-harm can challenge security. On the other hand, the potential risk associated with not taking such a threat seriously is grave. When clients do reveal that they want to hurt themselves, practitioners must be aware of their legal obligations for that specific state. Is inpatient hospitalization required if the client will not "contract for safety" (agree not to harm him/herself)? Who needs to be notified? In the event that a client does express suicidal intent, Lukas (1993, p. 122) recommended that practitioners explore six specific areas with the client:

1. When did she last have a thought about killing herself?
2. How often does she think about killing herself?
3. How comforting do these thoughts seem to her?
4. Has she made a previous suicide attempt?
5. Does she now have a plan to kill herself?
6. Can she carry out the plan?

"In discussing suicide plans, the *key factors* are the *lethality* of the method, the *availability* of the method, and the *likelihood of rescue*" (Waldinger, 1990, p. 451).

Suicide prevention programming is advocated for and supported by groups such as the American Correctional Association and the National Commission on Correctional Health Care. Using a combination of the 1990 and 1991 standards from the former and the 1995, 1996, and 1997 standards from the latter, Hayes (1995) developed a comprehensive suicide prevention policy. Readers are referred to these resources for a more detailed exposition on this critical topic.

> Most effective suicide prevention programs in correctional facilities have extended incident-free periods of suicide arguably related to their implementation of the following suicide prevention components: (a) suicide prevention training for correctional, medical, and mental health staff; (b) identification of suicide risk through intake screening; (c) procedures for referral to mental health or medical personnel, reassessment following crisis period; (d) effective communication between correctional, medical, and mental health staff when managing a suicidal inmate; (e) supervision and safe housing options for suicidal inmates; (f) timely medical intervention following a suicide attempt; (g) proper reporting procedures following an incident; and (h) administrative or clinical review of suicide, availability of critical incident debriefing to staff and inmates. (Hayes, 1998, as cited in Ivanoff & Hayes, 2001, pp. 322–323)

With such criteria in mind, Ivanoff and Hayes cited the Hamilton County Juvenile County Youth Center in Cincinnati, Ohio, and the Orange County Jail system in California as exemplary suicide prevention programs in which the focal point is zero-tolerance of suicide.

Suicidal ideation is also captured in some of the standardized assessment tools reviewed below.

STANDARDIZED ASSESSMENT INSTRUMENTS AND PROTOCOLS

Accurately recording a client's story through a semi-structured interview such as a psychosocial history is a critical component of any assessment.

EXHIBIT 2.3
The CAGE Questionnaire

1. Have you ever felt that you ought to CUT DOWN on your drinking?
2. Have people ANNOYED you by criticizing your drinking?
3. Have you ever felt bad or GUILTY about your drinking?
4. Have you ever had a drink first thing in the morning (EYE OPENER) to steady your nerves or get rid of a hangover?

Note. Scoring is either a 0 (no) or 1 (yes) for each item, and clinical significance is noted at total scores of 2 or greater. From "Detecting Alcoholism: The CAGE Questionnaire," by J. A. Ewing, 1984, *Journal of the American Medical Association, 252,* pp. 1905–1907. Copyright 1984 by American Medical Association. Reprinted with permission.

However, it is often useful to also administer standardized pencil-and-paper assessment tools. These tools are sometimes called rapid assessment instruments (RAIs) (Levitt & Reid, 1981) or scales. Today, RAIs are available to assess and monitor client progress across a broad range of problems (cf. Bloom, Fischer, & Orme, 1999; Corcoran & Fischer, 2000; Hudson, 1982; Shaffer et al., 1999). They are used as a method of empirical assessment and are easy to administer and score. A major benefit of RAIs is that they can be used as pretest–posttest measures to monitor an offender's attitudes, thoughts, feelings, and/or behaviors over the course of treatment. In this day of managed care and accountability, such monitoring is often crucial. We focus in this chapter on scales that assess a client's functioning as it relates to substance use. However, standardized scales exist for almost every problem that one might encounter with a client, from depression to anxiety to psychosis (cf. Corcoran & Fischer, 2000; Hudson, 1982; Sederer & Dickey, 1996; Shaffer et al., 1999).

We provide an overview of some of the scales that are available to practitioners below, along with guidelines on how to select the appropriate scale based on factors such as its psychometric properties (i.e., reliability and validity), clinical utility, and sensitivity. Screening tools are reviewed first, followed by assessment tools.

Screening Tools

CAGE

Substance abuse practitioners commonly use the CAGE Questionnaire (Ewing, 1984) to determine if a client has a problem with alcohol. CAGE is an acronym, with each letter representing a different question (see Exhibit 2.3). It can be administered either verbally or as a pencil-and-paper instrument with clients ages 16 and older.

Index of Drug Involvement

The IDI (Faul & Hudson, 1997) is a 25-item scale intended to measure the severity of a client's problem with drug abuse. Items are measured on a 7-

point Likert scale. Like many of Hudson's instruments, scores on the IDI range from 0 to 100. Higher scores indicate more problematic drug use. A clinical cutting score of 30 may be useful in interpreting the score and making clinical decisions; the higher the score, the more likely that inpatient treatment might be warranted. However, Faul and Hudson (1997) suggested that this cutting score be interpreted with caution until these study findings can be replicated with a larger clinical sample. Reliability estimates are excellent, with a coefficient alpha of .97 and a low *SEM* value (2.86), as are validity estimates at .60 or greater.

The IDI is available for a small fee from WALMYR Publishing Company, P.O. Box 12217, Tallahassee, FL 32317; 850-383-0045. WALMYR Publishing also has a Web site (www.walmyr.com) and can be contacted by e-mail (scales@walmyr.com).

Problem-Oriented Screening Instrument for Teenagers

The Problem-Oriented Screening Instrument for Teenagers (POSIT) was developed for use with adolescents. The POSIT was developed by a panel of experts as part of the comprehensive Adolescent Assessment/Referral System for use with 12–19-year-olds (Rahdert, 1991). The POSIT is a 139-item, self-administered tool. Items are measured on a dichotomous (yes/no) scale. The POSIT is intended to be used as a screening tool. It is not designed to measure treatment progress or outcomes. (A more complete diagnostic evaluation requires that the practitioner implement another component of the Adolescent Assessment/Referral System, the Comprehensive Assessment Battery.) The POSIT develops independent scores in 10 areas of functioning: substance use/abuse, physical health, mental health, family relations, peer relations, educational status, vocational status, social skills, leisure/recreation, and aggressive behavior and delinquency.

The National Clearinghouse for Alcohol and Drug Information offers the Adolescent Assessment/Referral System (NIDA, 1991), which contains the POSIT, free of charge. Contact the clearinghouse at P.O. Box 2345, Rockville, MD 20847; 800-729-6686.

Drug Use Screening Inventory–Revised

The Drug Use Screening Inventory–Revised (DUSI–R; Tarter & Hegedus, 1991) is a 159-item multidimensional pencil-and-paper instrument, measured on a dichotomous (yes/no) scale that has recently been created to assess the severity of problems of adolescents and adults. Like the ASI, this instrument addresses areas other than substance abuse. The 10 domains on the DUSI–R address the following areas: drug and alcohol use, behavior patterns, health status, psychiatric disorder, social competence, family system, school performance/adjustment, work adjustment, peer relationships, and leisure/recreation. A lie scale documents reporting validity. The information obtained from the completed DUSI–R can be used to develop an individualized treatment plan; however, scores do not indicate specific types of treatment. That decision is left to the clinical judgment of the practitioner. The authors of this instrument report that it is able to classify adults and adolescents with *DSM–IV* substance disorders and those with no psychiatric disorders.

Content validity has been established for some of the domains of the DUSI–R. Scores for each of the 10 life problem areas correlated with the number of substance abuse symptoms on the *DSM–III–R* (American Psychiatric Association, 1987), with the highest correlation (.72) on the DUSI–R Substance Use Behavior scale (NIDA, 1994). In a sample of 191 adolescents with alcohol and drug abuse problems, internal reliability coefficients averaged .74 for males and .78 for females across the 10 life problem areas. In a sample of polysubstance-abusing adolescents, the mean test–retest coefficients (1 week) were .95 for males and .88 for females (NIDA, 1994).

The developer of the DUSI–R is Ralph E. Tarter, PhD, Department of Psychiatry, University of Pittsburgh School of Medicine, 3811 O'Hara Street, Pittsburgh, PA 15213; 412- 624-1070. It is available from The Gordian Group, P.O. Box 1587, Hartsville, SC 29950; 803-383-2201. The DUSI–R is copyrighted and is available in three formats: paper questionnaire for manual scoring; computer administration and scoring system; and Opscan administration and scoring.

Michigan Alcoholism Screening Test

The MAST is a 24-item, dichotomous (yes/no) measure that addresses drinking habits with demonstrated empirical qualities (W. R. Miller, 1976; Selzer, Vinokur, & Van Rooijen, 1974). The MAST was originally designed to be administered orally by practitioners, but it is often completed as a pencil-and-paper instrument by the client and then scored. It takes approximately 7 minutes to administer the MAST. Two shorter versions of the MAST also exist: the Short MAST contains 13 items, and the Brief MAST contains 10 items (Pokorny, Miller, & Kaplan, 1972). These shorter versions are often used with slower readers, which may be relevant for those working with inmates.

Internal consistencies are excellent for both the long (alpha = .95) and short (alpha = .93) forms of the MAST (Corcoran & Fischer, 2000). Reported alpha coefficients from nine different studies ranged from .83 to .95. Zung (1982) reported test–retest reliability coefficients of .97 (1 day), .86 (2 days), and .85 (3 days) with a psychiatric population. In a study of 400 adult psychiatric inpatient clients, Moore (1972) found 78% agreement between the MAST and psychiatrists' opinion regarding whether the client was a "problem drinker" or "alcoholic." The instrument has excellent known-groups validity, being able to classify most respondents as either alcoholic or nonalcoholic (Corcoran & Fischer, 2000). Each item on the MAST is weighted on a 1-to-5 scale, with 5 considered diagnostic of alcoholism.

Those intending to use the MAST should be aware of one potential pitfall. It only takes 5 points to place someone in the alcoholic category. If a person responds affirmatively to question 8 ("Have you ever attended a meeting of Alcoholics Anonymous [AA]?"), for example, he or she is assigned 5 points. Most students who have been enrolled in a college course on chemical dependency have probably been required to attend an AA meeting as part of a class assignment; using this scoring scheme, they would be inappropriately categorized as an alcoholic by the MAST. Nevertheless, it is still a clinically useful tool that is widely used.

The MAST is available from Dr. Melvin Selzer, 6967 Paseo Laredo, La Jolla, CA 92037; 619-299-4043.

Substance Abuse Subtle Screening Inventory

The Substance Abuse Subtle Screening Inventory (SASSI; Miller, 1985; Miller, Miller, Roberts, Brooks, & Lazowski, 1997) is a 67-item pencil-and-paper instrument. There is also an updated adolescent version of the SASSI, referred to as the SASSI–A2, which is composed of 32 new items and 40 true–false items from the original adolescent version of the SASSI. The SASSI–A2 has been empirically validated as a screening tool for both substance dependence and substance abuse among adolescents, based on a sample of adolescents (N = 2,326) from treatment and criminal justice programs. Like the SASSI, an appealing feature of the SASSI–A2 is that it contains both face-valid items that directly address alcohol and drug use and subtle true–false items that do not inquire directly about alcohol or drug use. These items on the reverse side were formerly called the Risk Prediction Scales (Morton, 1978). Administering the subtle true–false items to a client before the more direct items related to alcohol and drug use may help minimize defensiveness and lead to more accurate responses. Research findings revealed that 95% of adolescents with a substance use disorder were correctly identified with a "high probability" result in the SASSI–A2 decision rule, and 89% of adolescents without a substance use disorder were correctly classified with a "low-probability" decision rule. The SASSI is accompanied by a set of decision rules to determine if the client fits the profile of a chemically dependent person, and other guidelines help determine if a respondent is an abuser but not dependent. An additional strength of the tool is that separate guidelines are used to score results for men and women; taking a client's gender into account during the assessment and treatment planning process is critical. All of the SASSI instruments are available from the SASSI Institute at www.sassi.com or 800-726-0526.

Assessment Tools

Addiction Severity Index

The ASI (McLellan, Luborsky, Woody, & O'Brien, 1980; McLellan, Luborsky, Cacciola, et al., 1985) is a 45-minute, 161-item structured interview that addresses the following areas of functioning: medical status, employment status, drug use, alcohol use, legal status, family/social relationships, and psychiatric status. It is one of few standardized instruments that addresses drugs other than alcohol. Although the ASI was not created to screen for mental illness, it does assess for psychiatric status (i.e., suicidal ideation, depression, anxiety, psychosis, and violence). In each of the seven areas of functioning, both the interviewer and the client rate the severity of problems, and each subscale score can be totaled to create an overall numeric score. The ASI has a follow-up version that has helped practitioners and researchers measure client progress and assess program effectiveness. Thus, the ASI helps monitor client progress over time. The fact that the ASI addresses legal status may make it particularly useful for practitioners working with substance-abusing offenders. It is not recommended for use with elderly clients or with adolescents and needs to be administered by trained clinicians or intake counselors to maximize its reliability (NIDA, 1994).

The psychometric properties of the ASI have been tested in many studies (Hodgins & El, 1992; McLellan et al., 1980, 1985). The interrater reliability coefficients on the ASI's subscales range from .84 to .93, with a reliability coefficient of .89 on the overall scale. It correlates highly with other instruments with which one would expect it to, such as the MAST, the Cornell Medical Index, and the Gunderson Drug Scale (NIDA, 1994), providing evidence of convergent construct and known-instruments criterion-related validity. The Psychiatric Status subscale correlates highly with the Symptom Checklist–90–R (SCL–90–R) (NIDA, 1994).

A. Thomas McLellan, PhD, at the Veterans Administration Medical Center of the University of Pennsylvania developed the ASI. There is no cost to use the ASI, as it is public domain. Copies of the ASI and related training materials are available from the Treatment Research Institute, founded and directed by Dr. McLellan, at 600 Public Ledger Building, 150 South Independence Mall West, Philadelphia, PA 19106-3475; 215-399-0980. The ASI can also be downloaded at no cost from the Web page of the Treatment Research Institute (www.tresearch.org). The National Institute on Drug Abuse has a technology transfer package on using the ASI that is available from the National Clearinghouse for Alcohol and Drug Information, 800-729-6686 (NIDA, 1994).

Child and Adolescent Functional Assessment Scale

The CAFAS (Hodges, 2000) is a popular standardized multidimensional assessment tool that is used to measure the extent to which the mental health/substance use disorders of youths ages 7–17 impair functioning. It is completed by the practitioner and requires specialized training. A major benefit of the CAFAS in helping practitioners determine a youth's overall level of functioning is that it covers eight areas: school/work, home, community, behavior toward others, moods/emotions, self-harmful behavior, substance use, and thinking. The youth's level of functioning in each of these eight domains is then scored as severe (score of 30), moderate (20), mild (10), or minimal (0). Additionally, an overall score can be computed. These scores can be graphically depicted on a one-page scoring sheet that provides a profile of the youth's functioning. This makes it easy to monitor progress over the course of treatment. An appealing feature of recent versions (Hodges, 2000) is that the CAFAS now includes strength-based items. Although these items are not included in the scoring, they are useful in treatment planning.

The psychometric properties of the CAFAS have been demonstrated in numerous studies (cf. Hodges & Cheong-Seok, 2000; Hodges & Wong, 1996). The interrater reliability of the CAFAS has been demonstrated by having 45 graduate and undergraduate psychology students and 9 clinical staff provide CAFAS ratings to 20 written case vignettes (Hodges & Wong, 1996). The concurrent and construct validity of the scale has also been demonstrated (Hodges & Wong, 1996). One study on the predictive validity of the CAFAS supported the notion that this scale is able to predict recidivism in juvenile delinquents (Hodges & Cheong-Seok, 2000). Higher scores on the CAFAS have been found to associate with previous psychiatric hospitalization, serious psychiatric diagnoses, restrictive living arrangements, below-average school performance and attendance, and contact with law enforcement (Hodges, Doucette-Gates, & Oinghong, 1999).

The CAFAS is available from Dr. Kay Hodges, 2140 Old Earhart Road, Ann Arbor, MI 48105; 734-769-9725; e-mail: hodges@provide.net.

The Voice Diagnostic Interview Schedule for Children (DISC–IV)

The Diagnostic Interview Schedule for Children (DISC) is a computerized respondent-based interview that assesses over 30 common diagnoses found among children and adolescents, including anxiety disorders, eating disorders, mood disorders, attention-deficit and disruptive behavior disorders, and substance use disorders (Shaffer, Fisher, & Lucas, 1999; Shaffer, Fisher, Lucas, Dulcan, & Schwab-Stone, 2000). It was developed to be compatible with the DSM–IV, DSM–III–R, and the *International Classification of Diseases* (ICD–10), and is organized into six diagnostic modules that measure the major Axis I Disorders and impairment. The DISC–IV includes assessment for three time frames—the present (past 4 weeks), the last year, and ever—with parallel versions existing for youth ages 9 to 17 (DISC–Y) and for parents or caretakers of youth ages 6 to 17 years (DISC–P). The DISC–IV is scored by algorithms that apply Boolean logic (i.e., "and" and "ors") to combine answers to component questions, and is "an ideal candidate for computerization, given the highly structured nature of the interview, the limited response options, the complicated branching and skipping instructions, and the need for the interviewer to keep close track of an informant's answers to numerous symptoms in order to ask onset and impairment questions correctly" (Shaffer, Fisher, & Lucas, 1999, p. 23). A recent voiced adaptation allows youth to hear the interview over headphones (while also reading questions on the computer screen) and key in responses via computer.

The Center for the Promotion of Mental Health in Juvenile Justice at Columbia University is spearheading efforts to administer the voice version of the DISC–IV. It has already been tested in three states (Illinois, South Carolina, and New Jersey) with youth recently admitted to juvenile correction institutions, with the primary aims to more accurately assess rates of mental health disorders among incarcerated juveniles, and to test the feasibility of using this type of structured, self-administered mental health assessment with this population (Ko & Wasserman, 2002). The Voice DISC–IV provides a "provisional" diagnosis for youth assessed. Findings from initial feasibility studies indicate that the instrument is tolerated well by youth, parents, and agency staff, and support its validity, revealing that information on psychiatric status matches existing justice system information regarding current substance offenses (Wasserman, McReynolds, Lucas, Fisher, & Santos, 2002). Adaptations for detention, correctional, and community juvenile justice sites are ongoing in ten other states.

For sites that are willing and capable, the Center for the Promotion of Mental Health in Juvenile Justice will provide the Voice DISC–IV assessment software program, provide training for key personnel, offer ongoing technical support through phone and e-mail, assist with data interpretation and preparation of reports/presentations, and provide guidelines for appropriate mental health referral. For more detailed information, Dr. Susan Ko, Clinical Director of the Center, may be contacted at kos@childpsych.columbia.edu.

The Psychopathy Checklist–Revised

The Psychopathy Checklist (PCL; Hare, 1980) and its revision (PCL–R; Hare, 1991) are probably the most widely used clinical rating scales that assess the degree of psychopathy. Although the PCL was originally intended for research with forensic populations, over the past two decades the PCL has gained widespread use. Any discussion of psychopathy without mention of the PCL–R would be incomplete. Indeed, the overwhelming majority of North American and European countries share a definition of psychopathy that is similar to Hare's Psychopathy Checklist (Cooke, 1998; Hare, 1991), and the "evolving worldwide consensus can be attributed to the empirical work of Hare and his colleagues" (Gacono, Nieberding, Owen, Rubel, & Bodholdt, 2001, p. 100). An increasing number of substance abuse programs use the PCL–R to detect psychopathic features in their clients (cf. Gerstley, Alterman, McLellan, & Woody, 1990; Hemphill, Hart, & Hare, 1994; S. S. Smith & Newman, 1990).

The PCL–R is composed of 20 items measured on a 3-point Likert scale. The ratings for most items involve some degree of judgment and inference, guided by the item description provided in the manual; however, for several items, fixed and explicit criteria are provided (Hart, Hare, & Harpur, 1992). PCL–R assessments are based on an interview and a review of collateral information. Hart, Hare, and Harpur recommended a 90- to 120-minute semistructured interview that allows the interviewer to obtain historical information (covering educational, occupational, family, marital, and criminal history) and to observe the individual's interactional style. To score the PCL–R, individual items are scored and then summed to produce a possible total score ranging from 0 to 40; a score of 30 or higher indicates psychopathy (Hart et al., 1992). When completed by a trained rater, intraclass correlations typically exceed .80 (Hare, 1998). In a review across several large-scale studies, average correlations were found between the PCL measures and general recidivism (.27), violent recidivism (.27), and sexual recidivism (.23), and individuals who scored 30 or greater on the PCL–R were found to be four times more likely to commit a future violent crime than were nonpsychopathic offenders (Hemphill, Hare, & Wong, 1998).

The PCL–R is made up of two stable, oblique factors. Factor 1 captures interpersonal and affective characteristics, such as lack of remorse, egocentricity, shallow affect, and callousness. Scores from this factor "are most closely correlated with classic clinical descriptions of psychopathy, prototypicality ratings of narcissistic personality disorder, and with self-report measures of machiavellianism, narcissism, empathy, and anxiety (negatively in the latter two cases)" (Hart et al., 1992, p. 111). Factor 2 captures aspects of psychopathy related to an impulsive, unstable, and parasitic individual, and is more strongly related to criminal behaviors, less education, lower socioeconomic background, conduct disorder, and substance abuse than is factor 1 (Gacono et al., 2001; Hart & Hare, 1989; S. S. Smith & Newman, 1990). "Although conceptual questions remain regarding its factor structure, among adult male samples the PCL/PCL–R has been shown to be a robust predictor of criminal behavior generally and violence specifically" (Edens, Skeem, Cruise, & Cauffman, 2001, p. 57).

The finding that factor 2 is more strongly associated with substance use lends support to the argument that in the course of substance abuse treatment, it is important to differentiate those clients who exhibit psychopathic features (score high on factors 1 and 2) and those whose abuse is part of a general pattern of antisocial tendencies (score high only on factor 2; Gerstley et al., 1990; Hart et al., 1992). Hemphill and colleagues (1994) examined the association between psychopathy, as assessed by the PCL–R, and substance use across studies. Although psychopathy diagnoses were not found to be significantly comorbid with substance use disorders, the findings did support the notion that substance use is associated with an unstable, antisocial lifestyle, but not necessarily with the interpersonal and affective characteristics of psychopathy as measured by factor 1 of the PCL–R. Based on their findings, Hemphill and colleagues (1994) recommended that clinicians working in forensic settings "assess for substance use given the presence of significant Factor 2-type personality traits, such as impulsivity, irresponsibility, poor anger controls, and criminality" but cautioned that "Factor 1-type traits will have little or no predictive efficiency with respect to substance use disorders in these settings" (p. 177).

There are additional psychopathy scales that are rational derivations from the PCL–R (Edens et al., 2001), including (a) a 12-item screening version of the PCL–R has been published (Hart, Cox, & Hare, 1995) that has demonstrated promise as a measure of psychopathic features in noncorrectional settings; (b) the PCL: Youth Version was designed to better represent adolescent life experiences (cf. Forth & Burke, 1998; Forth, Hart, & Hare, 1990), focusing more on peer, family, and school functioning; (c) the Psychopathy Screening Device (Frick & Hare, in press, as cited in Edens et al., 2001) is a 20-item scale also adapted for children and adolescents that, unlike the PCL: Youth Version, which must be completed by trained raters, can be completed by parents and teachers; (d) the Child Psychopathy Scale (Lyman, 1997), a 41-item measure that draws from the *Child Behavior Checklist* (Achenbach, 1991) and a version of the California Child Q–Set (Block & Block, 1980); and (e) the Hare P–Scan: Research Version (Hare & Herve, 1999), a 90-item scale available for use by researchers and nonclinicians (e.g., judges, law enforcement officers), that is intended to serve as a screening tool only (i.e., not a standardized diagnostic tool).

Not just anyone can administer and score the PCL measures described above. As outlined in the PCL–R Scoring Manual (Hare, 1991), certain qualifications and training are recommended, such as an advanced degree, registration with a state or provincial body that regulates the assessment and diagnosis of mental disorders, experience working with forensic populations, and adequate training in the use of the measure.

Information about the Hare PCL–R Training Program, which is coordinated and presented by Darkstone Research Group Ltd., can be found at www.hare.org.

Some Guidelines for Selecting Standardized Scales

Practitioners need to consider several factors when choosing an RAI or standardized protocol for use with clients. These factors include the tool's reliability, validity, clinical utility, directness, sensitivity, and availability (Corcoran & Fischer, 2000). To the extent that a scale has sound psychometric properties, it allows practitioners to measure a client's problem consistently (reliability) and accurately (validity). Practitioners using standardized scales should have some understanding of available methods for establishing reliability and validity so that they can become informed users of scales. Accordingly, a brief overview of reliability and validity is provided below; however, readers are referred to other sources for a more detailed exposition on this topic (cf. Hudson, 1982; Nunnally & Bernstein, 1994;

Springer, in press-a; Springer, Abell, & Hudson, 2002; Springer, Abell, & Nugent, 2002).

Reliability

A measurement instrument is reliable to the extent that it consistently yields similar results over repeated and independent administrations. In practical terms, a "measuring instrument is reliable to the extent that independent administrations of the same instrument (or a comparable instrument) consistently yield similar results" (Kyte & Bostwick, 1997, p. 173). There are various ways to compute a scale's reliability (cf. Allen & Yen, 1979; Crocker & Algina, 1986; Cronbach, 1951; Nunnally & Bernstein, 1994).

A tool's reliability is represented through reliability coefficients, which range from 0.0 to 1.0, with 0.0 representing the lowest degree of reliability and 1.0 representing the highest degree of reliability. Different standards are used to determine if a reliability coefficient has reached an acceptable threshold depending on how the tool is to be used. For use in nomothetic research such as scientific studies that seek to examine general phenomena, a reliability coefficient of .60 or greater is typically considered to be acceptable (Hudson, 1982). However, for use in guiding decision-making and treatment planning with individual clients, a higher coefficient is required. The reason for this standard is that when working with an individual, there is no opportunity to average out the inevitable measurement error contained in the scale as there is in nomothetic research.

Springer, Abell, and Nugent (2002) provided the following guidelines for acceptability of reliability coefficients for use with individual clients in treatment planning: <.70 = Unacceptable, .70–.79 = Undesirable, .80–.84 = Minimally acceptable, .85–.89 = Respectable, .90–.95 = Very good, and >.95 = Excellent. Using this criteria, the MAST would be considered to have an excellent internal consistency reliability coefficient (alpha = .95) and the Short MAST's reliability coefficient would be considered very good (alpha = .93; Corcoran & Fischer, 2000). Practitioners are encouraged to use these or similar guidelines when deciding if a scale is adequately reliable to guide clinical decision-making. The greater the seriousness of the problem being measured (e.g., suicidal risk), and the graver the risk of making a wrong decision about a client's level of functioning, the higher the standard to be adopted (Springer, 2002).

Validity

Reliability is a necessary, but not solely sufficient, condition for establishing the psychometric properties of a scale. If a scale measures something consistently from situation to situation, but does not measure what it is supposed to measure, it will not be of much use to practitioners or clients. Validity ensures the accuracy of a scale.

Where reliability represents a scale's degree of consistency, validity represents how accurately a scale measures the construct for which it was intended. The practitioner must make decisions about a scale's validity in relationship to its intended use. A measure may be valid for one client but not for another, and the practitioner must determine if a tool is valid for that particular client in a particular setting at a given time. Crocker and Algina (1986) have conceptualized validity in three basic ways: content validity, criterion-related validity (concurrent and predictive), and construct validity (convergent and discriminant). Many pencil-and-paper scales are now available as computer-based tools (Springer, in press-a), and it has been demonstrated that the use of computer-based clinical assessment does not compromise the validity of responses among clients receiving substance abuse treatment, even when legal issues are pending (Sarrazin, Hall, Richards, & Carswell, 2002). In addition to a scale's psychometric properties, the criteria outlined below are also important considerations in selecting an appropriate scale for a client.

Additional Considerations in Selecting Scales

Age and Reading Ability. Practitioners must consider the client's age and reading ability when selecting a scale. Scales are developed, validated, and normed for an intended population and for specific uses. If a scale is developed for use with adult clients, and a practitioner administers it to a 13-year-old client with a 5th-grade reading level, then this scale is not being administered properly, and the results obtained from the scale are meaningless.

Ethnic and Cultural Diversity. A second consideration is to fully respect a client's ethnic and cultural identity when using scales. Standardized measurement instruments may be biased against certain ethnic and cultural groups. For example, Mercer (1979) documented that African American children routinely scored 10 points lower than European American children on the Weschler Intelligence Scale for Children–Revised (WISC–R), indicating a cultural bias in the test. Practitioners should be alert to cultural differences throughout the assessment and treatment process with offenders (see chapter 3).

Overall Clinical Utility. The overall clinical utility of a scale refers to several factors, including those discussed above. Is the scale sensitive to changes in client functioning over time? Are the items direct and easy to understand? Is the length of the scale appropriate given its intended use by the practitioner? Lengthy scales may not be appropriate to administer in crisis situations, for example. Is the scale accessible at a reasonable cost? In addition to examining a scale's psychometric properties, practitioners must consider all these factors when selecting a scale for use with a given population in a given setting.

Having provided an overview of self-report standardized assessment tools, psychometric properties, and some criteria for selecting measurement tools, we now provide a word of caution. Practitioners should not rely solely on self-report measures when determining diagnostic impressions and a course of treatment, as it is relatively easy for respondents to present themselves on such measures as they wish to be perceived. Thus, clinical decisions should be supplemented by a thorough psychosocial history (which should include information gathered from collateral sources such as spouses or parents when at all possible), mental status exam (when appropriate), and direct observation of the offender.

Even with the advances made in standardized pencil-and-paper tools, such as those reviewed in this chapter, many measures of alcohol and drugs are scaled in such a way (e.g., uses three times or more per week) that precludes sensitivity when dealing with high levels of use (Liddle & Dakof, 1995; Waldron, 1997). For practitioners and researchers striving for measurement sensitivity in detecting change over time with heavy users, this creates a potential pitfall.

Waldron (1997) highlighted an alternative method that can be used to assess for substance abuse history, called the *timeline follow-back procedure* (Sobell & Sobell, 1992). This procedure is a structured interview technique that samples a specific period of time. A monthly calendar and memory anchor points are used to help the client reconstruct daily use during the period focused on. Whereas adult studies have found that direct self-report measures have high levels of sensitivity in detecting substance use problems and compare favorably to biomedical measures (blood and urine tests) (National Institute on Alcohol Abuse and Alcoholism, 1990), the timeline follow-back may offer the most sensitive assessment for adolescent substance abusers (Leccese & Waldron, 1994).

DIAGNOSIS

Following a complete assessment, the practitioner is in a position to make a diagnosis. Professionals can more easily communicate with one another about the issues a client faces by referring to a specific diagnosis to describe the client's problem. Additionally, a diagnosis can clarify the treatment plan; it identifies the problem and the client's appropriate goals and objectives.

One common diagnostic framework forensic clinicians and other helping professionals use is the *DSM–IV–TR* (American Psychiatric Association, 2000). The *DSM–IV–TR* operates on a multiaxial system. Although a client is evaluated on each of the five axes, below we focus our attention on the substance-related disorders that are recorded on Axis I and explore the differential diagnoses between conduct disorder, antisocial personality disorder, and psychopathy.

Substance-Related Disorders

The *DSM–IV–TR* lists approximately 120 substance-related disorders and clearly distinguishes among substance use, abuse, and dependence. "The essential feature of *Substance Dependence* is a cluster of cognitive, behavioral, and physiological symptoms indicating that the individual continues use of the substance despite significant substance-related problems" (American Psychiatric Association, 2000, p. 192, italics added). The symptoms of substance dependence are similar across the various categories of substances, of which there are 11: alcohol; amphetamine or similarly acting sympathomimetics; caffeine; cannabis; cocaine; hallucinogens; inhalants; nicotine; opioids; PCP or similarly acting arylcyclohexylamines; and sedatives, hyponitics, or anxiolytics.

In comparison to substance dependence, "the essential feature of *Substance Abuse* is a maladaptive pattern of substance use manifested by recurrent and significant adverse consequences related to the repeated use of substances" (American Psychiatric Association, 2000, p. 198, italics added). A key difference between the two diagnoses is that the criteria for substance abuse do not include physical tolerance, withdrawal symptoms, or a pattern of compulsive use.

Whereas substance abuse and substance dependence are classified as substance use disorders in the *DSM–IV–TR*, there are also substance-induced disorders which include two basic categories: substance intoxication and substance withdrawal.

Substance intoxication "results from overuse of a substance. Anyone can become intoxicated; this is the only substance-related diagnosis that can apply to a person who uses a substance only once. All drugs but nicotine have a specific syndrome of intoxication" (Morrison, 1995, pp. 62–63).

Substance withdrawal refers to symptoms that develop "when a person who has frequently used a substance discontinues or markedly reduces the amount used" (Morrison, 1995, p. 63). Substance withdrawal is typically associated with substance dependence (American Psychiatric Association, 2000).

Conduct Disorder and Antisocial and Psychopathic Personalities: Differential Diagnosis

Psychopathy is not synonymous with the *DSM* diagnostic category of antisocial personality disorder (ASPD; Losel, 1998), as "the *DSM–IV* criteria for antisocial personality disorder underestimate the individual differences in psychopathy-related traits found in criminal and forensic psychiatric populations" (Hare, 1998, p. 101, italics added). *Sociopathy*, used in the original *DSM* (American Psychiatric Association, 1952), is an outdated term lacking contemporary clinical meaning (Gacono et al., 2001) that is also inappropriately used interchangeably with the terms *psychopathy* and *ASPD*. The *DSM–IV–TR* defines *conduct disorder* and ASPD using behavioral criteria, in which a juvenile diagnosis of conduct disorder is a prerequisite for an adult diagnosis of ASPD.

Behaviors associated with a diagnosis of conduct disorder include aggressive behavior toward others, using a weapon, fire setting, cruelty to animals or people, vandalism, lying, truancy, running away, and theft (American Psychiatric Association, 2000). The *DSM–IV–TR* allows for coding a client with one of two subtypes of conduct disorder: childhood-onset type (at least one criterion characteristic occurs before age 10) and adolescent-onset type (absence of any criteria before age 10). A poorer prognosis is associated with the childhood-onset type. Conduct disorder may be diagnosed in people older than age 18, but only if the criteria for ASPD are not met (American Psychiatric Association, 2000). It is important to highlight the difference between juvenile delinquency and conduct disorder. An adolescent may be considered a "juvenile delinquent" after only one delinquent act. However, to warrant a diagnosis of conduct disorder, an adolescent must be engaged in a pattern of behavior over time that consistently violates the rights of others and societal norms.

Following their extensive review and critique of the literature examining the construct of psychopathy as it relates to children and adolescents, Edens and colleagues (2001) reached the following conclusion:

> Although we are aware of ongoing research that will improve upon our existing knowledge base, at present there are several reasons to exercise caution in applying the construct of juvenile psychopathy in clinical/forensic settings. In our opinion, clinicians may appropriately use validated measures of juvenile psychopathy to *aid* in making *short-term* predictions of violent behavior among adolescents if they clearly acknowledge the measures' limitations (e.g., unclear long-term stability and factor structure). However, measures of juvenile psychopathy should not be used to make long-term predictions of violent behavior, nor to make clinical decisions with long-term implications . . . . To date, there have been no published longitudinal studies of the stability of psychopathy, as assessed by the PCL or other assessment tools, from early adolescence through adulthood. (pp. 73–74)

It is critical that forensic clinicians and researchers take painstaking care in their diagnostic assessments of conduct disorder, ASPD, and psychopathy, as both false positives and false negatives could have serious consequences for both the offender and society. For additional information on the effective and differential diagnosis of psychopathic personalities, readers are referred to the following sources (Cooke, Forth, & Hare, 1998; Edens et al., 2001; Gacono, 2000; Gacono et al., 2001; Hare, 1998).

Comorbidity

In addition to assessing for the presence of a substance use problem or psychopathy, practitioners must be aware of the potential for other co-existing disorders in their work with clients (also referred to as *dual diagnosis, comorbidity,* or *co-occurrence*). For a variety of reasons, dual diagnosis warrants more attention in substance abuse treatment efforts with offenders than is usually paid. Mood disorders can contribute to a client's need to self-medicate with drugs or alcohol, which can lead to substance abuse or dependence (Khantzian, 1997). Additionally, other psychiatric disorders (e.g., post-traumatic stress disorder) might be aggravated by substance use, and substance-related and mental disorders can arise from shared biological vulnerabilities (Leukefeld & Walker, 1998). In fact, we believe that the topic of working with dually diagnosed offenders is important (and urgent) enough to warrant its own chapter (see chapter 8).

Once the practitioner has conducted a thorough assessment and has developed a diagnostic impression, a decision must be made as to what type of treatment modality and treatment setting is most appropriate for the offender. Conducting a thorough assessment with a client is a time-consuming process that is part art and part science. The practitioner must use counseling skills, such as active listening, while synthesizing a wealth of information into a format that guides clinical decision-making and treatment planning. We recommend using a variety of assessment strategies whenever possible to get the most complete picture of an offender.

SUMMARY

This chapter has reviewed assessment methods with substance-abusing offenders, providing an overview of the psychosocial interview. We amplified and discussed the importance of assessing for suicidal ideation among offenders and reviewed several standardized scales, including their psychometric properties and availability. Additionally, we provided criteria for selecting standardized scales with adequate psychometric properties for use with individual clients. Finally, we briefly reviewed diagnosing clients using *DSM* criteria, including the substance-related disorders, conduct disorder, and psychopathy. (Working with dually diagnosed offenders is reviewed at length in chapter 8.) It is critical to conduct a comprehensive assessment, as a good assessment serves as a roadmap for implementing the various treatment modalities and approaches discussed in the remainder of this book.

Certainly, the context in which the substance use occurs must be tapped by the practitioner, which makes some of the multidimensional tools reviewed in this chapter particularly appealing when compared to those that capture only substance use. Of course, validity is maximized when multiple measures, such as self-report, urinalysis, and collateral reports all converge to give similar results (Waldron, 1997), which in turn, leads to a greater degree of confidence in the ensuing treatment plan. It is to treatment that we now turn our attention.

3

INDIVIDUAL TREATMENT

Although group treatment is the most commonly used mode of intervention with substance-abusing offenders (Bureau of Justice Statistics, 2000; see chapter 5), individual treatment can address targeted areas such as depression, faulty cognitions, dual diagnoses, and "using" behaviors. This modality usually takes place between an offender and psychologist, social worker, or substance abuse counselor. It is rare that individual treatment is the only modality delivered with substance-abusing offenders. Rather, individual treatment is often combined with group or family treatment, pharmacotherapy, and case management. Additionally, many practitioners have a developed style of practicing and draw selectively from various approaches such as cognitive therapy, behavior therapy, and so on. Indeed, research consistently demonstrates that integration or eclecticism is the most popular theoretical orientation of U.S. psychotherapists (cf. Jensen, Bergin, & Greaves, 1990; Norcross & Newman, 1992; Norcross, Karg, & Prochaska, 1997, as cited in Prochaska & Norcross, 1999). Accordingly, rather than attempt to provide an overview of a multitude of treatment approaches and modalities in this chapter, we focus instead on a model of change and corresponding treatment recommendations that practitioners can use as a guide while integrating techniques across different treatment models.

Regardless of practitioners' theoretical orientation in working with offenders, we advocate that they operate from a stance of nonpossessive warmth and empathic understanding. We assert that a practitioner can be both client-centered and directive in his or her approach with an offender (cf. W. R. Miller & Rollnick, 2002).

Hokanson (1983) described *nonpossessive warmth* as the

> quality of relating to clients as worthwhile human beings, with unconditional acceptance of them as persons (although not necessarily condoning all their behavior). Relating to a client as simply a member of a diagnostic category, or in an overly judgmental fashion, or essentially as a nonperson who happens to display certain problems, all run counter to this principle. (p. 40)

Empathic understanding refers to the extent to which the practitioner understands what the offender is experiencing from the offender's frame of reference. Exercising these traits is sometimes easier said than done, especially when working with substance-abusing offenders who are manipulative or angry. Nevertheless, these components serve as the foundation of any practitioner–client relationship, on which everything else rests.

Beutler, Machado, and Neufeldt (1994) reviewed the literature that examines the relationship between therapist factors, the nature of the therapeutic relationship, and therapy outcomes and concluded that "Collectively, the quality of the therapeutic relationship, by its various terms, has consistently been found to be a central contributor to therapeutic progress. Its significance traverses theoretical schools, theory-specific concepts, and a diversity of measurement procedures" (p. 244). Beutler and colleagues went on to emphasize that "the therapeutic relationship is not a therapist quality but is a set of processes that are dependent on both therapist and client" (p. 244). Additionally, Lambert and Bergin (1983) found that the emotional well-being of practitioners facilitates positive treatment outcomes and, conversely, that practitioners with poor emotional health inhibit client progress. The degree of therapeutic alliance has been cited as important when working with substance-abusing offenders (Dansereau, Joe, & Simpson, 1995).

Gendreau and Ross (1987) provided specific guidelines for work with the offending population. In their survey of the correctional treatment literature from 1981 to 1987, Gendreau and Ross identified factors associated with successful programs, which include use of cognitive problem-solving interventions, rehearsal of prosocial behavior, matching interventions to client characteristics, and substance abuse treatment. By contrast, factors associated with unsuccessful programs include insufficient interaction between staff and clients, use of the medical model, poorly trained staff, a focus on punishment or psychopathology, and use of Rogerian treatment principles.[1]

---

[1]We assert that core Rogerian treatment principles, such as empathetic understanding, serve as a foundation for any therapeutic relationship, but must be coupled with more directive interventions to realize positive treatment effects with substance-abusing offenders.

Such findings are critical in guiding the work between practitioners and offenders. For example, suppose a practitioner tries to match an intervention with an offender's specific sets of needs and characteristics. (We expand on this process at length below.) A juvenile offender arrested for his or her first drug-related offense requires a very different intervention than the adult male prisoner who has a long rap sheet and scores high on Hare's Psychopathy Checklist (see chapter 2). The practitioner's efforts to strike a balance between being too compassionate versus too controlling will look quite different with these two offenders. One size does not fit all when it comes to treating the complex needs of substance-abusing offenders. In other words, "start where the client is." Accordingly, we focus much of our attention in this chapter on considering where the offender falls along a stages-of-change continuum and then matching interventions to that specific offender's needs. Additionally, we encourage practitioners to integrate a strength-based approach into their work with substance-abusing offenders (cf. Van Wormer & Davis, 2003), appreciating the bio–psycho–spiritual nature of addiction. In recovery treatment vernacular, "Addicts are not bad people getting good but instead sick people having the courage to get well."

We cover four primary topics related to work with individuals in this chapter: (a) a model of client change, called the individuals, families, organizations, and communities in an ecological context (IFOCEC) model; (b) gender- and culture-sensitive therapy; (c) pharmacotherapy; and (d) case management.

INDIVIDUALS, FAMILIES, ORGANIZATIONS, AND COMMUNITIES IN AN ECOLOGICAL CONTEXT MODEL

Many practitioners view substance use disorders through a biopsychosocial lens. An ecological perspective views individuals, families, organizations, and communities in the context of multiple social systems. These systems can be categorized as micro, mezzo, and macro as defined by the following list.

- INDIVIDUAL: Person, family, organization, community, and other entities such as legislative bodies subject to the change process in the context of the ecological system.
- MICRO LEVEL: Family (nuclear, extended, other), peers, and other immediate social contacts that encourage or discourage the use of drugs and promote or inhibit recovery.
- MEZZO LEVEL: Organizations, communities, neighborhoods and cultural, religious, social, athletic, and civic groups. Includes

shared cultural values and beliefs such as the appropriate/inappropriate use of drugs; the times and places (if any) that alcohol or other drugs are used; forms of substance use by youth, adults, and older adults; the role of churches and other cultural institutions in preventing or treating drug use; and the use of informal and formal helping resources to address drug problems.

- MACRO LEVEL: Societal prescriptions/proscriptions/prohibitions, governmental policies, institutional policies and their effects such as institutional discrimination, cultural values and norms that promote or diminish drug use and encourage or discourage participation in treatment and promote recovery; general population characteristics such as urban/rural, age, isolation, impoverishment, education, and income levels.

The ecological perspective (Bronfenbrenner, 1979; Gitterman & Germain, 1976) explains the etiology and treatment of human behavior as interrelated with the multiple social systems in which individuals interact. The ecological metatheory assumes that change strategies must be proactively planned and implemented across multiple systems to be effective. Thus, this model serves practitioners who work with substance-abusing offenders, as this population almost always experiences problems across multiple areas of functioning and across settings. Because the ecological perspective serves as a metatheory, it offers few specific change strategies. However, other empirically based models can be integrated with the ecological perspective to provide the change strategies needed to impact differing social systems.

Barber (1995) initially integrated the ecological metatheory with the transtheoretical model (TTM) developed by Prochaska, DiClemente, and Norcross (1992). The TTM is a dominant intervention model in health promotion and is widely applied in the chemical dependency field (Prochaska, 1999). Much of the original and continuing research on the model focuses on addictive behaviors. It offers an integrative framework for understanding and designing interventions for human intentional behavior change.

The TTM focuses on how individuals and populations adapt and maintain behavioral change. It is based on important assumptions about behavioral change and the types of interventions that can promote such change. Prochaska (1999) argued that behaviors change when practitioners proactively apply stage-matched interventions across multiple systems, which will increase participation, retention, and progress, and impact change rates in entire populations at risk for unhealthy behaviors. The stages-of-change model is the most frequently applied construct of the TTM model, and it offers the most research concerning the validity of TTM constructs (cf. Prochaska, Norcross, Fowler, Follick, & Abrams, 1992; Prochaska, Velicer, et al., 1994; Velicer, Norman, Fava, & Prochaska, 1999).

The IFOCEC model[2] demonstrates that individuals, families, organizations, and communities may be the targets of change and that each of these entities may influence change in other entities. In addition, though the stages-of-change model has been used to describe changing undesirable behaviors like drug use, we propose that it can also be used to identify factors that can prevent and mitigate substance abuse. For example, an adolescent may never seriously contemplate adopting drug use behaviors because of micro influences (e.g., family support and supervision), mezzo influences (e.g., community youth activities and church and cultural activities), and macro influences (e.g., laws that punish drug users).

Borrowing liberally from Prochaska, DiClemente, and Norcross (1992), the IFOCEC model contains six stages that individuals, families, organizations, or communities go through in changing an undesirable behavior, adopting a new behavior, or implementing an innovation. Each stage of change is reviewed below. The IFOCEC model does not prescribe intervention techniques that practitioners can use in their individual work with offenders, but it is flexible enough that practitioners can integrate treatment approaches with which they are already familiar into the IFOCEC model. Some techniques are illustrated below to demonstrate how common treatment approaches can be integrated with the IFOCEC model. Of course, these illustrations are by no means exhaustive. They are simply meant to encourage readers to think about integrating appropriate interventions or techniques at various points in the therapeutic process as represented by the IFOCEC model.

Stage 1: Precontemplation

In the precontemplation stage, individuals are unaware that they have a problem, and they have no intention of changing their behavior. "In order to move ahead, they need to acknowledge or 'own' the problem, increase awareness of the negative aspects of the problem, and accurately evaluate self-regulation capacities" (Prochaska & Norcross, 1999, p. 496). To use a familiar term, these offenders are *in denial*.

Prochaska and Norcross (1999) suggested that consciousness-raising interventions, such as sharing observations with clients, or confronting them, may help clients become more aware of the causes and consequences of their problem behavior. For example, a process known as *The Intervention* (V. Johnson, 1986) is familiar to most substance abuse counselors. The Intervention is based on the notion that substance abusers in denial will resist attempts to engage them in treatment; it consists of helping professionals and significant others (e.g., family members, friends) confronting a loved one in

---

[2]The IFOCEC model was developed by faculty (Dr. Clayton Shorkey and Dr. Diana M. DiNitto) at the University of Texas at Austin, School of Social Work. Barber (1995) initially integrated the ecological metatheory with the transtheoretical model developed by Prochaska, DiClemente, and Norcross (1992), on which the IFOCEC model is based.

a nonjudgmental and caring manner. The purpose is to make clients aware of the impact that their substance abuse (and other problem behaviors) has on their lives and how it affects people close to them.

Clients in this stage may also benefit from catharsis (expression of emotion; Prochaska & Norcross, 1999), indicating that practitioners must balance confrontation and observations with empathy and active listening skills.

Motivational Interviewing

A specific approach that practitioners may use to help clients in this early stage is known as *motivational interviewing* (W. R. Miller & Rollnick, 2002). TTM, and in particular the stages of change aspect of the model, has informed the development of motivational interviewing (cf. DiClemente, 1999; DiClemente & Velasquez, 2002; Rollnick, Mason, & Butler, 1999). W. R. Miller and Rollnick (2002) defined motivational interviewing as a "client-centered, directive method for enhancing intrinsic motivation to change by exploring and resolving ambivalence" (p. 25). This approach is client-centered *and* directive and is a method of communication rather than a set of techniques that focuses on eliciting a person's intrinsic motivation for change while resolving ambivalence toward change. Motivational interviewing rests on four general principles: express empathy, develop discrepancy, roll with resistance, and support self-efficacy (W. R. Miller & Rollnick, 2002).

Research during the past decade, such as the secondary findings from Project MATCH (Project MATCH Research Group, 1997), suggest that the authoritarian approach to prompt behavior change is less effective than are interventions like motivational interviewing that target internal motivation (Ginsburg, Mann, Rotgers, & Weekes, 2002). To date, three published reviews have critically examined the efficacy of motivational interviewing or adaptations of motivational interviewing (AMI; Burke, Arkowitz, & Dunn, 2002; Dunn, DeRoo, & Rivara, 2001; Noonan & Moyers, 1997).

Noonan and Moyers (1997) reviewed 11 clinical trials of AMIs (9 of which involved problem drinkers and 2 involved drug abusers) and concluded that 9 of these studies supported the efficacy of AMIs for addictive behaviors. In their review, Dunn and colleagues (2001) systematically reviewed 29 randomized trials of AMIs, examining the efficacy across four domains (substance abuse, smoking, HIV risk reduction, and diet and exercise), with the strongest evidence for efficacy found in the substance abuse domain. Finally, Burke and colleagues (2002) reviewed 26 studies that met their criteria for inclusion (e.g., controlled clinical trial), and they provide some of the following conclusions regarding the efficacy of AMIs:

- In the areas of alcohol problems and drug addiction, relatively brief AMIs (1–4 sessions) have yielded moderate to large effects and good maintenance over time.

- In general, AMIs are more efficacious than no treatment, and they are not significantly different from credible alternative treatments.
- AMIs are efficacious, both as stand-alone treatments and as preludes to other treatments.
- Many of the outcomes of AMIs, especially for alcohol problems, not only have been statistically significant but also appear to be clinically significant. (pp. 241–242)

To date, the most comprehensive application of motivational interviewing with substance-abusing offenders is a group program Graves and Rotgers developed called *motivational enhancement treatment* (Jamieson, Beals, Lalonde, & Associates, 2000). In its early stages of development, the outcome literature pertaining to substance-abusing offenders provides equivocal evidence for the efficacy of motivational interviewing, with some reporting null findings (cf. Amrod, 1997; Ferguson, 1998) and others modest findings (cf. Harper & Hardy, 2000, as cited in Ginsburg et al., 2002).

Node-Link Mapping

One other innovative intervention that has been used to enhance treatment readiness is called *node-link mapping* (Pitre, Dansereau, Newbern, & Simpson, 1998; Simpson, Chatham, & Joe, 1993; Simpson, Dansereau, & Joe, 1997). Simpson and colleagues have developed a series of treatment readiness interventions as part of the Cognitive Enhancements for the Treatment of Probationers Project supported by the National Institute on Drug Abuse (NIDA). These interventions are designed for use with offenders throughout the treatment process and are ideally used in groups of 5 to 7 participants.

Essentially, node-link mapping is a visualization tool, in which elements of ideas, feelings, actions, or knowledge contained within "nodes" (circles, squares) are connected to each other by "links" (lines) that are named to specify relationships between the nodes (Dees, Dansereau, & Simpson, 1997; Pitre, Dansereau, & Simpson, 1997). These maps are usually drawn by practitioners in collaboration with their clients during group or individual sessions.

Node-link mapping has produced modest positive effects across studies. Mapping appears to increase counseling efficiency, help clients focus their attention, and facilitate the development of the therapeutic relationship (cf. Czuchry, Dansereau, Dees, & Simpson, 1995; Dansereau, Joe, & Simpson, 1995; Pitre et al., 1997). Mapping has been found effective in outpatient methadone clinics (Dansereau, Joe, & Simpson, 1993) and in a residential criminal justice treatment setting that uses a modified therapeutic community approach with large-group sessions (Pitre et al., 1998). More specifically, an examination by client subgroups indicates that the following types of individuals benefit the most strongly from mapping-enhanced counseling: clients with attention difficulties (Czuchry et al., 1995; Dansereau et al., 1995), cocaine-using opioid addicts (Joe, Dansereau, & Simpson, 1994), African American and Mexican American clients (Dansereau, Joe, Dees, & Simpson, 1996), and clients who do not have a high school degree or GED certificate (Pitre, Dansereau, & Joe, 1996; cited in Pitre et al., 1997).

Treatment Readiness Manuals are available through Lighthouse Institute, a part of the Chestnut Health Systems (see more information at http://www.chestnut.org). The manuals are also available for downloading from the Web site of the Institute of Behavioral Research of the Texas Christian University (http://www.ibr.tcu.edu), where Simpson and his colleagues are based.

Approaches such as motivational interviewing and node-link mapping would also be appropriate for use in the second stage, contemplation.

Stage 2: Contemplation

Individuals are aware of the problem, and think about changing but have made no commitment to change. Clients in this stage are the most open to consciousness-raising interventions such as those mentioned above and are likely to be receptive to bibliotherapy and educational interventions (Prochaska & Norcross, 1999).

Presuppositional questions (Selekman, 1993) and miracle questions (de Shazer, 1988; Selekman, 1993) may prove useful to clients in this and the following (preparation) stage, as it invites clients to examine and evaluate their situation. Both of these techniques are derived from solution-focused therapy (SFT; Berg & de Shazer, 1991; de Shazer, 1985, 1991), which has been used with substance-abusing clients (Berg & Gallagher, 1991; Berg & Miller, 1992; Selekman, 1991), prisoners (Lindforss & Magnusson, 1997), and antisocial adolescent offenders (Seagram, 1997).

Presuppositional questions can be used to invite clients to think about change in a less threatening way. Selekman (1997, p. 61) provided the following illustration of presuppositional questions: "Let's say that . . . you were driving home from today's session and it proved to be highly successful, what will have changed with your situation?" Alternative phrasing for incarcerated offenders could also be used, such as "How will you know when you're ready to be released?"

Circular questions are often nonthreatening to clients because the questions are posed in such a way that one comments on a situation from the view of an outside observer (cf. Fleuridas, Nelson, & Rosenthal, 1986; C. O'Brien & Bruggen, 1985). Consider the following illustration: "How will I (or others, such as the judge or your probation officer) know when you know that you're ready to be released?"

The miracle question can assist clients with imagining change and with goal setting. For example, the practitioner might ask, "Suppose you go to bed tonight, and while you are sleeping a miracle happens and all of your problems are solved. When you wake up in the morning, how will you know that this miracle happened? What would be the first thing that you notice?"

The types of questions illustrated above may help offenders move into the next stage, preparation.

Stage 3: Preparation

Individuals in this stage take steps such as setting goals and priorities to change in the near future. These individuals are usually ready to change and need to set goals and priorities to help them do so.

Clients in this stage are going to be more receptive to treatment plans that outline goals, objectives, and plans of action. Stimulus control may also be used effectively with clients in this stage, which "involves managing the presence or absence of situations or cues that can elicit problems, such as not stopping at a bar after work" (Prochaska & Norcross, 1999, p. 502).

The scaling question (Berg & de Shazer, 1993) is a useful technique from SFT that can be used to set realistic goals for clients in the preparation (or an earlier) stage. Scaling questions are useful for getting a quantitative measurement of a client's problem at various points during treatment. Clients are asked to rate their problem on a scale from 1 to 10. For example, a practitioner might ask a client, "On a scale from 1 to 10, with 1 being terrible and 10 being fantastic, how would you rate your current ability to manage your anger?" Suppose a client provided a rating of 6. A possible follow-up question might be "Over the next week, what can you work on to get from a 6 to a 7?" This series of questions accomplishes three objectives: (a) the initial rating serves as a baseline measure so that progress can be tracked (and even graphed) over time; (b) the client is invited to set a treatment goal when he or she has to state what it will take to get from a rating of 6 to 7; (c) it encourages the client to take incremental steps toward change because he or she is being asked to think in one-week and one-point increments. Techniques such as the scaling question also encourage clients to "buy into" the treatment process. This is critical because it is important that clients feel a sense of self-liberation as they prepare for the action stage. Self-liberation is "the belief that one's own efforts play a critical role in succeeding in the face of difficult situations" (Prochaska & Norcross, 1999, p. 502).

In a critical review of all of the controlled outcome studies of SFT to date (N = 15; Gingerich, 2000), five well-controlled studies were identified, all of which showed positive outcomes. Two of these studies are particularly relevant here.

The first is a randomized study (Lindforss & Magnusson, 1997) that examines the effectiveness of an SFT network intervention in reducing recidivism for prisoners. Prisoners were assigned to an SFT treatment group (n = 30) or a control group (n = 30). Treatment lasted for an average of five sessions. The recidivism rate for prisoners in the treatment group was lower than that of the control group at 12 months (53% compared to 76%, respectively) and at 16 months (60% compared to 86%, respectively) postrelease. The cost-effectiveness of SFT in this study is supported, as the prisoners in the control group "incurred an expenditure of 2.7 million Swedish crowns more in prison costs than the experimental group during the follow up year" (p. 102).

The second study (Seagram, 1997) examined the efficacy of SFT in improving attitudes and behaviors, and reducing antisocial thinking and behavior among adolescent offenders in a secure facility. A matching design was used, whereby 40 youths were rank-ordered according to sentence and then alternately assigned to the treatment (n = 21) or control (n = 19) group. The majority of the sample (85%) had a history of violent behavior. Augmenting traditional services, the SFT treatment consisted of a group orientation session and three individual assessment sessions followed by 10 weekly SFT sessions, each lasting 45 to 60 minutes. Among the key findings were that the treatment group had significantly fewer reported antisocial tendencies and substance abuse. Despite these positive trends, the overall outcome findings in this study appear modest (Gingerich, 2000).

Gingerich (2000) cautioned that SFT is still in the process of moving from an "open trial" phase of investigation to an "efficacy" phase. Much more research needs to be conducted on the effectiveness of SFT before it can truly be held up as an evidence-based approach. Nevertheless, SFT techniques, such as those illustrated above, may be useful to practitioners in their work with offenders.

Stage 4: Action

Individuals in this stage make successful efforts to change and develop strategies to address barriers. This stage requires considerable effort on part of the client and is often where the noticeable behavioral changes take place. According to Prochaska and Norcross (1999), clients are in this stage if they have "successfully altered a problem behavior for a period of one day to six months. Successfully altering a problem behavior means reaching a specific criterion, such as abstinence" (p. 497). It is in this stage that one would most expect a client to stop drinking or using.

Cognitive–behavioral approaches to treatment are based on the proposition that behavior is modifiable through the systematic application of empirically supported learning principles (J. Smith, 1990). Beck, Wright, Newman, and Liese (1993) developed a theory regarding the cognitive processes of people who have substance abuse problems: They possess characteristics such as an exaggerated sensitivity to unpleasant feelings, inadequate motivation to control behavior, impulsivity, excitement seeking, low tolerance for boredom, low tolerance for frustration, inadequate prosocial alternatives for acquiring pleasurable feelings, and a sense of despair in obtaining those feelings.

Using tools from cognitive therapy (cf. Beck et al., 1993; Ellis & Dryden, 1996), clients in the action stage are likely to accelerate their efforts (hopefully begun in the preparation or contemplation stage) to explore faulty cognitions that contribute to their problem behavior. Examples of faulty cognitions that clients may address include the following:

- *Catastrophizing*—clients anticipate the worst happening and often take relatively minor events and blow them out of proportion.
- *Overgeneralizing*—clients believe that if it is true in one situation, it is true in any similar situation.
- *Magnification*—clients exaggerate the personal importance of current or past experiences, which increases emotional arousal.
- *Excessive responsibility*—clients believe that they are responsible for anything bad that happens.
- *Dichotomous thinking*—also referred to as *black-and-white thinking*, clients believe that everything is either all good or all bad.
- *Selective abstraction*—clients believe that the only events that matter are the failures, and this is often how they measure their sense of self-worth.

Toneatto (1995) has developed a cognitive–behavioral method for treating substance abuse called the *regulation of the cognitive state*, which attempts to treat substance abuse through the modification of "undesirable cognitive states subsequent to such consumption" (p. 93). Using this model, the practitioner's task is to assist clients to

- Become more cognizant of the parameters of their cognitive states. (This is done by developing an awareness of thoughts, feelings, memories, perceptions, and sensations regardless of whether these cognitive states are desirable, uncomfortable, disturbing, or pleasurable.)
- Correctly understand the nature of cognition. (The counselor accepts that these cognitions are real to clients but emphasizes that these subjective experiences are extremely temporary, unstable, difficult to control, and mostly harmless—although they may be unpleasant.)
- Learn to recognize the contents of awareness that are related to substance abuse. (The client learns to recognize which combination of cognitive states and environmental factors lead to substance use.)

- Learn to deal with unpleasant feelings without changing them with drugs or alcohol. (This involves learning that these cognitive states should not be viewed as dangerous and do not require a solution with drugs or alcohol; R. Alexander, 2000).

Toneatto (1995) determined treatment effectiveness by monitoring the extent to which a client uses substances following treatment. Where abstinence may be the desired goal, a substantial reduction in substance use is also considered evidence of treatment effectiveness. Equally important is a person's ability to cope with distressing cognitions without using drugs. Thus, both behavioral and cognitive indicators are used.

The NIDA-funded Correctional Drug Abuse Treatment Effectiveness project coded reported studies of treatment programs in prison, jail, probation, or parole settings from 1968 through 1996 (Pearson, Lipton, Cleland, & Yee, 2002). Meta-analyses were conducted on 69 primary research studies, demonstrating the effectiveness of behavioral and cognitive–behavioral treatment in reducing recidivism among offenders. The project findings confirm those from Izzo and Ross's (1990) meta-analysis of cognitive–behavioral treatment, revealing that cognitive–behavioral programs can significantly reduce recidivism rates. This was the case both for "the overall collection of cognitive–behavioral studies and also for the subcategories social skills development training and cognitive skills training" (Pearson et al., 2002, p. 490). However, like Whitehead and Lab (1989), their findings did not permit them to reject the null hypothesis for standard behavior modification interventions (e.g., contracting, token economies). Pearson and colleagues (2002) went on to speculate that "behavioral reinforcement programs will be verified effective if and only if they can develop and maintain strong contingencies of reinforcement in the natural environment of the clients, for example, maintained by parents (or spouses) and teachers (or employers)" (p. 493).

Stage 5: Adaptation/Maintenance

Individuals in this stage work to adapt and adjust to facilitate maintenance of change. This is the final stage in Prochaska and Norcross's (1999) stages-of-change model. Substance-abusing offenders work to prevent relapse in this stage and to continue to make changes in their lives. In this stage a practitioner and offender might work together to create a discharge (relapse prevention) plan for the offender, and more focused work on concurrent issues (e.g., trauma, marital difficulties, substitute addictive behaviors) can be explored and addressed more fully.

Stage 6: Evaluation

Individuals in this stage assess results and obtain feedback to continue the dynamic change process. Prochaska and Norcross (1999) noted that "relapse is the rule rather than the exception with problems such as addictions" (p. 497). This is why their model and the IFOCEC model are presented as spirals. Clients do not simply pass through these stages in a linear fashion. An offender that has successfully completed one treatment program may relapse and have to revisit an earlier stage. Indeed, in one study (Prochaska & DiClemente, 1984), approximately 15% of smokers who relapsed went back to the precontemplation stage, and 85% went back to the contemplation or preparation stage.

Selected Studies on the Stages of Change

There have been several research studies on the stages-of-change construct that speak to the construct's clinical utility and predictive validity (Prochaska & Norcross, 1999). Some of these are reviewed below.

In one study of 570 smokers, Prochaska and DiClemente (1992) found that success was directly associated with the stage of change that clients were in prior to beginning treatment. They found that clients that progressed from one stage to the next during the first 6 months of treatment doubled their chances of taking action (stage 4 above) during the initial 6 months of the treatment program and concluded that treatment programs that are set up to help clients progress through just one stage in a month can double the chances that clients will take action (cited in Prochaska & Norcross, 1999).

The stages-of-change construct can also predict who will remain in psychotherapy (Medieros & Prochaska, 1993, as cited in Prochaska & Norcross, 1999). In the Medieros and Prochaska study, 93% of clients that terminated prematurely were correctly identified, lending support to the predictive validity of the stages-of-change construct. The profile of the 40% of the clients that dropped out of treatment prematurely was that of precontemplators. "Action-oriented therapies may be quite effective with individuals who are in the preparation or action stage. These same programs may be ineffective or detrimental, however, with individuals in the precontemplation or contemplation stage" (Prochaska & Norcross, 1999, p. 500).

El-Bassel and colleagues (1998) have examined the psychometric properties and utility of the University of Rhode Island Change Assessment Scale (URICA), a 32-item assessment tool for people with substance abuse problems, on a sample of female inmates (N = 257) from a New York prison. Nearly two-thirds (63%) of the sample was African American. A focus of the study was to determine whether the URICA identified stages of change among substance-using female inmates. The URICA was found to have five subscales that correspond to the stages-of-change model: Precontemplation, Contemplation, Determination for Action, Action, and Maintenance. The findings from this study suggest that female inmates who are actively involved in the change process and those who have tried to change are more likely to be depressed, and thus, in greater need of support and treatment.

The URICA may be helpful to practitioners in their attempts to tailor interventions to an offender's current place along the stages-of-change continuum, including treatment matching (El-Bassel et al., 1998).

The development of systems change models emphasizes the importance of working with individuals in their environmental contexts as the most effective method of intervention. The ecological model, the TTM, and the IFOCEC model share several common assumptions that are helpful in formulating interventions and research studies. First, each can be used with many treatment philosophies, such as cognitive, behavioral, and cultural (e.g., Afrocentric) perspectives, as well as various other treatment modalities, such as therapeutic community and drug diversion programs. The three models may also augment and strengthen the 12-step or self-help approach that many offenders use in their recovery. Second, these models permit consideration of cultural factors which can influence drug usage by minority populations—for example, ethnic identification that can buffer ethnic minority youths from drug abuse (Brook et al., 1998; Oetting, Beauvias, & Goldstein, 1982). Third, they allow for clinical practice interventions as well as policy, organizational, and administrative interventions that might reduce the ill effects of addictive behavior, and they allow for systems other than the individual to be the target of the intervention. Thus, integrating the ecological perspective with the TTM in the IFOCEC model provides a useful theoretical framework to guide the work of practitioners, researchers, administrators, and policymakers.

GENDER- AND CULTURE-SENSITIVE THERAPY

Given the increasing number of female offenders and the disproportionate number of African American and Hispanic offenders in the justice system, it is critical that practitioners engage in gender- and culture-sensitive therapies with offenders across all stages of change.

Gender

The increasing incarceration of female offenders has had a particularly grave impact on women of color in poverty. By 1994, the proportion of African American women incarcerated in the United States was seven times higher than for White women. The rising use of crack cocaine among minority women in poverty, combined with Congress setting mandatory minimum sentences and "three strikes and you're out" laws, appear to be major factors.

The good news is that effective substance abuse treatment programs can empower these women to overcome their substance abuse, to lead crime-free lives, and to become productive citizens. Treatment is also cost-effective. It costs considerably less to treat a woman than to build a jail cell to incarcerate her or to pay for foster care placement for her child (see Exhibit 3.1; Kassebaum, 1999).

EXHIBIT 3.1
Potential Health and Social Savings From Successful
Treatment of Substance Abuse Among Women

- **Preventing new cases of HIV/AIDS:** An average lifetime cost for treating a person with HIV/AIDS is now at least $102,000, up from $85,000 in 1991 (Hooker & Bryant, 1993).
- **Preventing fetal alcohol syndrome:** up to $1,400,000 is spent on lifetime care costs for each case (Center for Substance Abuse Treatment, 1995, p. 19).
- **Preventing drug-exposed infants:** It costs from $48,000 to $150,000 to treat complications of infants born to addicted mothers (Health Insurance Association of America, 1994). The costs of caring for a boarder baby,[a] even if the infant has no medical complications, range from $200 to $500 per day, or up to $15,000 per month (CSA, 1996).
- **Reducing welfare costs:** An average of $6,000 per year is saved for each woman who leaves welfare and gains employment (Children's Defense Fund, 1995).
- **Reducing foster care costs:** An average of $3,600 per year is saved for each child removed from foster care and reunited with his or her family (American Public Welfare Association, 1995).

Note. From *Substance Abuse Treatment for Women Offenders: Guide to Promising Practice,* (DHHS Publication No. SMA 99-3303) by P. A. Kassebaum, 1999, Rockville, MD: U.S. Department of Health and Human Services, Substance Abuse and Mental Health Services Administration, Center for Substance Abuse Treatment.
[a]Boarder babies are infants under 12 months of age who remain in the hospital past the date of medical charge because parental care is not available. More than three-fourths of these babies are drug-exposed and over half are of low birth weight.

Influenced by the work of Quinney (cf. 1977, 2000), Radosh (2002) asserted that "women's crime is grounded in exploitation. Without exploitation there would not be crime. Nearly all of women's crime is related to sexual exploitation, abuse, poverty, and structural inequality" (p. 303). Women in prison are more likely than their male counterparts to arrive with a history of addiction to drugs, child care responsibilities, mental illness, sexual or physical abuse, and trauma (cf. Greenfeld & Snell, 1999; Morash, Bynum, & Koons, 1998; Radosh, 2002). Accordingly, treatment programs need to be tailored to meet the special needs of incarcerated women.

Consider the finding that in one NIDA-funded study (Rosenbaum, Washburn, Knight, Kelley, Irwin, 1995), women viewed pregnancy as a motivating force for entering treatment, to "clean up the baby" and to make other positive changes in their lives (cited in Rosenbaum, 1997). In working with such a client, the practitioner who can simultaneously operate from a strength-based perspective while viewing the treatment process through a stages-of-change lens would recognize the pregnancy as a potential factor for enhancing treatment engagement.

CSAT (Kassebaum, 1999) provides recommendations for tailoring treatment for substance-abusing female offenders, with the aim to provide the most effective service delivery system possible (see Exhibit 3.2).

In addition to providing gender-sensitive interventions, practitioners should also be familiar with and engage in culturally competent practice with offenders.

EXHIBIT 3.2
Recommendations for Tailoring Treatment for Female Offenders

1. **Each woman should receive a thorough assessment of her needs that is female specific and culturally relevant.** Very few instruments exist that are specific for women or even women focused. The important issue is to be aware that the assessment needs to be comprehensive and to include domains that are particularly relevant to women. Appropriate instruments, as woman focused as possible, should be used to obtain a complete criminal history; medical history; history of substance abuse; physical, emotional, and sexual abuse history; psychological history; and educational level.

2. **While a woman is incarcerated, a treatment team should do an in-depth assessment to identify the range of her medical, substance abuse, criminal justice, and psychosocial problems and develop an individualized treatment plan.** That plan should address all the needs identified in the assessment, including homelessness. Treatment services should begin in the institution.

3. **Each woman should be tested for HIV/AIDS and be provided with pre- and posttest counseling** as appropriate to state law, regulations, and administrative guidelines. In prison and jail programs for women, HIV testing should be available. The women need to be educated about HIV and encouraged to undergo HIV/AIDS testing. Counseling should be provided for all women tested for HIV/AIDS.

4. **Medical care should be provided for the woman through formal arrangements with community-based health care facilities.** This care should include screening and treatment for infectious diseases, including sexually transmitted diseases and hepatitis, and immunizations. It should also include obstetrical and gynecological care, including prenatal obstetrical services for pregnant clients.

5. **Substance abuse education and counseling, psychological counseling (where appropriate), and other women-specific and culturally appropriate therapeutic activities should be provided throughout the continuum of care.** Services should be offered in the context of family and other interpersonal relationships, including individual, group, and family counseling. Counseling based on individualized treatment plans should be provided for women who have experienced physical, sexual, psychological, and emotional abuse and trauma. Counseling based on individualized treatment plan should also be provided for relapse prevention.

6. **Family planning counseling should be provided.** This needs to include information on prenatal care, birth control options, adoption, and education on perinatal transmission of HIV.

7. **Training in parenting skills should directly involve the mother–child dyad and, whenever possible, involve other family members.** Women in treatment should be permitted and encouraged to participate in programs for their children, such as Head Start and Parent and Child Centers that incorporate parent participation.

8. **Interagency agreements should be developed with relevant child welfare agencies** to address the needs of the children whose mothers are in local correctional facilities and to help make possible regular visits from children to the mothers who do not have custody of their children.

9. **Formal linkages should be established with community providers for provision of all necessary services.** The services should include basic needs of food, clothing, housing, and finances; assistance in legal matters, family planning, and vocational/educational needs; transportation; health care; mental health services; and support services.

10. **Specialized services should be provided for the children of female offenders.** Children and other family members should be included in all levels of the

(continues)

EXHIBIT 3.2
(Continued)

services delivery network—in the continuum of prevention, treatment, and recovery. The program should provide therapeutic child care and child development services, including supervision of children while their mothers are engaged in treatment and other rehabilitative activities in the community.

Note. From *Substance Abuse Treatment for Women Offenders: Guide to Promising Practice*, (DHHS Publication No. SMA 99-3303) by P. A. Kassebaum, 1999, Rockville, MD: U.S. Department of Health and Human Services, Substance Abuse and Mental Health Services Administration, Center for Substance Abuse Treatment.

Culture

Groups vary widely in their vulnerability, their attitudes, and their methods of resistance to drugs (R. L. Collins, 1995; Korzenny & McClure, 1990). For example, in some parts of the country, Mexican American youths have reported receiving drug offers at a significantly higher rate than have White Americans or African Americans (Hecht, Trost, & MacKinnon, 1997). Holleran, Reeves, Dustman, and Marsiglia (2002) emphasized that approaches to drug intervention are more effective when they are grounded in the culture that they target. Research in this area must strive to avoid fostering stereotypes about traditionally oppressed groups (Holleran et al., 2002). Historically, when the "culturally neutral" interventions fail with certain populations, the underrepresented community, rather than the intervention, is often blamed (Marsiglia, Cross, & Mitchell, 1998).

Afrocentrism, a cognitive framework that is an ongoing process (Asante, 1988; Meyers, 1988), has been used with offenders. The Afrocentric framework goes beyond some of the culturally sensitive writings that appear in the literature. It incorporates the key elements of spirituality that are so central to treating addiction, as well as respect for tradition, life as a series of passages, importance of community ("we"), and importance of elders. Through the Afrocentric worldview, the offender is "encouraged to consider every aspect of his life, and to transpose the strengths of his historical roots into his present situation" (Jackson & Springer, 1997, p. 236). Meyers (1988) proposed a therapeutic process called *belief systems analysis*. Based on an Afrocentric worldview, this process is "a form of cognitive therapy in that it involves the process of knowing, and knowing involves both awareness and judgment" (R. Alexander, 2000, p. 83).

The Afrocentric approach has been applied with African American juvenile and adult offenders across settings (cf. Harvey & Coleman, 1997; Jackson & Springer, 1997; King, 1994, 1997; Longshore, Grills, Annon, & Grady, 1998). The approach has been implemented with African American juvenile gang members (Jackson & Springer, 1997) and with juvenile offenders referred for issues such as abuse and neglect, mental health problems, and delinquent behavior (Harvey & Coleman, 1997). It has also been applied with incarcerated and young violent (King, 1994) African American males, and with drug-addicted African American women.

Longshore and colleagues (1998) have integrated an Afrocentric approach with the stages-of-change model and motivational interviewing, as presented above, to treat drug-addicted African American women in the Engagement Project. This project assumes that its clients are in the early stages of change (precontemplation or contemplation) and works hard to engage the client in the first session. In addition to the Engagement Project, Jackson (1995) asserted that CSAT has underwritten a residential treatment program, called *Iwo San* (Swahili for "house of healing"), which was based primarily on an Afrocentric perspective. The Iwo San program entails a multistage treatment program for the women and their children.

Although progress has been made in recent years, little research has been done that examines the best practices for substance-abusing female and minority offenders (Longshore et al., 1998). As additional research in this area is conducted, it is critical that the findings be disseminated in a format that practitioners can apply in their efforts to become culturally competent helpers. Summaries of ethnic variables related to substance abuse can be found at http://www.samhsa.gov/oas/oas.html. Additionally, the Drug and Alcohol Services Information System, compiled by the Office of Applied Studies at the Substance Abuse and Mental Health Services Administration, is a primary source of national data on substance abuse treatment.

Pharmacotherapy is often used in conjunction with individual therapy and has received considerable attention in recent years by researchers interested in the neurobiology of addiction. As a result, we know more now than ever before about the neurobiology of addiction and the effectiveness of pharmacological treatments. It is this expanding area of treatment to which we now turn our attention.

PHARMACOTHERAPY

Some drugs are used to assist in the detoxification process, and several types of drugs may be used to help substance abusers recover from their addiction following detoxification. Such drugs include, but are not limited to, Antabuse, opioid antagonists, opioid agonists, and several somewhat unrelated drugs used to treat cocaine addiction or the side effects of cocaine use. These four types of drugs are briefly reviewed below, as are some available outcome studies regarding their use in treatment. First, a brief summary of the current status of knowledge on brain chemistry and addiction is provided.

Neurobiology of Addiction

There is a growing interest in neurological or neurobiological theories of addiction. There are about 100 types of neurotransmitters in the central nervous system (Abadinsky, 2001). A neurotransmitter is a chemical found in nerve cells that acts as a messenger by carrying electrical impulses between cells and along cell pathways—more than 40 chemical neurotransmitters have been discovered (Bentley & Walsh, 2001). Neurotransmitters that are associated with addiction include dopamine, serotonin, endorphins, gamma-aminobutyric acid (GABA), glutamate, and acetylcholine (Erickson, 2000). Some scientists now believe that impaired control over drug use may be caused by a dysfunction of the medial forebrain bundle, or "pleasure pathway," in the brain (Erickson, 2000).

The neurotransmitter dopamine has been given special attention in recent neurological research on addiction because of its role in the regulation of mood and affect and in the reward and motivation processes. There are several dopamine systems in the brain, but the mesolimbic dopamine system appears to be the most important in motivation (Volkow et al., 1999). Repeated use of stimulants (e.g., cocaine) or depressants (e.g., heroin) produces changes in the mesolimbic dopamine system. For example, repeated use of either cocaine or heroin can deplete dopamine from this system. Such a depletion causes normal rewards to lose their motivational power (Erickson, 2000).

Abstinence from cocaine or heroin after prolonged use may further decrease dopamine levels, and this may lead to a craving response associated with withdrawal in drug-dependent people. Relapse into drug-taking behavior is thought to be directly associated with this subjective craving experience, which results from decreased levels of dopamine (Abadinsky, 2001).

Agonist drugs are substances that stimulate receptor sites, mimicking the action of neurotransmitters and "fooling" the receptor into accepting it. Antagonist drugs inhibit the action of a receptor site and can counteract the effect of an agonist drug by occupying receptor sites without stimulating neurotransmitter activity. Thus, both agonist and antagonist drugs may be used in treatment.

Treating Addiction With Drugs

Treating a drug problem with other drugs has always been somewhat controversial, especially for people in the criminal justice system. Several of the pharmacotherapies described below are in experimental stages, and others are more likely to be used with offenders who are on probation or parole. The potential for abuse in a prison or jail setting eliminates some of them from being realistically considered as a part of inmate therapy. However, according to the White House's Office of National Drug Control Policy (ONDCP, 2001), methadone, naltrexone, buprenorphine, and levo-alpha-acetylmethadol (LAAM) are currently being used to treat inmates in some jails and prisons and thus warrant discussion here.

Antabuse

Disulfiram, better known by its trade name Antabuse, is perhaps the least controversial of the pharmacotherapies. Used to treat alcoholics, it is neither an agonist nor an antagonist. Clients usually take Antabuse once a day. It does not reduce the desire to drink. Rather, it deters those taking it from drinking because they know that they will become extremely ill if they consume alcohol. Even products that contain alcohol, such as mouthwash, can bring about symptoms. Antabuse-alcohol reactions might include increased pulse, sweating, a severe headache, and vomiting. Some deaths have even been reported. Thus, it is important that a client is completely detoxified before starting Antabuse. Criminal justice system staff have supported use of the drug, ordering many offenders to take Antabuse when appropriate. Offenders report to their probation or parole officer to take the drug under supervision, and some are required to crush the aspirin-size pill and mix it with a liquid so that they cannot hold the pill inside their cheek ("cheek their meds") until leaving the office and then spitting it out. Outcome studies on the use of Antabuse have been equivocal, with some authors (Fuller et al., 1986) doubting its usefulness and others (McNichol & Logsdon, 1988) giving a more positive review of its benefits in treatment.

Opioid Antagonists

Opioid antagonists are substances that bind with opiate receptor sites, either displacing an opiate already at that site or blocking or counteracting their effects, thereby preventing stimulation. Naloxone and cyclazocine are effective antagonists but also have significant side effects, such as anxiety, hallucinations, sweating, nausea, and a feeling of intoxication. Because of their side effects, these drugs would have to be used under medical supervision, a factor that makes their use with offenders unlikely in many situations.

Neither of these drugs reduces the craving of heroin addicts (DeLong, 1972). Naloxone is frequently recommended as a test for opiate dependence before admission to a methadone maintenance program. It has no effect on the nondependent person but causes immediate withdrawal symptoms in a heroin addict.

An improved version of the drug naloxone (Witters & Venturelli, 1988), naltrexone (trade name ReVia) is useful in treating narcotic overdose because it reverses respiratory depression produced by narcotics. Unlike methadone, which is a substitute for narcotic drugs, naltrexone reverses their effects. Also unlike methadone, it is nonaddicting. It defeats the effects of opiates by occupying their receptor sites in the brain. Witters and Venturelli (1988) stated that

> Naltrexone is best suited for adolescent heroin users with relatively short experience with heroin, for recently paroled prisoners who have been abstinent while incarcerated, and for persons who have been on metha-

done maintenance who wish to go off, but who are afraid of relapsing to heroin. (p. 331)

Naltrexone may cause nausea and vomiting; less frequently it may cause headaches, anxiety or depression, low energy, skin rashes, and decreased alertness. The manufacturer recommends it for use as an adjunct in the treatment of opioid abuse (Ginzburg, 1986, p. 5). Naltrexone has recently been found to enhance treatment outcomes of alcoholics and cocaine addicts (University of Florida College of Medicine, 1992), but more long-term studies are needed.

Buprenorphine, a drug currently used in the experimental treatment of opiate dependence, has a mixture of antagonist and agonist qualities. A powerful analgesic, it is related to the drug morphine but is much more potent. It blocks the effects of opioid drugs, but it can also create a physical dependence and mild withdrawal symptoms. Strain and colleagues generally found it as effective as methadone and argued that clients should have a choice between methadone and buprenorphine (Strain, Stitzer, Liebson, & Bigelow, 1994).

Other studies (Ling, Rawson, & Compton, 1994, p. 126) have noted that "some patients will have a level of opioid tolerance higher than can be achieved by buprenorphine because of its ceiling effect," suggesting that methadone or LAAM may be a better choice for them. Tests on buprenorphine are currently under way at Columbia University in New York in a program that is authorized to dispense government-provided heroin as a component of the experimental trials (Wren, 1999).

Opioid Agonists

Methadone was approved by the U.S. Food and Drug Administration in 1972 for treating opioid addiction (Rettig & Yarmolinsky, 1995). It is a synthetic narcotic drug that appears to be helpful in deterring addicts from pursuing illegal activities to support their drug habits, although it produces similar analgesic and sedative effects as heroin and is no less addictive. However, with "repeated administration of a fixed dose, methadone loses its sedative and analgesic effects. The subject becomes tolerant" (Dole, 1980, p. 146). There are approximately 750 to 800 methadone clinics operating in the United States (Ling et al., 1994). Nevertheless, methadone treatment remains highly controversial. Because the potential for abuse is so high, great care must be taken in using it in a correctional setting. Hanson and Venturelli (1995) summarized some advantages and disadvantages of methadone maintenance:

> The advantages of methadone over other forms of maintenance therapy are (1) It can be administered orally. (2) It acts in the body 24 to 36 hours, compared to heroin's action of 4 to 8 hours. (3) It causes no serious side effects at maintenance doses. (4) At sufficient dose levels, metha-

done will almost completely block the effects of heroin. (5) When taken orally, it does not produce substantial euphoric effects. Disadvantages of methadone maintenance include (1) The person taking it may develop dependence. (2) It will not prevent the addict from taking other drugs that may interfere with treatment and rehabilitation. (p. 486)

Methadone prevents a person from becoming "high" on heroin because it creates a cross-tolerance, that is, a person who becomes tolerant to methadone will be tolerant to heroin. However, it does not prevent the euphoric rush that comes by taking heroin. Many methadone clients have been found to abuse heroin as well as other drugs (Abadinsky, 2001).

Methadone is considered cost-effective in the sense that it may contribute to reduced crime (Ling et al., 1994). Nevertheless, some communities refuse to allow the use of methadone in a clinic setting for fear of attracting heroin users to their area. There are more outcome studies available about the effectiveness of methadone maintenance than about other types of pharmacotherapy, and in spite of controversies surrounding this treatment, it generally produces positive outcomes (Gerstein & Harwood, 1990), as these programs tend to be effective in reducing drug use and criminality (Snair, 1989), especially when combined with psychosocial services (McLellan, Grossman, Blaine, & Haverkos, 1993).

Approved by the U.S. Food and Drug Administration in 1993, LAAM is a methadone analog with longer-lasting effects (up to 72 hours) than methadone used to treat narcotic addicts (Gerstein & Harwood, 1990), and clients generally take it three days a week (Prendergast, Grella, Perry, & Anglin, 1995). However, LAAM takes longer to take effect, and this makes it less effective for diverting addicts on the street. Thus, LAAM may be best used with clients who warrant fewer clinic visits or who are in residential programs, whereas methadone might be better suited for clients in need of daily clinical contact. Long-term studies on the effectiveness of LAAM are sparse, but it has generally been found to be as effective as methadone in terms of reduced heroin use, employment rates, and arrest rates (McNeece & DiNitto, 1998). It appears that clients feel "more normal" when taking LAAM in comparison to methadone. A 1997 study of heroin-dependent people taking LAAM over a 17-week period indicated that they reduced their heroin use by up to 90% (NIDA, 1997).

Pharmacotherapies for Cocaine Dependence

No drug has been discovered that effectively treats cocaine dependence. Dopamine antagonists are available, but they "can produce serious and permanent motor disorders, unpleasant subjective effects, or increases rather than decreases in cocaine self-administration in experimental animals" (Winger, 1988, p. 125). However, medication may be used in adjunctive therapy with cocaine abusers as a way of dealing with the deleterious effects of the cocaine use itself or treating the underlying motivations for using cocaine.

Cocaine use itself may be a form of self-medication by people with certain deficiencies, especially deficiencies in neurotransmitters that affect mood and activity levels. Tricyclic antidepressants (TCAs), such as imipramine, may be used to treat cocaine depression in clients whose cocaine use appears to be a form of self-medication to ward off depression. TCAs are believed to act as cocaine antagonists by displacing or blocking cocaine receptors in the central nervous system (Spitz & Rosecan, 1987).

Because chronic cocaine use may deplete the neurotransmitter dopamine, causing a craving in dopamine receptors, a dopamine agonist, bromocriptine, is sometimes used to bind the dopamine receptors and reduce craving. Used primarily as a treatment for Parkinson's disease, bromocriptine does have serious side effects, including nausea, headaches, dizziness, abnormal involuntary movements, and psychosis. Rosecan and Nunes (1987) believed that its use is justified only in treatment-resistant cases in which recovery is hampered by severe craving. In laboratory animals the chronic administration of bromocriptine has produced toxic effects, including preconvulsive symptoms (Winger, 1988).

Desipramine was patented as a cocaine substitute by the National Institute of Mental Health in 1990. Used to wean users off cocaine, it does not have any of the serious side effects of cocaine and is believed to reduce craving (Kosten, 1993). It is most effective with people who also experience depression (McCance, 1997).

Lithium, a standard drug for certain mood disorders, is sometimes used with cocaine abusers with mood swings (either cyclothymia or bipolar disorder) that preceded their cocaine use (Abadinsky, 2001). Several other frequently used medications that are used for depression or bipolar disorder are used to treat cocaine abusers for those conditions.

New Pharmacotherapies

Acamprosate is one of several medications aimed at helping alcoholics curb their habit. Disulfiram blocks alcohol metabolism and, therefore, causes toxicity when an alcoholic takes a drink. Naltrexone (ReVia) is an opioid blocker that binds with the pleasure receptors in the brain, effectively blocking the rewarding effects of alcohol. Acamprosate, however, affects an entirely different system in the brain, the glutamate system, which becomes hyperactive during alcohol withdrawal and can remain hyperactive for up to a year of abstinence.

Acamprosate appears to function as a neuromediator, normalizing the activity of that system, specifically by inhibiting the release of GABA, in turn reducing the ill-effects of withdrawing from alcohol. The drug also seems to be tolerated better by a wider range of clients. Whereas naltrexone is processed in the liver and can possibly exacerbate already existing liver disease, acamprosate can be taken by clients with reduced hepatic function. Also, because acamprosate does not interact with opioids like naltrexone does, even those receiving methadone treatment for heroin addiction can take it.

A new opioid antagonist drug, nalmefene, which is structurally similar to naltrexone, also shows promise in helping to cut down on relapses in clients attempting to abstain from alcohol (Mason et al., 1999). Unlike naltrexone, nalmefene reportedly has no dose-related association with liver toxicity. Also, the new drug is said to have greater oral bioavailability as well as longer duration of action.

Mason and colleagues (1999) randomized about 100 patients to either oral nalmefene (20 or 80 mg/day) or placebo for 12 weeks. Besides drug therapy, all participants in the study also participated in cognitive–behavioral therapy. The investigators concluded that, compared with placebo, both doses of nalmefene produced significant benefits, beginning as early as the first week of therapy. Overall, the authors found that about 59% of patients on placebo relapsed during the 12-week study, compared with only about 37% of patients randomized to nalmefene.

Hundreds of other new pharmacological approaches to treating addiction are under investigation, and scientific advances are being made almost on a daily basis. Any practitioner working with substance-abusing offenders would be well advised to keep abreast of current research reports in the medical journals—and to seek advice from trained physicians concerning appropriate pharmacotherapies for clients.

Each of the drug therapies presented above should not be used in isolation. Rather, they should be used in conjunction with other treatment modalities. Clients should be closely monitored when participating in these drug therapies, especially in the early stages of treatment. One means of monitoring the progress of drug therapy is through case management services.

CASE MANAGEMENT

The adjunctive services of coordination and monitoring are called *case management, care management,* or *managed care.* A systems or multidimensional approach to providing services to offenders requires the remediation of employment, legal, family, health, and other problems. Many agencies have special case management units to assist clients with multiple problems. The clients served by these units generally (a) have problems that are severe and persistent; (b) have a history of involvement with the chemical dependency or mental health service delivery systems, or both; and (c) have had difficulty in utilizing available services (McNeece & DiNitto, 1998). According to Marlow, Marlowe, and Willetts (1983), case management typically consists of assessment, planning, linking, monitoring, and advocacy.

The monitoring function is especially valuable, because the early identification of new problems and the recognition of recurring problems can frequently prevent a crisis (Weil & Karls, 1985).

Case management activities originated in early-20th-century social work practice that provided services to disadvantaged clients. Most descriptions of case management include at least six primary functions: (a) identification and outreach to people in need of services, (b) assessment of specific needs, (c) planning for services, (d) linkage to services, (e) monitoring and evaluation, and (f) advocacy for the client system (Ridgely, Morrissey, Paulson, & Goldman, 1996). Workers are increasingly engaging in case management activity in their work with substance-abusing offenders.

Case management with substance abusers has gained more attention in the past decade, particularly among populations who have multiple, long-term needs. NIDA (Ashery, 1992) published a monograph on several case management models that have been used with various drug-abusing populations: intravenous drug users, methadone clients, HIV-positive drug users, drug-abusing pregnant women, formerly homeless women, youths, and parolees. Many other creative models of case management techniques, such as those described by Levy, Gallmeier, and Wiebel (1995), have been used to reach out to active drug users in a combined program of case management and support.

The most controversial aspect of case management is related to the cost control objectives of social services agencies. In addition to providing services to clients with multiple needs, public and private providers use case management as a tool to control the services used by clients and thereby the costs of providing those services (McNeece & DiNitto, 1998).

A wealth of recent literature indicates that case management services, when applied to most mental health or substance abuse treatment programs, are effective both in retaining clients in treatment longer and in leading to better outcomes for clients. Bigelow and Young (1991) found that, in Oregon, case-managed clients with a mental illness received more services, had fewer unmet needs, had a better quality of life, and required less frequent institutional care than did clients without case management services. In a study of severely mentally ill individuals who were also at risk for homelessness, Wolff et al. (1997) compared the cost-effectiveness of three different approaches to case management. Clients who were assigned to "assertive community treatment" (small case loads, advocacy, assistance with daily living activities) experienced a greater reduction in their psychiatric symptoms and were more satisfied with their treatment than those receiving "brokered" case management (purchase of services). However, there were few differences in the costs of treating clients. The assertive community treatment approach spent less money on inpatient services but more on case management and maintenance (food stamps, housing subsidies, Supplemental Security Income).

Gorey et al. (1998) reviewed the findings of 24 published studies in the United States and Canada dealing with the effectiveness of case management with the severely and persistently mentally ill. Overall, these studies showed that 75% of the clients who received case management services did better than clients who did not. Clients who received intense case management services (caseloads of 15 or fewer) were 30% less likely to require rehospitalization.

In research on substance abuse treatment, Siegal, Fisher, et al. (1996) concluded in a study of 632 veterans that a strength-based case management approach improved employment status, as measured by increased income and increased days of employment. Laken and Ager (1996) studied 225 pregnant, substance-abusing women and concluded that case management services (including transportation) improved treatment retention. Another study of substance-abusing women found that case management services improved retention in substance abuse treatment during pregnancy (Laken, McComish, & Ager, 1997). Similarly, a study (Siegal, Rapp, Li, Saha, & Kirk, 1997) of 632 substance-abusing veterans using random assignment found that strength-based case management services also improved retention in treatment.

Mejta, Bokos, Mickenberg, Maslar, and Senay (1997) studied a cohort of 306 intravenous drug users and concluded that case management services improved treatment access, retention, and outcomes. A study (Cox et al., 1998) of 298 homeless chronic public inebriate clients found that case-managed clients fared better than a control group on income, homelessness, and drinking. A six-month follow-up of clients in eight Philadelphia outpatient substance abuse treatment programs by McLellan, Hagan, et al. (1999) concluded that clinical case management resulted in decreased alcohol use along with improvements in medical status, employment, family relations, and legal status.

A five-year prospective study of homeless addicted veterans (Conrad et al., 1998) found that a case-managed residential care program reduced substance abuse, increased employment, decreased homelessness, and improved health during the year of treatment. However, differences between the program group and control group diminished during the next year. A review of the literature on "comprehensive services" by Platt, Widman, Lidz, Rubenstein, and Thompson (1998) found case management services to be effective in improving entry into treatment, retention in treatment, and treatment outcomes. They concluded, "case management is the most valuable of adjunctive services for substance abusers in treatment" (p. 1053).

Only one recent article (Volpicelli, Markman, Monterosso, Filing, & O'Brien, 2000) found case management to be less effective than another approach, called psychosocially enhanced treatment (PET). In this study, 84 cocaine-dependent mothers were randomly assigned either to case management services or to PET. The PET clients demonstrated increased retention and decreased cocaine use, compared to the case management clients. However, in this study, case management service was limited to a single 15-minute appointment per week, primarily to check up on clients and to make referrals. PET clients were provided access to a parenting class, GED classes, a staff psychiatrist, and unlimited access to an individual therapist. When the psychosocial needs of PET clients could not be met on site, referrals were made to outside services such as legal counseling. Thus, one might reasonably assert that this was not a fair comparison of case management services.

The importance of practitioners providing case management services for substance-abusing clients in the criminal justice setting is supported by Martin and Inciardi (1993), who stated that

> Drug-involved criminal justice clients often face a wider spectrum of problems than other populations targeted by case management, including the life disruptions associated with police and court processing, the perceived stigma of a criminal record, the possibility of lost freedom through incarceration, and the disruptions caused in work, school, and family activities. (p. 89)

They went on to argue that, if case management is combined with legal sanctions to enforce participation in treatment, it is more likely that clients will remain in treatment and thus receive needed services. Treatment Alternatives to Street Crime programs (see chapter 7) have successfully implemented this notion (Inciardi & McBride, 1991). Others also support the use of case management services, as it has been shown to encourage substance abusers to remain in treatment and reach treatment goals (Kofoed, Tolson, Atkinson, Toth, & Turner, 1986).

One recent study (Jenson et al., 1994, as cited in Jenson, 1997) followed 93 delinquent youths who received case management services in the Utah corrections system, indicating that the most common activity of case managers was the coordination of substance abuse services. Although case management has been found to be effective with dually diagnosed youths (Evans & Dollard, 1992) and with juvenile delinquents (Enos & Southern, 1996), little is known about its effectiveness in juvenile justice settings (cited in McBride et al., 1999).

As the prevalence of HIV increases in the drug-abusing population, it is imperative that case managers address this multifaceted problem in their work with clients. One study (Batki, 1990, as cited in Beeder & Millman, 1997) revealed improved outcomes in clients whose case management included interdisciplinary communication and treatment procedures, such as medical treatment of HIV symptoms and treatment of neuropsychiatric syndromes associated with AIDS. Beeder and Millman responded to controversy around HIV testing in early stages of substance abuse recovery by noting their experience, which suggests that if the need for the test is presented in a tactful, empathic manner, then clients do not leave treatment prematurely. They go on to highlight that making the diagnosis of HIV or AIDS early on in treatment can help clients utilize their resources and live an abstinent, responsible life.

SUMMARY

This chapter covered four primary topics related to work with substance-abusing offenders individually. Although these four topics were covered separately for clarity of presentation, it is important to note that, in reality, there is much overlap among these approaches.

First, we presented a model of client change, the IFOCEC model. It is based on the stages-of-change construct Prochaska and his colleagues developed. We amplified the need to recognize where an offender falls along the stages-of-change continuum so that treatments may be matched to his or her needs and strengths. Regardless of one's theoretical orientation, it is critical that practitioners operate from a stance of nonpossessive warmth and empathy. Certainly, the extent to which a practitioner experiences emotional well-being impacts treatment outcomes (Lambert & Bergin, 1983), and the therapeutic alliance is an important element when working with this population (Dansereau et al., 1995). We urge practitioners against developing such a "thick skin" that they cannot connect with offenders in a therapeutic context. Start where the client is.

Second, we reviewed gender- and culture-sensitive therapies, such as an Afrocentric approach. To date, racial and ethnic composition and gender have been given scant attention in the literature. In terms of treatment effectiveness, the majority of meta-analyses do not even mention these factors in the studies that are being examined. One of the few exceptions is the well-known review of the literature by Catalano, Hawkins, Wells, Miller, and Brewer (1991), in which out of 34 studies reviewed, only three mention findings on Mexican American juveniles and three report findings on African American juveniles. As additional research in this area is conducted, relevant findings must then be disseminated in a practitioner-friendly format that encourages helping professionals to become culturally competent.

Third, we provided a review of pharmacotherapy treatments, including Antabuse, opioid antagonists, opioid agonists, and some of the newer pharmacotherapies such as naltrexone. Given that methadone, naltrexone, buprenorphine, LAAM, and other pharmacotherapies are increasingly being used to treat inmates (ONDCP, 2001), this is an area that warrants further examination so that the challenges of using pharmacotherapies with offenders can be identified and solutions recommended.

Finally, the role of case management with substance-abusing offenders was addressed. It appears that case management is a cost-effective way to enhance treatment effects that should be considered for practitioners and administrators who desire a holistic treatment approach. Case management is valuable not only in augmenting individual treatment but also in family and group treatment.

4

FAMILY-BASED TREATMENT

A truism in substance abuse treatment is that the family is a critical factor to consider in the development of a treatment plan for the client (Springer, in press-b). Although incarcerated offenders may not have the opportunity to include their family members in their treatment, many community-based programs for offenders offer opportunities for family participation. Working with the individual client without examining the family structure, dynamics, and roles that are influenced by and influence the client's substance abuse is often insufficient. For example, the relationship between adolescent substance use and family system characteristics or parental behaviors is supported in the literature (A. R. Anderson & Henry, 1994; Denton & Kampfe, 1994), revealing that family drug use, family conflict, lack of parental monitoring, and rigid family rules are all correlated with an increased risk of adolescent substance use. The same is certainly true of adult substance-abusing clients. In some situations, particularly cases in which family members are also using, it may not be advisable to include them as a part of the treatment. However, when family members are not substance abusers and are willing to be involved, they can be used as a source of support to the person in treatment.

The practice of involving the spouses of alcoholics in treatment began in the 1940s, and by 1948 the spouses of AA members formed Al-Anon.

Subsequently, family systems theory, an extension of general systems theory (Bertalanffy, 1968), emerged in the 1950s. Throughout the 1960s, family treatment for alcoholism typically consisted of a concurrent program for the nonalcoholic spouse. Not until the 1970s and 1980s did family treatment gain the momentum that continues to date. As families of alcoholics gained more attention in the literature, concepts such as codependency (Cermack, 1986) and therapy for children of alcoholics (Ackerman, 1983) and adult children of alcoholics (ACOAs; Black, 1981; Woititz, 1983) gained popularity. ACOA support groups originally emerged in the 1970s under the auspices of Al-Anon. Today, independent ACOA and Co-dependents Anonymous groups continue to flourish.

In this chapter we discuss the importance of involving family members in the treatment process to examine family structure, roles, rituals, and so on as they relate to substance abuse. We present structural–strategic family therapy to illustrate an applied family systems model. Additionally, we present an effective family preservation model, multisystemic therapy (MST; Henggeler & Borduin, 1990), which has been used with substance-abusing juvenile offenders. Finally, we examine parent management training (PMT) approaches as a way to help offenders who are parents of young children.

FAMILY DYNAMICS AND STRUCTURE

This chapter rests on the assumption that families are systems and should be viewed as such by the practitioner. According to W. Snyder (1994), family systems theory "sees all aspects of a person's environment as a 'context' that creates meaning and influences the person even as it is redefined and influenced by him or her" (p. 13). A practitioner using a family systems perspective involves family members of the substance-abusing offender because of the belief that the interactions in the family are among the most powerful forces in a person's life. Another central assumption is that substance abuse, like any other behavior, takes place in a larger context of family and society. Accordingly, family systems theory encourages practitioners to assess the structure and dynamics of the family system.

The importance of examining the family structure and dynamics is supported in the literature. For example, exposure to family violence and parent criminality or antisocial personality have been cited as risk factors for the development of conduct disorder and delinquency (Kruttschnitt, 1996, as cited in Hoyt & Scherer, 1998). Additionally, L. E. Wells and Rankin (1991) concluded from their meta-analytic review of the literature that coming from a "broken home" or single-parent family had a modest effect ($phi = .05-.15$) on the prevalence of delinquency for males and females. Child abuse and neglect and ineffective parental discipline have been associated with both delinquent behavior and substance abuse (Hawkins, Catalano, & Miller, 1992; Huizinga, Loeber, & Thornberry, 1994).

EXHIBIT 4.1.
Questions to Ask of a Family With an Alcoholic Member

1. **Who is most affected by the drinking or drug use?** Is a son or daughter more anxious than a spouse? Is one parent more upset by a child's drug use?
2. **Is it really an addiction?** This question is always in the back of the family's mind, and while only the alcoholics/addicts themselves can make that determination, the clinician must also make this assessment and use the decision strategically.
3. **In what lifecycle stage is the individual who is drinking?** An adolescent drinker represents different family dynamics and requires different treatment approaches than an elderly drinker.
4. **In what generation of the family is the individual who drinks, and in what stage of the lifecycle is the family this drinker is affecting?** What developmental tasks have been accomplished by the drinker/family, and which seem to be arrested by the drinking?
5. **What is the time lapse between the onset of the early-warning signals of alcoholism and the presentation of the family for treatment?** How many lifecycle phases have occurred since the drinking began, and how have they been or not been resolved?
6. **How does the family think about the drinking or drug use?** Do they deny that it is a problem or think that it is the only problem?
7. **To what degree has the family isolated itself?**
8. **What is the family history of both addiction and recovery?**
9. **Make a detailed and careful assessment of the patterns of overresponsibility and underresponsibility in the marriage or family.**

Note. From "Alcohol Problems and the Family Life Cycle," by J. Hudak, J. Krestan, and C. Bepko, 1999, in *The Expanded Family Life Cycle: Individual, Family, and Social Perspectives* (3rd ed., pp. 455–469), B. Carter and M. McGoldrick (Eds.), Boston: Allyn & Bacon. Copyright 1999 by Allyn and Bacon. Reprinted with permission.

Bepko and Krestan (1985, as cited in Hudak, Krestan, & Bepko, 1999, pp. 466–467) provided a series of questions or issues that the practitioner should consider in assessing a family with an alcoholic member, some of which are provided to help readers think about alcoholism and addiction from a family systems perspective (see Exhibit 4.1).

It is also critical to assess for the presence of domestic violence. Over half of battering men have alcohol or drug problems (Hamilton & Collins, 1981; Pernanen, 1991). If the substance abuser has threatened the spouse or if there has been a violent incident, then the practitioner should make the appropriate referral (e.g., treatment program for batterers). The couple should not be seen together. Additionally, Al-Anon is not an appropriate referral until the spouse or partner is safe, because Al-Anon's message of "giving up control" is dangerous to battered women (Hudak et al., 1999).

The list of questions in Exhibit 4.1 is by no means exhaustive. However, it illustrates the types of questions that practitioners should consider when using a family systems perspective in their work with substance-abusing offenders and families.

Three points of family systems theory warrant mention. First, the term *alcoholic family* is used below because much of the relevant literature on families is about alcoholism. However, it is reasonable to assume that these concepts can be generalized to other drug addictions (C. A. Hawkins, 1998).

Second, the term *family* as it is used in this chapter is inclusive rather than exclusive. That is to say, it applies to all forms of families (e.g., nuclear, extended, gay/lesbian, stepfamilies, single parent). The client determines who is considered "family," not the practitioner. Finally, although we advocate that family treatment is a critical component of an effective and holistic treatment approach, we also believe that only those practitioners who have received training in family therapy should practice this modality.

C. A. Hawkins (1998) discussed three important areas of family systems theory as it relates to substance abuse: rituals and routines, shame, and rules and roles. Each is briefly explored below.

Rituals and Routines

Rituals are an important part of our lives. They include those "big" events such as holidays, birthdays, weddings, and other celebrations. However, families also have more frequent rituals, such as eating dinner together, going to church, and so on. Rituals and routines are key to helping families establish boundaries, roles, rules, values, and structure—in short, their identity. When these rituals are disrupted, as they inevitably are in families with a substance-abusing offender, it hinders the family's ability to function as a healthy system. When alcoholic families organize their functioning around the alcoholic member, the rituals are in a sense being invaded by alcoholism (i.e., ritual invasion). Ritual invasion has been demonstrated to play a role in the development and maintenance of alcoholism in a family (Wolin, Bennett, & Jacobs, 1988). Thus, the practitioner should explore with the family rituals that have been lost but that they may want to re-establish. The practitioner may also want to work with the family to establish new rituals and routines. For example, a homework assignment for the family might be to eat dinner together at least two nights a week as a way to help them establish this as a ritual for their family.

Shame

The theoretical and clinical literature on the relationship between shame and substance abuse for families has advanced in recent years (cf. Fossom & Mason, 1986; Potter-Efron, 1989). What is shame, and how does it differ from guilt? According to Fossom and Mason (1986), *shame* is "an inner sense of being completely diminished or insufficient as a person . . . [It] is the ongoing premise that one is fundamentally bad, inadequate, defective, unworthy, or not fully valid as a human being" (p. 5). People experience *guilt* when they feel regret about something that they have done, whereas shame is a painful feeling about one's self as a person. Fossom and Mason described a shame-bound family as one that functions according to a set of rules and injunctions demanding control, perfectionism, blame, and denial. The pattern inhibits or defeats the development of authentic intimate relationships, promotes secrets and vague personal boundaries, unconsciously instills shame in the family members, as well as chaos in their lives, and binds them to perpetuate the shame in themselves and their kin. (p. 8)

Thus, alcoholic families that are shame-bound are often cloaked in secrecy because they try to hide the alcoholism from others outside of the family (and from each other). "Secrets serve to perpetuate the addiction as well as the shame of the people involved" (C. A. Hawkins, 1998, p. 234).

Rules and Roles

"All families, over time, establish rules and roles that determine the values and goals of the family, regulate power and authority, specify how the family will deal with change, and establish patterns of communication" (C. A. Hawkins, 1998, p. 235). In alcoholic families, these rules and roles are often unhealthy.

All family members have roles, and they may have more than one. Some roles are obvious (e.g., mother, spouse, child); others may be less clear (e.g., enabler, scapegoat). The roles that family members assume help define the family's identity. When family roles become too toxic or rigid, family members and the family system as a whole suffer. Additionally, when a family member is incarcerated or in treatment because of substance abuse, other family members may have to take on new roles to allow the family to function. This can lead those members feeling frustrated, angry, or resentful because of added responsibilities and expectations.

A schema of family roles familiar to most readers is Wegscheider's (1981, p. 85) depiction of family roles in alcoholic families:

- Dependent (the substance abuser)
- Enabler (the powerless spouse or partner)
- Family hero (the overachieving child)
- Scapegoat (the "problem" child)
- Lost child (the isolated child)
- Mascot (the immature child or "class clown").

Of course, in large families, one role may be assumed by more than one family member, while in small families, one person may assume more than one role (C. A. Hawkins, 1998). The roles depicted above serve different purposes for the family system. For example, the family hero (frequently the oldest child) provides a sense of self-worth to the family through overachieving and perfectionistic behavior. In contrast, the scapegoat often acts out the family's problems. Such patterns of interacting and behaving come at no small cost. The scapegoat child may end up in the juvenile justice system due to repeated encounters with law enforcement. Accordingly, the roles that family members assume should be addressed in family treatment, with a focus on exploring what purposes those roles have served for individual family members and the family system. Where indicated, the practitioner may support family members as they struggle with relinquishing these fixed and rigid roles.

Now that we have reviewed some of the key concepts integral to family systems theory, an important question remains—How does one "wrestle family systems theory to the ground" so that it can be applied to actual families? There are several models of family therapy available. Reviewing all of them is beyond the scope of this chapter. Rather than gloss over several models of family therapy, we selectively review two promising family intervention approaches that are widely used with substance-abusing clients: structural–strategic family therapy and multisystemic therapy (MST). Our rationale for focusing on these two approaches is twofold: their popularity and their demonstrated effectiveness with substance-abusing offenders.

STRUCTURAL–STRATEGIC FAMILY THERAPY

A commonly used family treatment approach with substance-abusing clients is structural–strategic family therapy (Springer, in press-b). The structural and strategic family therapy approaches complement one another very nicely. They are commonly referred to together and represent a major school of therapy within which several specific models can be categorized. Structural family therapy was developed by Salvador Minuchin and his associates (Minuchin, 1974; Minuchin & Fishman, 1981) at the Philadelphia Child Guidance Clinic, including Jay Haley, whose work with Cloe Madanes subsequently led to the strategic approach (Haley, 1976; Madanes, 1981).

Like other family therapists, structural–strategic therapists view the interactive behaviors of family members as forms of communication. The therapy is goal-oriented and short-term, typically lasting 10 to 20 sessions over 4 to 6 months (Todd & Selekman, 1994). Therapeutic goals are consistently related to drug abuse, but they also should relate to broader issues, such as family roles and interaction patterns. A basic assumption of this approach is that problems are maintained by dysfunctional family structures and rules. Accordingly, a major goal of family therapy is to alter the family structure that maintains the substance abuse and offending behavior. For example, with juvenile substance abusers, a goal might be to restructure the family so that the parents are in charge. Some paradoxical techniques might be used, such as recommending that the family "goes slow," or predicting relapse. Paradoxical techniques give the client information or instructions that are contradictory to what the client expects (Goldenberg & Goldenberg,

1991), such as asking the family to continue or exaggerate their current behavior (Jordan & Franklin, 1999). A classical structural intervention is an enactment, wherein the family is encouraged to act out its problems in the session so that the therapist can intervene directly to help resolve conflict. Structural–strategic interventions aim to challenge the family's view of the problem (W. Snyder, 1994). One way to accomplish this is through reframing the family's situation. For example, a practitioner might point out that an adolescent's delinquent behavior resulted in getting the family help. Strategic techniques tend to be very direct.

When working with juveniles, structural–strategic therapists avoid the use of labels such as *addict* or *alcoholic* for various reasons. These labels can actually be harmful to an adolescent, particularly early in treatment before the practitioner knows how responsive the adolescent may be to treatment (Todd & Selekman, 1994), and studies have demonstrated that adolescents do not accept such static labels because of where they are in the developmental life cycle and what they value (Glassner & Loughlin, 1987). Adolescent development is typically marked by an impaired ability to realize that one's ideals are not shared by all others, seeking peer approval while simultaneously separating from the family of origin, and struggling with the dynamic question, "Who am I?" In implementing a structural–strategic model with substance-abusing adolescents, Todd and Selekman (1994) did not routinely refer adolescents to 12-step recovery groups when they believe that an *addict* or *alcoholic* label may be harmful. However, they did recommend making such a referral when an adolescent needs the support of such a group or when an adolescent is immersed in the drug culture.

In the early phase of treatment, the practitioner engages all of the family members in the therapeutic process. Stanton and Todd (1982) emphasized the importance of using a "nonblaming message" in the recruitment of families of heroin abusers into treatment. A couple of specific strategies that can be used accordingly are (a) to stress the need for an active and coordinated helping effort on the part of everyone involved in the substance abuser's life and (b) to talk about the effect that substance abuse has on the entire family system, such as family roles that family members may unknowingly assume (e.g., enabler, family hero).

Todd and Selekman (1994) have found that providing adolescent substance abusers one-on-one time with the practitioner early in treatment is helpful in establishing rapport. By joining with the adolescent substance abuser, the practitioner will not lose him or her when it comes time to empower the parents to set limits. Empathy and humor go a long way in helping the practitioner join with the adolescent client. It is also helpful if the practitioner has a good grasp of street language used by adolescents to describe various types of drugs and drug paraphernalia.

Goal setting, a critical task early on in family treatment, must be done with each family member. Each family member should be allowed to state what he or she would like to get out of family therapy. It is the practitioner's job to help the family see how their stated goals overlap and to point out common threads among their stated goals. It is also the practitioner's job to help the family establish goals in two major areas: substance use and interpersonal relationships, with a clear relationship between the two sets of goals (Todd & Selekman, 1994). Additionally, when working with adult or juvenile substance-abusing offenders who have been incarcerated, it is critical that the practitioner work with the family to help the offender and the family with the offender's re-introduction to family life.

Often, as therapy progresses, the family will experience difficulty translating its goals into action. Should the substance abuser achieve abstinence, other problems (e.g., marital) that the family has been "pushing aside" will begin to surface. It is crucial for the focus of therapy sessions to gradually shift toward such interpersonal issues. If the family is allowed to focus solely on the abuser, then the chances that the abuser will relapse increase substantially. To the extent that the practitioner is able to view the family as a system, these interpersonal issues will be addressed because the practitioner will be able to guide the sessions in that direction. By contrast, if a practitioner is stuck in a linear mode of thinking, that is, if a practitioner helps only the abuser, it is probable that the family will remain stuck in its old patterns of interacting and relating to one another.

Should the "identified abuser" relapse, a crisis will most likely follow. It often takes a crisis to make people change, so the practitioner may want to mobilize the family to meet the challenges associated with the relapse. It is important to utilize the family's strengths. If the family has made considerable progress, and a member relapses or reoffends, then the practitioner should point out that they have demonstrated their ability to cope with tough problems in the past and instill a sense of hope that they will overcome this obstacle as well. In other words, it may be more therapeutic to view the relapse later on in treatment as a temporary slip rather than as a permanent reversion to drug use (Todd & Selekman, 1994).

As the termination of treatment approaches, practitioners should consider longer intervals between sessions. The final sessions may even be treated as maintenance sessions that the family attends once a month to report on how things are progressing. We refer readers interested in this approach to working with families to several comprehensive sources (cf. Haley, 1976; Minuchin, 1974; Minuchin & Fishman, 1981; Todd & Selekman, 1991).

In the past decade, "considerable advances have been made in researching the effectiveness of family treatments for alcohol- and substance use problems generally and adolescent substance abuse in particular" (Waldron, 1997, p. 199). There are several recent reviews and meta-analyses of well-controlled family therapy outcome studies (cf. Liddle & Dakof, 1995; Stanton & Shadish, 1997; Waldron, 1997), but some of the earliest research examining the effectiveness of family therapy with substance-abusing adolescent can be traced back to Stanton, Todd, and their colleagues (cf. Stanton & Todd, 1979; Stanton, Todd, & colleagues, 1982) and to the work of Szapocznik and his colleagues (cf. Szapocznik, Kurtines, Foote, Perez-Vidal, & Hervis, 1983, 1986).

Stanton and colleagues (1978) studied the impact of a structural–strategic family therapy approach with drug addicts in a methadone program. African American and white lower-class male clients were randomly assigned to one of three treatment conditions (a family therapy group compensated for their participation, a noncompensated family therapy group, or a group that received methadone and individual counseling). The paid family therapy group demonstrated the highest number of days free from drugs at a 6-month follow-up. Interestingly, reduced drug use was found to correlate with changes in behavioral interactions among family members.

Structural family therapy has been found effective with drug addicts and their families. Stanton and Todd (1979) compared structural family therapy with a family placebo condition and individual therapy. Sixty-five families with a heroin-addicted son and 25 control, nonaddict families were studied. Structural family therapy resulted in a significant reduction in symptoms. The degree of positive change was more than double that obtained in the other two conditions. Furthermore, these positive changes lasted at 6- and 12-month follow-ups.

Alexander and Parsons (1973) compared strategic family therapy with client-centered family therapy, eclectic–dynamic therapy, and a no-treatment control group for treatment of delinquent behavior. Recidivism rates for clients receiving strategic family therapy were half that of the other two treatment conditions. Siblings of the strategic group exhibited fewer problems over a 3-year follow-up period.

Overall, however, the findings of outcome studies that have been conducted with alcoholic families have been mixed. L. Collins (1990) reviewed outcome studies of family treatment for alcoholism using behavioral marital therapy, systems-oriented marital therapy, and Al-Anon groups. The results were inconclusive, due mostly to methodological limitations of the studies reviewed.

Edwards and Steinglass (1995) reviewed the results from 21 studies that examined the efficacy of family therapy in treating alcoholism. They found support for the effectiveness of involving family members at all phases of treatment; however, no single family therapy approach was shown to be more effective than another. Family-based models of intervention have been found to engage and retain client systems in substance abuse treatment (Joaning, Quinn, Thomas, & Mullen, 1992; Santisteban et al., 1996). Marital or couples counseling has also shown promising effects for alcohol-using clients, but the short-term benefits appear to outweigh any long-term changes (National Institute on Alcohol Abuse and Alcoholism, 1990).

The effectiveness of family-based interventions with adolescents has been demonstrated in outcome research (cf. J. F. Alexander & Parsons,

1973; Aponte & VanDeusen, 1981; Gutstein, Rudd, Graham, & Rayha, 1988; Klein, Alexander, & Parsons, 1976; Liddle et al., 2001; Szapocznik et al., 1989; Waldron, 1997; Williams & Chang, 2000), demonstrating that "family therapy leads to decreased substance use and, when compared to alternative, nonfamily interventions, family therapy appears to emerge as the superior treatment" (Waldron, 1997, p. 229). The approach we review next, multisystemic therapy, has also produced positive outcomes with substance-abusing juvenile offenders.

MULTISYSTEMIC THERAPY

Scott Henggeler and his colleagues at the Family Services Research Center, Department of Psychiatry and Behavioral Sciences at the Medical University of South Carolina in Charleston developed MST (Henggeler & Borduin, 1990; Henggeler, Schoenwald, Borduin, Rowland, & Cunningham, 1998). MST is a family- and community-based treatment approach that is theoretically grounded in a social–ecological framework (Bronfenbrenner, 1979) and family systems (Haley, 1976; Minuchin, 1974). In fact, this overview of MST is included in this chapter because the "provision of MST is consistent with the family preservation model of service delivery" (Schoenwald, Borduin, & Henggeler, 1998, p. 488). MST is one of few scientifically based approaches for adolescent substance abuse treatment recommended by the National Institute on Drug Abuse (1999b) and the Center for Substance Abuse Treatment (2000). The social–ecological model views human development as a reciprocal interchange between the client and "nested concentric structures" that mutually influence each other (Henggeler, 1999). Furthermore, the ecological perspective asserts that one's behavior is determined by multiple forces (e.g., family, school, work, peers)—a perspective that has been confirmed by causal modeling of delinquency and substance abuse (Henggeler, 1997).

A basic foundation of MST is the belief that a juvenile's acting out or antisocial behavior is best addressed by interfacing with multiple systems, including the adolescent's family, peers, school, teachers, neighbors, and others (T. L. Brown, Borduin, & Henggeler, 2001). Thus, the MST practitioner interfaces not just with the adolescent, but also with various individuals and settings that influence the adolescent's life.

More specifically, there are nine guiding principles of MST (Schoenwald et al., 1998, pp. 488–489) that the MST practitioner should follow (see Exhibit 4.2). These principles can be used to guide practice with substance-abusing juvenile offenders.

Henggeler (1999) has summarized the MST model of service delivery. The MST practitioner typically carries a low caseload of 5 to 6 families, which allows him or her to work more intensively with the client than in tradi-

EXHIBIT 4.2.
Guiding Principles of Multisystemic Therapy

1. The primary purpose of assessment is to understand the "fit" between the identified problems and their broader systemic context.
2. Therapeutic contacts should emphasize the positive and should use systemic strengths as levers of change.
3. Interventions should be designed to promote responsible behavior and decrease irresponsible behavior among family members.
4. Interventions should be present-focused and action-oriented, targeting specific and well-defined problems.
5. Interventions should target sequences of behavior within and between multiple systems.
6. Interventions should be developmentally appropriate and fit the developmental needs of the youth.
7. Interventions should be designed to require daily or weekly effort by family members.
8. Intervention efficacy is evaluated continuously from multiple perspectives.
9. Interventions should be designed to promote treatment generalization and long-term maintenance of therapeutic change.

Note. From "Multisystemic Therapy: Changing the Natural and Service Ecologies of Adolescents and Families," by S. K. Schoenwald, C. M. Borduin, and S. W. Henggeler, 1998, in *Outcomes for Children and Youth with Emotional and Behavioral Disorders and Their Families: Programs and Evaluation Best Practice* by M. H. Epstein, K. Kutash, and A. Duchnowski (Eds.), pp. 485–511. Austin, TX: Pro-Ed. Copyright 1998 by Pro-Ed. Reprinted with permission.

tional approaches (2–15 hours per week rather than 1 hour per week). The practitioner is available to the client system 24 hours a day, 7 days a week. Services are delivered in the client's natural environment, such as the client's home or a neighborhood center. Treatment is typically time-limited, lasting 4 to 6 months. For a detailed exposition on implementing MST with high-risk youths, readers are referred to sources that describe MST in detail (cf. Henggeler & Borduin, 1990).

An appealing aspect of MST is that it is driven by evidence-based practice. The choice of modality for a given client system is based largely on the empirical literature supporting its efficacy. According to Henggeler (1999), MST utilizes treatment approaches that are pragmatic, problem-focused, and have some empirical support, including, but not limited to, strategic family therapy (Haley, 1976), structural family therapy (Minuchin, 1974), behavioral parent training (Munger, 1993), and cognitive–behavior therapy (Kendall & Braswell, 1993).

MST is being used in approximately 25 sites across the United States and Canada (cf. Schoenwald & Rowland, 2002; Schoenwald et al., 1998). It remains to be seen whether the treatment fidelity (consistent implementation) of MST can be maintained across sites. Accordingly, a recently initiated study funded by the National Institute of Mental Health includes an examination of the transportability of MST to real-world practice settings, and the U.S. Department of Justice's Office of Juvenile Justice and Delinquency Prevention has funded research aimed at the successful dissemination of MST (Schoenwald & Rowland, 2002).

Numerous studies have been conducted on the effectiveness of MST. Three early clinical trials (Borduin, Henggeler, Blaske, & Stein, 1990; Brunk, Henggeler, & Whelan, 1987; Henggeler et al., 1986) demonstrated the initial effectiveness of MST with high-risk youths, including inner-city juvenile offenders and adolescent sexual offenders.

Two well-known randomized controlled studies (Borduin et al., 1995; Henggeler, Melton, & Smith, 1992) examined substance abuse–related outcomes with juvenile offenders (Henggeler et al., 1991). The first, the Simpsonville, South Carolina, study (Henggeler et al., 1992) involved violent and chronic juvenile offenders ($N = 84$). Findings from this study revealed that MST significantly reduced adolescent reports of alcohol and marijuana use following treatment. The results from this study also showed that MST was effective at reducing rates of criminal activity. At follow-up (59 weeks), juvenile offenders who received MST had significantly fewer arrests than did juveniles who received traditional services. Additionally, families receiving MST reported greater cohesion, whereas families involved in traditional services reported decreased cohesion. Finally, a 2.4-year follow-up found that MST doubled the percentage of youths who did not relapse when compared to traditional services (Henggeler, Melton, Smith, Schoenwald, & Hanely, 1993).

The second study (Borduin et al., 1995), the Columbia, Missouri, project, compared the effectiveness of MST with individual therapy. Juvenile offenders were assigned to receive either MST ($n = 92$) or individual treatment ($n = 84$). Families receiving MST demonstrated more positive changes in family interactions than did the comparison group families. Results from a 4-year follow-up of recidivism revealed that youths who completed MST ($n = 77$) were significantly less likely to be rearrested (22.1%) than were those youths who completed individual therapy ($n = 63$, 71.4% rearrested). More specifically, substance-related arrests at this 4-year follow-up were 4% for MST youths, compared to 16% for the individual therapy youths.

More recently, Henggeler, Clingempeel, Brondino, and Pickrell (2002) reported the findings of a 4-year outcome study from a randomized clinical trial of MST that was conducted in the mid-1990s. Henggeler and colleagues used a multimethod (self-report, biological, and archival measures) assessment battery to monitor criminal behavior, illicit drug use, and psychiatric symptoms among substance-abusing juvenile offenders ($n = 80$, with 68% of original sample participating in this 4-year follow-up). Juveniles receiving MST demonstrated significant long-term treatment effects for aggressive criminal activity but not for psychiatric symptoms or property crimes. A plausible explanation for the null findings with regard to property crimes is that family-based interventions exert differential effects on overt (e.g., aggressive crimes) and covert (e.g., property crimes) behaviors (Eddy, Dishion, & Stoolmiller, 1998). Findings regarding illicit drug use were mixed, with biological measures (urine and head hair samples) indicating a (statistically significant) 100% increase in marijuana abstinence and a (nonstatistically significant) 33% increase in cocaine abstinence. However, self-report measures failed to differentiate the treatment conditions. Such mixed findings amplify the need to promote treatment fidelity, potentially with a heavier focus on drug use (Henggeler et al., 2002).

According to T. L. Brown and colleagues (2001),

> To date, MST is the only treatment for serious delinquent behavior that has demonstrated both short-term and long-term treatment effects in randomized, controlled clinical trials with violent and chronic juvenile offenders and their families from various cultural and ethnic backgrounds. (p. 458)

MST has been found to reduce substance use, as well as arrests for substance-related offenses (Henggeler et al., 1991).

Finally, the potential cost-savings of MST have been demonstrated with substance-abusing juvenile offenders. Schoenwald, Ward, Henggeler, Pickrel, and Patel (1996) demonstrated that the costs associated with delivering MST to substance-abusing and substance-dependent juvenile offenders were nearly offset by the savings incurred as a result of reductions in out-of-home placement days. In its evaluation of 16 programs, the Washington State Institute for Public Policy (1998) cited MST as the most cost-effective intervention for juvenile offenders.

TRAINING FOR INCARCERATED PARENTS WITH YOUNG CHILDREN

Children of incarcerated parents are five to six times more likely to go to prison than their peers (Johnston, 1995). In 1999, at least 126,100 children had mothers in prison, with a mean age of 8 years for all children with parents in prison (Mumola, 2000, as cited in Radosh, 2002).

The impact of a mother or father being incarcerated can be traumatic for the child of the offender. Children may experience a variety of problems, including but not limited to, profound sadness, a sense of loss similar to a death in the family, a drop in school performance, stigma associated with the imprisonment of a family member, a loss of self-esteem, eating problems, attachment disorders, and aggressive behavior (Gabel, 1992; Johnston, 1995; Sack, Seidler, & Thomas, 1976; Springer, Pomeroy, & Johnson, 1999).

Various modalities and programs are available to help this special population (cf. Springer, Lynch, & Rubin, 2000). Here our focus is on parent management training (PMT) approaches. *PMT* is a summary term that describes a therapeutic strategy in which parents are trained to use skills for managing their child's problem behavior (Kazdin, 1997). PMT programs may differ in focus and therapeutic strategies used, but they all share the goal of enhancing parental control over children's behavior (Barkley, 1987; Eyberg, 1988; Forehand & McMahon, 1981; Patterson, Reid, Jones, & Conger, 1975; Webster-Stratton, 1987).

Although an extensive review is not possible, we briefly cover four well-known parenting training programs, namely behavior management parent training (BMPT), child relationship enhancement family therapy (CREFT), responsive parent therapy (RPT), and Systematic Training for Effective Parenting (STEP). Both BMPT and CREFT began approximately 30 years ago as interventions designed to extend to parents with emotionally disturbed children parenting skills originally used by therapists (Cavell, 2000).

Behavior Management Parent Training

BMPT has dominated the parent training literature, with one review of parent-training research finding that 89% of studies emphasized a behavioral approach (Rogers Wiese, 1992). Although there are variations of BMPT programs (cf. Barkley, 1987; Eyberg, 1988; Forehand & McMahon, 1981; Patterson et al., 1975; Webster-Stratton & Herbert, 1994), most follow a two-stage model based on the work of Hanf (1969). The first stage consists of training parents to attend to their child's desired behaviors in a positive manner and to describe it in a way that is free of questions, commands, and criticism. The second stage focuses on teaching parents to give effective, direct commands to their child and how to use timeout (Cavell, 2000).

Some findings support the effectiveness of BMPT, and others do not (cf. Dumas, 1989; Hughes & Cavell, 1994; Kazdin, 1987; Patterson, 1985). Nevertheless, the effectiveness of BMPT is well documented and in many respects, impressive. In a recent meta-analysis, Serketich and Dumas (1996) concluded that "the results of the meta-analysis largely provide support for the effectiveness of [BMPT] in comparison to no intervention" (p. 181). However, most parent-training outcome studies lack any follow-up data (Cavell, 2000).

Child Relationship Enhancement Family Therapy

CREFT, originally named *filial therapy* (B. Guerney, 1964), was designed to teach parents the skills of child-centered play therapists (L. F. Guerney, 1983). Intended for use with children ages 3 to 10 years, CREFT is composed of four phases: (a) training in play therapy, (b) home play sessions, (c) transfer and generalization, and (d) phase out. To date, the empirical support for CREFT is scant, with most studies being either anecdotal or quasi-experimental in nature. "Without stronger empirical support for relationship enhancement approaches to parent training, clinicians cannot afford to rely solely on CREFT to meet the needs of aggressive children and their families" (Cavell, 2000, p. 47).

Responsive Parent Therapy

Cavell (2000) has blended key aspects of BMPT, CREFT, attachment theory, and structural family therapy to form RPT. This appears to be a promising approach in working with parents whose children are aggressive and difficult. RPT is similar to MST (described earlier in this chapter) in that it is based on the assumption that problem behaviors in children should be addressed through more than one system.

"In RPT, parenting goals, parenting skills, parent–child relationship issues, family system variables, and parents' overall level of health and well-being are all considered grist for the therapeutic mill" (Cavell, 2000, p. 55). The focus of RPT is to teach parents the skills needed to enhance the quality of the parent–child relationship while simultaneously establishing and maintaining an appropriate family structure. The RPT approach to working with parents involves seven components: acceptance, containment, prosocial values, parenting goals, family structure, parental self-care, and the establishment of a strong therapeutic alliance between practitioner and parents. For a detailed description of RPT, readers are referred to Cavell's (2000) book covering this approach.

In a preliminary trial examining the effectiveness of RPT compared to a BMPT video modeling condition, Cavell (2000) reported generally positive findings favoring the RPT approach. Although the findings should be interpreted with caution given the small sample size and the lack of external measures of improvement, RPT appears to be a promising PMT approach.

We found no studies that examined the effectiveness of BMPT, CREFT, or RPT with incarcerated parents with children. However, one other well-known parenting education approach, STEP, has been successfully implemented with both incarcerated female (Showers, 1993) and male (Wilczak & Markstrom, 1999) parents.

Systematic Training for Effective Parenting

STEP (Dinkmeyer & McKay, 1976) is a group-oriented, Adlerian-based parent education program. The necessary group leadership skills are provided in the leader's manual and include structuring, universalizing, linking, providing feedback, focusing on the positive, and task setting. Topics for the curriculum include understanding children's behavior and misbehavior, understanding more about your child and about yourself as a parent, providing encouragement, communicating, applying natural and logical consequences, having family meetings, and developing confidence. It is recommended that

STEP groups have no more than 12 members, with each session usually lasting 1 1/2–2 hours.

Showers (1993) examined the effectiveness of a parenting education curriculum based on the STEP program by comparing women who completed the 10-week curriculum ($n = 203$) with women who were released without taking the classes ($n = 275$). Using the Child Management Behavior Survey, which assesses knowledge about child development and child behavior management techniques, Showers noted significant improvements for both White and African American women in the experimental group but not those in the comparison group. Additionally, recidivism rates were markedly lower for the experimental group (1%) than for the comparison group (19%).

Wilczak and Markstrom (1999) found that an 8-session STEP program had a positive impact on inmate fathers' parental knowledge and efficacy. Inmate fathers in the STEP program experienced an overall increased satisfaction with their parenting, whereas inmate fathers in the control group showed no significant changes.

In recent years, practitioners and researchers have certainly given more attention to incarcerated parents and their children. Despite these gains, research regarding the effectiveness of parent training approaches with incarcerated parents is in its infancy.

SUMMARY

This chapter has reviewed family dynamics, structures, and rules that are commonly found in families with a substance-abusing family member. It is critical that practitioners include these factors in any family assessment. Given that more than half of battering men have alcohol or drug problems (Pernanen, 1991), practitioners should always assess for the presence of domestic violence as well as other forms of abuse (e.g., sexual, physical).

We presented two promising approaches to family treatment with substance abusers: structural–strategic family therapy and MST. Empirical evidence supports the effectiveness of both approaches with substance-abusing juvenile offenders over any other family-based intervention. Accordingly, we encourage practitioners to consider integrating these modalities into their work with families of juvenile offenders.

Additionally, we reviewed PMT approaches. Although BMPT and RPT have potential as interventions for incarcerated parents with aggressive children, STEP is the only parent training approach to date that has been demonstrated effective specifically with the offending population. We encourage PMT researchers to continue their efforts to demonstrate the effectiveness of this modality across populations and settings.

Although family therapy is a critical component to the effective treatment of substance-abusing offenders, it should be practiced only by practitioners with specialized training. An additional word of caution for agencies that are primarily individual oriented: There may be challenges to introducing family therapy as a modality into the therapeutic milieu, including disorientation of staff and problems with administrative procedures (Haley, 1975), as well as obtaining third-party reimbursement for family treatment.

5

GROUP INTERVENTION

Group counseling is often chemical dependency counselors' treatment of choice; it can take the form of support groups, psychoeducational groups, and interactional therapeutic groups. Such groups can be conducted in out-patient and inpatient settings, including settings within the criminal justice system, and can be closed-ended or open-ended. While approaches to group therapy may vary, according to Flores (1988),

> Most professionals who work with alcoholics and addicts on a sustained basis agree that group therapy offers the chemically dependent individual unique opportunities (1) to share and to identify with others who are going through similar problems; (2) to understand their own attitudes toward addiction and their defenses against giving up alcohol and drugs by confronting similar attitudes and defenses in others; and (3) to learn to communicate needs and feelings more directly." (p. 7)

Working with group members in the criminal justice system takes on a different connotation than working with members in the community. In the criminal justice setting, the group worker is bound by structural constraints, policies, and laws, as we illustrate below. Nevertheless, the primary objective remains the same. The worker should focus on the strengths of the indi-vidual, consider group exercises that will emphasize these strengths, and fos-ter cohesion within the group.

87

This chapter provides guidelines for and illustrations of conducting interactional group therapy with substance-abusing offenders, with a focus on controlled settings. We address a common approach used with juvenile delinquents in therapeutic community settings, positive peer culture (PPC), along with two other approaches, Equipping Youth to Help One Another (EQUIP) and aggression replacement training (ART). EQUIP incorporates into the PPC approach a multicomponent skills training (ART) to provide a more structured format for developing a positive youth group culture. Additionally, we explore the use of psychoeducational and multifamily therapy groups approaches with substance-abusing offenders. Finally, we cover self-help programs such as Alcoholics Anonymous (AA).

GROUP THERAPY

We feel it important to begin this section by addressing the often-asked question, "Why group therapy?" Yalom (1995) has conducted research that examines what group members actually get out of participating in group therapy. He identified 11 *therapeutic factors of group therapy* (see Exhibit 5.1) which, in part, answer the question, "How does group therapy help clients?"

It is the group worker's responsibility to encourage the development and functioning of the 11 therapeutic factors, according to Yalom. For offenders who have been sentenced to life without parole, the therapeutic factors may help them with their emotional well-being as they realize that they are not alone in their struggle (universality). "Warden Duffy, a legendary figure at San Quentin Prison, once claimed that the best way to help a man is to let him help you" (Yalom, 1995, p. 13). Duffy's comment reflects the therapeutic value of altruism. For offenders who will be released, or those in community-based settings, all of the therapeutic factors are relevant to help them live functional, healthy, meaningful lives with those who are important to them. Recognizing that life is at times unfair and learning that we must take ultimate responsibility for the way we live our lives (existential factors) are particularly relevant concepts offenders need to learn to cope with their trials and tribulations. Readers not already familiar with the therapeutic factors are referred to Yalom's (1995) classic text.

Stages of Group Development

It will take time for a group to experience all 11 therapeutic factors. As groups meet over time, the members will begin to experience each other in different ways. The structure and functioning of the group will change. Determining what stage of group development a group most closely resembles can aid practitioners in delivering appropriate interventions to help the group move forward (cf. Garland, Jones, & Kolodny, 1973; Tuckman, 1965). Gar-

EXHIBIT 5.1
Therapeutic Factors of Group Therapy

1. Instillation of hope
2. Universality
3. Imparting information
4. Altruism
5. Corrective recapitulation of the primary family group
6. Development of socialization techniques
7. Imitative behavior
8. Interpersonal learning
9. Group cohesiveness
10. Catharsis
11. Existential factors

Note. From *The Theory and Practice of Group Psychotherapy,* by I. D. Yalom (4th ed.), 1995, New York: Basic Books. Copyright 1995 by Basic Books. Adapted with permission.

land and colleagues (1973) offered five stages of group development: preaffiliation, power and control, intimacy, differentiation, and separation.

Stage One: Preaffiliation

This stage is marked by members becoming familiar with one another and with the group situation. They are generally anxious about the group experience, and not sure what to make of it. An approach and avoidance pattern of behavior by the members is typical at this stage.

Stage Two: Power and Control

This stage is marked by considerable testing of limits by the group members as they struggle for their position in the status hierarchy of the group. "The behavior of members reflects the ambiguity and turmoil associated by change from a nonintimate to an intimate system of relationships. The basic issues to be coped with are rebellion against the leader, individual and group autonomy, acceptable norms, protection, and support" (Northen, 1988, p. 175). These issues around power and control must be worked through if the group is to move forward.

Stage Three: Intimacy

This stage is where group members begin to become more personally involved in the group. Self-disclosure will likely increase, and group members begin to understand and accept how the group can be helpful to them.

Stage Four: Differentiation

This stage is marked by even a stronger sense of cohesion among members. They relate to and accept each other as distinct persons, and respect one another as autonomous individuals. It is this stage where members feel comfortable enough to "tell each other like it is" because they are comfortable and natural with one another.

Stage Five: Separation

As the group nears its end, members will begin to separate from one another emotionally. Group members may revert back to earlier behaviors and patterns of interacting as their anxiety increases around termination. Members will often use various defensive and coping mechanisms to avoid dealing with termination.

Groups may fluctuate between these stages as new members join and veteran members leave the group. Additionally, Glassman and Kates (1983) pointed out that two themes—power and intimacy—permeate all stages of groups. When groups are composed of involuntary clients such as substance-abusing offenders, the initial stages (i.e., preaffiliation, power and control) may be prolonged due to resistance or deficits in the members' ability to develop relationships and to communicate effectively, and because it will take additional time to test limits and accept the group's purpose (Northen, 1988). Groups with frequent and extensive membership turnover are very likely to remain at a formative stage of group development (Toseland & Rivas, 2001). Many other factors can impact a group's development and functioning, some of which are explored below.

Group Work in Controlled Settings

In addition to being cognizant of the therapeutic factors and what stage of development a group is in, the practitioner must also be aware of special considerations that are of particular importance when facilitating groups with substance-abusing offenders in controlled settings.

Many substance-abusing offenders participating in group therapy are there involuntarily. Rooney (1992) described an involuntary relationship as one that consists of at least one of the following elements: (a) a person feels forced to remain in it because of physical or legal coercion, (b) the cost of leaving the relationship for the person is too high, or (c) the person feels pressured to act differently in the relationship than he or she wishes to act.

Practitioners should be aware of legal issues associated with involuntary clients in groups (and other modalities). One such issue is *due process,* which means that individuals "are entitled to due process of law before they can be deprived of life, liberty, or property" (Rooney, 1992, p. 40). According to Garvin (1997), it can be argued that requiring or mandating group treatment deprives a person of liberty unless all the protections ensured by due process have been observed.

Offenders must give *informed consent* to participate in treatment (Garvin, 1997). This means that offenders must be provided with a clear explanation of group treatment, and they must consent to participate. Garvin raised an important ethical issue that must be addressed when working with juvenile offenders in controlled environments. Juveniles are not legal adults, and some

EXHIBIT 5.2
Principles for Group Work With Involuntary Clients

1. Respect the client's right to reject group work, and "take the consequences."
2. Explain the rationale for group work, the group work methods to be utilized and the evidence for the effectiveness of group work as fully as possible. Many of these clients have not been treated as intelligent beings; reinforcement of their awareness of their own abilities to learn and understand will help them approach future situations as opportunities to learn effective and socially acceptable solutions to problems.
3. Choose as many ways as possible to involve the involuntary client in decision making in the group, such as prioritizing issues for consideration, selecting problems on which to focus, or selecting among group approaches.
4. Recognize the right of group members to work toward changes designed to improve the relevant systems such as the service agency or other agencies.
5. Above all, recognize that the group member is an individual and not a clone of every other prisoner or patient (or whatever other term applies).

Note. From *Contemporary Group Work* (3rd ed., pp. 248–249) by C. D. Garvin, 1997, Boston: Allyn & Bacon. Copyright 1997 by Allyn and Bacon. Adapted with permission.

may have severe mental or emotional problems in addition to their substance abuse problems. When clients are incapable of establishing therapeutic goals for themselves, the practitioner is obligated to communicate with their legal guardians. First, informed consent for such communication should be obtained from the juveniles whenever possible.

Group leaders should be familiar with a set of principles for group work with involuntary clients (see Exhibit 5.2; Garvin, 1997). The group worker's primary consideration when composing a group should be its cohesiveness. In other words, how well will these offenders be able to work together in a meaningful way over the life of the group? For example, including too many juvenile offenders with a diagnosis of conduct disorder can be countertherapeutic. Thus, group composition becomes critical to the success of the group. Scott (1993) echoes this sentiment but noted that an ideal group composition is impossible to implement in the prison setting.

During the first meeting, the rules and sanctions for the entire group should be established in a group contract. These rules and sanctions should be written and posted at subsequent meetings and should include the need for confidentiality and corresponding consequences for breaking the rules. Physical violence cannot be tolerated under any circumstance, and group members must understand this if they are allowed to participate in the group.

When the group is beginning (i.e., in the power and conflict stage), there will be a considerable amount of conflict and distrust directed at the group worker and the institution in which the group is held. Consider the comments of a group member who participated in a group for substance-abusing male inmates in a prison setting (Albert, 1994):

> After a silence, Kevin, an inmate leader who was serving his fifth "bid" (sentence), said, "How is one little group gonna make a difference in this

place? Everything in jail is talk, and everyone talks shit. Everyone has a game. You say something here, next thing you hear it from the parole people. Fuck that." (p. 204)

The worker cannot simply ignore such concerns in hopes that they will disappear on their own. If not addressed, dysfunctional roles and norms that emerge will continue throughout the life of the group. Accordingly, "the concern of a group leader should be fostering interaction among group members and instilling some confidence that it might eventually be effective and rewarding" (Empey & Erickson, 1972, as cited in Jackson & Springer, 1997, p. 242). The group leader must be focused on involving members in the group process, placing a certain amount of responsibility on the members for the success of the group.

Of course, achieving the ideal situation in controlled settings is practically impossible. Group members will challenge the rules and encourage deviant behavior from one another. Group workers have the responsibility to establish norms (unwritten rules of behavior) for the group. The group worker can address deviant behavior by constructively confronting members about various values and belief systems that lead to such behavior. It may be helpful to have veteran group members challenge new members on such behavior.

Scott (1993) reported generally positive group therapy results with mentally and emotionally disturbed adult prisoners, including lower functioning offenders (e.g., those with low IQ, extensive criminal record, frequent periods of psychosis) and those who were higher functioning (e.g., bright, verbal, unit leaders). He recommended the following guidelines for group leaders to use when conducting prison therapy groups with offenders: (a) "when in doubt, talk it out," as opposed to acting it out; (b) the offender must practice the painful task of self-observation; and (c) offenders must change both their behavior and their attitude. Because he provides only anecdotal evidence, not statistical support, for his conclusions, Scott's work cannot be considered evidence-based. However, drawing on his experience, Scott has listed statements and topics he has used successfully to guide group discussion:

- Once an offender, always an offender.
- All offenders are alike.
- Offenders don't know themselves.
- Offenders make poor choices.
- Most offenders wouldn't have committed a crime, if not on alcohol or drugs (love my excuses).
- Six different ways to not commit a crime.
- Old hatred can keep you alive, but it's not much of a life.
- What does an offender mean when he says, "I've learned my lesson"? (pp. 143–145).

At a minimum, practitioners conducting groups with offenders may find Scott's list to have clinical heuristic value.

Ferrara (1992) has written a useful guide to conducting effective group work with juvenile delinquents. Informed by programs and interventions found to be effective in treating juvenile delinquents, his "limit and lead" approach to group work is marked by an integration of traditional (e.g., guided group interaction) and contemporary (e.g., cognitive–behavioral interventions) influences. In this approach, two major tenets are recognized: that the behavior of juvenile delinquents needs to be limited because they hurt people, and that they can be led toward prosocial behavior through rehabilitation. Various types of groups address different needs, and Ferrara provided the following definitions:

- *Called Groups*. Spontaneous problem-solving groups designed to prevent program disruption or physical aggression.
- *Daily Groups*. Problem-solving groups designed to help youth develop an understanding of their delinquent and nondelinquent behavior and allow them to modify their behavior so it is more positive and appropriate.
- *Special Groups*. Groups designed to focus on specific topics, e.g., improving self-esteem, dealing with sexual victimization, or aggression control. Youths are assigned to these groups based on common characteristics. (p. 8)

Each of these types of groups is in Ferrara's guide, which includes a philosophical overview of the limit and lead group program, an orientation and in-service training program for group leaders, training modules and a training workbook, as well as an orientation program for the youths. Additionally, the means for establishing and monitoring administrative support at the facility and agency level are addressed. Practitioners conducting groups with juvenile delinquents are referred to this comprehensive hands-on source.

Jackson and Springer (1997) described a special type of group that can be formed in juvenile justice settings, the *therapeutic gang*, which is a group approach to work with incarcerated juvenile gang members. This approach is informed by guided group interaction (cf. Empey & Erickson, 1972). Although one reason for the worker to form a therapeutic gang may be to improve security within the facility, the major purpose is to assist these offenders in finding positive alternatives to the negative attitudes, behaviors, and values that they are typically accustomed to. To effectively implement the therapeutic gang, the practitioner must have a working knowledge of both group and gang dynamics, including, but not limited to, how a gang handles disloyal members, a gang's agenda (e.g., maintain and expand turf, sell drugs for profit), and the hierarchical organization of a gang (cf. Goldstein & Huff, 1993; Hopps & Pinderhughes, 1999).

In their description of the S Street Lions in the Boston area, Hopps and Pinderhughes (1999) explain that the "vertical structure for distribution of drugs allows leaders to maintain control because there is competition among the lower echelons. Some members are always willing to do more work and expand drug sales. And there are always people at the lower levels hoping to earn a greater volume of drug sales, obtaining more and higher status" (pp. 151–152).

It is important to highlight the proliferation of adult prison gangs (e.g., Aryan Brotherhood, Mexican Mafia, Bloods, Crips), which tend to form along racial lines (Buentello, 1992). The serious concern among criminal justice administrators regarding adult prison gangs is illustrated by the Texas Department of Criminal Justice's solution to the problem. First, administrators identify which inmates are gang members and then separate them from the general population. It is worth noting, however, that a cognitive restructuring program implemented with adult prison gang members was found to have a positive impact on level of gang involvement (Toller & Tsagaris, 1996) and that gang members have been hired to counsel youths about the negative impact on one's life of joining a gang as well as to mediate gang conflicts (Gibbs, Potter, Barriga, & Liau, 1996). Practitioners should be aware of the gang dynamics for their particular setting and geographic region before implementing any interventions with adult or juvenile offenders.

Albert (1994) presented the Straight Ahead substance abuse group that he and a colleague facilitated in a prison setting with male inmates over a four-year period. Straight Ahead was mandated to provide group treatment to a population of approximately 250 male inmates, of which 150 or so were substance abusers, including alcoholics (45%); cocaine addicts (25%); heroin addicts (25%); and marijuana, PCP, and hallucinogen users (5%). Most of the inmates were serving sentences of less than two years for substance-related charges. The Straight Ahead group was open-ended, and met for two 90-minute sessions each week.

Albert (1994) discussed major themes that emerged during the course of the Straight Ahead group, including attitudes toward authority in general and correctional officers in particular, attitudes toward peers and friendship, and using drugs and sex to deal with loneliness and powerlessness. The key practitioners' skills that were helpful in addressing the major themes were as follows:

1. Mediating between the group and the agency staff.
2. Refusing to join scapegoating or to side with conflicting subgroups.
3. Empathizing with difficulties and ambivalence and reaching for unspoken feelings.
4. Modeling moderation and realism.

5. Extracting specifics from generalities and abstracting general guidelines from specifics.
6. Demanding work while providing support. (p. 212)

Working with substance-abusing offenders in criminal justice settings requires the practitioner to assume a different role than when working in community-based settings. It is imperative that the group worker act as a mediator between the institution and the group to ensure that the group's needs are being met. Albert (1994) described his experience with this phenomenon in conducting the Straight Ahead group described earlier, as he met resistance from staff members.

> The sources of resistance included: a) cynicism about services provided from the outside, which partly derived from a history of oversold services and partly from territoriality; b) lack of information about the nature of substance abuse and its treatment; c) fear that group members would belittle staff members and con the leader; d) hostility toward substance abusers resulting from personal or family substance-abuse issues. The staff's ambivalence was complicated by an institutional ambivalence that mirrored and amplified the ambivalence of the inmates. (p. 202)

Albert (1994) went on to describe his struggle early on in the life of the group with getting space for the group on a consistent basis, being kicked out of the space for scheduled GED exams, or finding an available correctional officer to unlock the doors and supervise the area in which the group was to be held. In an attempt to mediate between the correctional staff and the group, Albert invited one of the influential officers, Carl, to a group session with the inmates (after first obtaining permission from the group). Albert also attended a staff training meeting to discuss the group with the staff. These efforts proved to be worthwhile. This mediation improved communication between correctional officers and group members, reduced administrative interference with the group's meeting space, and increased the number of referrals to the group by correctional officers. "Mediating between the group and the staff deserves special emphasis, because avoiding it can be both tempting and disastrous" (pp. 212–213).

Another challenge for the group worker in the juvenile or criminal justice setting is what Garvin (1997) referred to as the *inmate code* (or *convict code*). This norm demands that inmates maintain their respective status with other inmates by maintaining secrecy within their natural circle and aligning with one another against staff. This norm can be addressed in the group setting. Albert's ability to humanize the institutional setting for the group members as he mediated between the group and the officers is an excellent example of how to challenge the inmate code. Albert (1994), Garvin (1997), and Scott (1993) have each had success challenging this norm by actually training prison guards as group workers and then having them help colead groups. Consider the following excerpt from one correctional officer's account of working with Scott (1993) in a prison group therapy setting with dually diagnosed offenders:

> I do believe that group has been helpful. My group is composed of the hard cases and the manipulators. In group, the barriers come down. It helps the tough guys to get to know each other better, instead of just trying to be top dog. Even the toughest one has the same feelings as others—deep down. Group appears to function as a neutral place where exchanges occur. (p. 141)

Outcome Studies on Group Therapy

There are many forms of group treatment with chemically dependent clients. Brandsma and Pattison's (1985) review of about 30 studies generally indicated a positive outcome of using group therapy in a chemical dependency treatment program as well as a need to further empirically demonstrate the effectiveness of this modality. This is further supported by Solomon (1982), who noted a lacuna in the literature comparing group with individual treatment for alcoholics and comparing different approaches to conducting groups. More recently, however, group work has been shown to reduce offending behavior by 10–20%, with cognitive–behavioral methods scoring high in meta-analyses that examine what works with offenders (Lipton, 1998, as cited in Dixon, 2000).

Towberman (1993) examined the impact of group versus individual treatment with incarcerated female juvenile offenders on perceptions of the treatment environment (as measured by the Correctional Institutions Environment Scale [CIES]). The CIES measures three dimensions of the environment, including the treatment program, interpersonal relationships, and emphasis on institutional order and control. Towberman found that female offenders in the group treatment condition reported more favorable ratings on perceptions of interpersonal relationships and the treatment program than did their counterparts in the individual treatment condition. One plausible explanation for these results is the effect of the therapeutic factors provided through group treatment.

Additional resources cover evidence-based group work with offenders (Chapman & Hough, 1998; Dixon, 2000).

STRUCTURED GROUP-ORIENTED APPROACHES

Positive Peer Culture

In the case of work with juvenile substance abusers in agency and juvenile justice settings, forms of PPC are often used to facilitate group treatment. Positive peer culture, developed by Harry Vorrath, was heavily influenced by a peer-oriented treatment model, Guided Group Interaction (McCorkle, Elias, & Bixby, 1958). According to Vorrath and Brendtro (1985), "PPC is a total system for building positive youth subcultures" (p. 20). In a typical PPC meeting, each group member might report a recurring problem. The group then "awards" the meeting to a particular group member for further discussion of his or her problem (Leeman, Gibbs, & Fuller, 1993). Consider the following case example taken from Vorrath and Brendtro (1985), which illustrates how PPC might work for youths with substance abuse problems:

> A group home for troubled girls had severe drug abuse problems. The result of the many attempts to suppress the activity was a cold war between staff and youth. Suspicion, searches, and restriction became commonplace. That was a year ago. Now staff members no longer police students for drugs, and the climate of intrigue is gone. As a new girl enters, her peers confiscate any drugs she may have and tell her, "We don't have to use dope around here." Drug problems are dealt with openly in a helpful, matter-of-fact way. Group members state with strong conviction that when a person has good feelings about herself she no longer needs to get high on drugs. (p. xix)

PPC is a holistic approach to working with youths in a therapeutic setting. It is not simply a set of techniques but rather attempts to change the culture in the therapeutic setting.

> PPC is designed to "turn around" a negative youth subculture and mobilize the power of the peer group in a productive manner . . . In contrast to traditional treatment approaches, PPC does not ask whether a person wants to receive help but whether he is willing to give help. (Vorrath & Brendtro, 1985, p. xxi)

Proponents of PPC view troubled youths not as rebellious or "bad seeds" but rather as youths that with nurturing have much to contribute. Here we have attempted to synthesize and highlight some of the key aspects and assumptions of the PPC approach discussed by Vorrath and Brendtro (1985) (see Exhibit 5.3).

The summary listing in Exhibit 5.3 is by no means exhaustive, and it does not do justice to the comprehensiveness of the PPC approach. It is merely intended to provide readers with a basic understanding of some of the assumptions that drive the PPC approach.

Vorrath and Brendtro (1985) did not recommend composing a PPC group of both sexes because coeducational groups present barriers to a relaxed and open interaction pattern; male and female adolescents often engage in courtship behavior that masks honest communication. Vorrath and Brendtro also recommend a group size of nine youths.

EXHIBIT 5.3
Key Aspects and Assumptions of Positive Peer Culture

- PPC does not seek to enforce a set of specific rules but to teach basic values.
- The peer group has the strongest influence over the values, attitudes, and behavior of youths.
- Adults have much to offer youths but should not attempt to control or surrender to them.
- Youths feel positive about themselves when two conditions exist: the youth feels accepted by others, and the youth feels deserving of this acceptance.
- Youths are experts on their own lives.
- Youths are resilient.
- Youths possess strengths that should be recognized by practitioners and tapped throughout the treatment process (i.e., a strengths perspective). When these strengths are tapped, youths are better able to help one another.
- PPC focuses on the "here-and-now" of what is happening.
- PPC views problems as opportunities rather than as trouble.
- Youths must accept responsibility for their behavior and be held accountable.
- Both youths and adults must care for and help one another.

Note. From *Positive Peer Culture* (2nd ed.), by H. H. Vorrath and L. K. Brendtro, 1985, New York: Aldine de Gruyter. Copyright 1985 by Harry H. Vorrath and Larry K. Brendtro. Adapted with permission.

Simply stated, the essence of PPC is captured in the following statement: "If there were one rule, it would be that people must care for one another" (Vorrath & Brendtro, 1985, p. xxi). Those readers wishing to learn more about PPC are referred to Vorrath and Brendtro's (1985) classic text on the subject.

Despite the positive aspects of the PPC approach, it is not without its critics. "Peer group programs such as positive peer culture generally have had only mixed success, perhaps because they do not sufficiently counteract the negative youth culture and the helping-skill limitations of antisocial youth" (Gibbs et al., 1996, p. 283). To address such limitations, EQUIP incorporates into the PPC approach a multicomponent skills training (i.e., aggression replacement training) to provide a more structured format for developing a positive youth culture.

EQUIP

EQUIP (Equipping Youth to Help One Another; Gibbs, Potter, & Goldstein, 1995) is a comprehensive, multimodal treatment approach to help youths with antisocial behavior problems. EQUIP incorporates a psychoeducational program—ART (Goldstein, 1988; Goldstein & Glick, 1987), which aims to teach youths how to replace aggression with interpersonally responsible behaviors. EQUIP became multicomponent in two senses.

> First, it helped youths develop skills in order to render the mutual help group approach more effective (in other words, it combined skills training with mutual help approaches). Second, the skill development was

itself multifaceted, focusing on moral judgment, anger management (including the correction of thinking errors), and social skills. (Gibbs, Potter, & Goldstein, 1995, p. xii)

Herein lies the appeal of EQUIP. It comprehensively integrates several treatment approaches, including guided group interaction, PPC, ART, social skills training, and moral judgment. The basic premise is that antisocial youths can motivate one another, if they are appropriately "equipped" through a psychoeducational curriculum to do so.

Gibbs, Potter, & Goldstein (1995) outlined the typical EQUIP program as follows. EQUIP consists of approximately seven youths meeting daily for 1 to 1 1/2 hours, Monday through Friday. These "equipment meetings" are based on coordinated curriculum components that address moral education, anger management, the correction of thinking errors, and social skills. Before introducing the 10-week EQUIP curriculum, each session should begin as a mutual-help meeting. A weekly sequence of anger management—social skills—social decision making is recommended for three primary reasons: (a) this provides group members with anger management tools needed to navigate the mutual-help group process and "sells" the need for equipment meetings, (b) social skills is the easiest component to split across two meetings, and (c) social decision making seems to have the most impact when it follows social skills training. The 10-week agenda can be tailored to meet the specific needs of the population or it can be setting targeted (e.g., the course may take 15 weeks for a group that has more than 7 or 8 members and does not have two equipment meetings per week, or for groups that become engaged in certain elements).

> Our message to young people . . . is not direct help to each youth but rather help to the *group* so that the group can help its *members*. The spirit of EQUIP, then, is adult guidance and empowerment of youths toward more effective mutual help—just as an athletic coach, in teaching various skills, guides and empowers team members to help one another by using their complementary strengths and thereby to succeed. (p. 218)

Because many offenders exhibit aggressive behavior and because EQUIP integrates ART as a central component of its treatment approach, a brief overview of ART is warranted here.

Aggression Replacement Training

ART is based on the premise that "much of the outcome variance associated with efforts to change [aggressive] behavior would occur in the domains of enhanced skill proficiency, heightened anger control, and more advanced levels of moral reasoning" (Glick, 1996, p. 196), and accordingly, consists of three components: structured learning training, anger control training, and moral education.

Structured learning training is a small group psychoeducational intervention (Glick & Goldstein, 1987) consisting of a 50-skills curriculum of prosocial behaviors, which is broken down into the following six components:

- Beginning social skills (e.g., starting a conversation, giving a complaint)
- Advanced social skills (e.g., asking for help, apologizing)
- Skills dealing with feelings (e.g., dealing with someone else's anger)
- Skill alternatives to aggression (e.g., responding to teasing, helping others)
- Skills for dealing with stress (e.g., dealing with an accusation)
- Planning skills (e.g., goal setting, decision making).

These skills are demonstrated and practiced in the group setting using various techniques, including modeling, role playing, performance feedback, and transfer training (Glick, 1996).

The second component, anger control training, initially developed by Feindler, Marriott, and Iwata (1984) and based in part on anger control and stress inoculation research (cf. Meichenbaum, 1977; Novaco, 1975), aims to teach youths skills to inhibit aggressive responses. For 10 weeks, group members bring to each session a description of a recent anger-arousing experience (a hassle), which they record in their hassle log. They are trained to cope with the hassles using a variety of skills, including how to identify triggers and cues, and using reminders, reducers, and self-evaluation (Glick, 1996).

Finally, the third component, moral education, consists of a set of procedures that are designed to raise each group member's sense of fairness, justice, and concern with the needs and rights of others. For each group session, two group leaders, or trainers, choose and prepare the moral dilemmas and then initiate and guide group discussion around the dilemma (Glick, 1996).

Effectiveness of PPC, EQUIP, and ART

Positive Peer Culture

The earliest recorded study of PPC was conducted by the Minnesota Department of Corrections (1973), which studied more than 700 youths who had been paroled from a Minnesota PPC program. Their findings were favorable, indicating a success rate of 81.5% and less than one-fifth (18.5%) recidivism rate in a two-year follow-up. Subsequent analysis of the Minnesota study revealed problems with the research methodology (Sarri & Selo, 1974). Since that time, other studies have found that PPC is an effective modality across different problem areas, including increased feelings of self-worth and reduced delinquent values and attitudes (Michigan Department of Social

Services, 1983) and a reduction in asocial behavior (McKinney, Miller, Beier, & Bohannon, 1978).

A facility called the Laker Group in Duluth, Minnesota, operates a treatment program for delinquent girls that utilizes principles from PPC. Quigley and Steiner (1996) conducted an outcome study of the group by comparing the outcomes of the Duluth program to a range of outcome findings in relevant literature. Quigley and Steiner reported that the group had a better success rate (93%) when compared to adolescent residential programs in Minnesota (69%) from 1991 to 1995. Lending further support to the program's effectiveness, Quigley and Steiner found that, on entering treatment with the group, more than half (57%) of the female delinquents presented with the problem of running away, but only a fraction (6%) of the girls ran away during the course of treatment. Furthermore, more than one-third (37%) of the girls presented with the problem of physical aggression, but only 15% were physically aggressive during the course of treatment.

The findings on the effectiveness of the PPC approach are equivocal to date. There is a dearth of adequately controlled studies and, when implemented, many PPC programs do not operate as intended (Brendtro & Ness, 1982). According to Gibbs and colleagues (1996),

> It might be argued that evaluations of the peer-helping approach might be more consistently favorable if institutions more often implemented and operated guided peer group programs as intended. Yet, the widespread abuse of confrontation and "helping" may signal a problem more central than that of insufficient staff training: The central issue may be whether the peer-helping approach as typically applied has adequately addressed the challenges represented by the negative culture and helping-skill limitations of antisocial youth. (p. 285)

EQUIP

Preliminary evidence for the effectiveness of EQUIP was demonstrated in a controlled outcome study conducted at a medium-security juvenile correctional facility (Leeman et al., 1993). Incarcerated young men ($n = 57$), ages 15 to 18, were randomly assigned to either the EQUIP experimental unit or to one of two control groups—a simple passage-of-time control and a control group that received a motivational message. The EQUIP group experienced a highly significant improvement in institutional conduct gains, relative to the control groups, as captured by self-reported misconduct, staff-filed incident reports, and unexcused absences from school. At 12 months following release, the recidivism rate for EQUIP participants remained low and stable (15%), compared to a 12-month mean recidivism rate of 40.5% for the control groups. Additionally, the EQUIP group evidenced significant gains in social skills relative to the control groups (Gibbs et al., 1996).

With regard to the moral education component of EQUIP, it was found that moral judgment was weaker than social skills as a mediator of overt behavior change, and the EQUIP group's gains in moral judgment were not significant. Leeman and colleagues (1993) asserted, however, that "it would be premature to discard the moral judgment component from the EQUIP program. Although not proximal to situational behavior, mature moral judgment may serve as a foundation for mature social behavior in a general and long-term sense" (p. 290).

Overall, however, findings on the effectiveness and importance of moral education included in curricula such as EQUIP and ART are mixed. Some studies support the notion that moral reasoning can be improved among troubled and delinquent juveniles (cf. Gibbs, Arnold, Ahlborn, & Cheesman, 1984; Niles, 1986); however, others have obtained mixed results from moral reasoning training with incarcerated delinquents (Goldstein & Glick, 1987) or failed to find improvement on moral reasoning with emotionally disturbed junior high students (Swarthout, 1988). Indeed, Arbuthnot and Faust (1981) have suggested that advanced moral reasoning may be a necessary but not sufficient condition to impact moral behavior (cited in Coleman, Pfeiffer, & Oakland, 1992).

Aggression Replacement Training

The available research on the effectiveness of ART is equivocal to date, although generally positive and encouraging. Goldstein and Glick (1987) examined the efficacy of ART with two samples of incarcerated juvenile offenders.

The first study was conducted with males ($N = 60$) ages 14 to 17 at the Annsville Youth Center incarcerated for offenses such as burglary, auto theft, and assault. Participants were randomly assigned to an ART treatment group ($n = 24$), an attention control group ($n = 24$), or a control group ($n = 12$). Various dependent measures were used to measure the efficacy of ART. The findings revealed significant gains on selected social skills accompanied by decreases in impulsive and aggressive behavior for the ART group. Findings from the 3-month follow-up (17 ART participants and 37 control participants) indicated that ART recipients were rated as better adjusted in three of five areas (home/family, peer, and legal). The second study by Goldstein and Glick replicated the first with juvenile offenders ($N = 51$) ages 13 to 21 incarcerated at MacCormick Youth Center for more serious crimes, such as murder, rape, and arson. Results of the ART training at MacCormick were very similar to those at Annsville. However, no follow-up data were available from the MacCormick study due to lengthy incarceration periods.

Coleman and colleagues (1992) examined the effects of a 10-week ART program with adolescents ($N = 39$) in residential treatment. Two-thirds of the sample had a *DSM–III–R* (American Psychiatric Association, 1987) diagnosis of conduct disorder. Participants were assigned to the treatment group ($n = 25$) or the control group ($n = 14$). The findings were less supportive of ART than those reported by Goldstein and Glick. Coleman and colleagues found that participants in the treatment group improved over control participants on only one measure: knowledge of social skills. However, no impact on observable behavior was noted. Coleman and colleagues questioned whether 10 weeks is an adequate amount of time to effect behavior change in such a high-risk population. In fact, they attempted to have a second treatment group that received a 20-week ART curriculum but were unable to continue the 20-week program due to attrition. Coleman and colleagues also suggested that "individualizing both behavioral goals, and to some extent the treatment, would maximize the probability of demonstrating favorable treatment gains" (p. 64).

Finally, Nugent, Bruley, and Allen (1999) examined the effectiveness of ART on antisocial behavior with male and female adolescents in a residential runaway shelter. Using an interrupted time series design, they reviewed case records (which included measures of antisocial behavior) of 552 adolescents in the facility during a period of 519 days. The traditional ART curriculum was condensed into a 15-day program and did not include the moral reasoning component of the curriculum. A key finding was that ART was effective in reducing female antisocial behavior regardless of how many male or female residents were in the facility. However, for the male adolescents, more positive findings were realized when there were fewer young men living in the facility (Nugent et al., 1999). This finding is consistent with the notion that having too many antisocial males in a group setting has a potentially detrimental effect on outcomes.

Both EQUIP and ART use a psychoeducational component to help structure the PPC approach, which seems to enhance the effects of PPC. Practitioners frequently use psychoeducational approaches with substance-abusing offenders. Accordingly, other psychoeducational approaches to group work are reviewed below.

PSYCHOEDUCATIONAL GROUPS

In many corrections settings, adult and juvenile offenders are required to complete educational classes as a part of treatment, and in other instances, a psychoeducational component may be integrated into an interactional group intervention. Among the specific types of substance abuse programs provided in jails, about 30% provide education or awareness programs (Bureau of Justice Statistics [BJS], 2000). In the justice system, two main types of educational programs for offenders exist: didactic educational programs and psychoeducational programs.

Didactic educational programs closely resemble a seminar or class. In these programs, offenders are presented with information about substance abuse and its effects. Offenders may learn about topics such as the physical effects of drug and alcohol abuse or the impact of substance abuse on family members, or they may be provided information about substance abuse treatment. In didactic educational programs, offenders are expected to listen to the information provided and, although there may be some interaction, the presenter is the focus of the program, and interaction is generally minimal.

Psychoeducational programs combine "the presentation of didactic information to increase knowledge with a variety of other techniques to help clients make desired changes and to provide support" (McNeece & DiNitto, 1994, p. 117). In these programs, the emphasis is not solely on the facilitator; group interaction is also encouraged. Structured exercises such as role plays, group discussion on specific topics, and homework assignments are generally a part of psychoeducational programs.

The major objectives of psychoeducational approaches include development of motivation and commitment to treatment through recognition of the addiction history, stages of recovery, and the impact of drug use on physical health and vocational and social functioning; the enhancement of life skills (e.g., managing a checkbook, time management) and communication skills; AIDS education and prevention activities; relapse prevention skills, including recognition of signs and symptoms of relapse, avoidance of active drug users, identification of high-risk situations, and strategies for managing a lapse or relapse; and development of an aftercare plan that incorporates use of community treatment resources (Peters, 1993, p. 53).

Literature examining the effectiveness of psychoeducational approaches with offenders is scant. However, we did find a couple of relevant studies. Pomeroy, Kiam, and Green (2000) conducted a quasi-experimental, pretest–posttest study examining the impact that an HIV/AIDS psychoeducational approach had on the emotional well-being of male inmates. The purpose of the 10-session psychoeducational group intervention was to reduce the amount of depression, anxiety, and trauma symptoms among male inmates while increasing their knowledge of HIV/AIDS. The first part of each session lasted approximately 45 minutes and consisted of a presentation or discussion concerning HIV/AIDS-related topics. The second half of each session (also 45 minutes) focused on supportive group processes using cognitive–behavioral and task-centered techniques (Pomeroy et al., 2000).

The participants were nonviolent offenders. The total sample ($N = 53$) consisted of 25 inmates in the experimental group and 28 inmates in the comparison group. The findings revealed that the intervention had small to moderate effects on depression (.37) and anxiety (.59), and an even greater impact on trauma symptoms (.71) and HIV/AIDS-related knowledge (1.13). Overall, the findings suggest that this psychoeducational group intervention had a meaningful effect in reducing the emotional distress of the inmates while increasing their knowledge of HIV/AIDS. The authors also point out that

> the group facilitators' nonjudgmental and supportive attitude and behavior . . . may have been an unusual experience for many of these men.

The group facilitators perceived much less resistance than expected in terms of the men discussing their feelings of low self-esteem, loss, anxieties, and traumatic experiences. (Pomeroy et al., 2000, p. 164)

Anderson and Reiss (1994) reported on a family psychoeducational model that was developed in Pittsburgh for treating adolescents who were seriously emotionally disturbed. The research project randomly assigned schizophrenic individuals with "high expressed emotion" families to one of four treatments: family therapy; social skills training; family therapy and social skills training; and medication alone (with all four treatments including medication management). Clients and their families from each treatment modality were followed over a two-year period. Various measures of individual and family functioning were taken at periodic intervals. The results demonstrated that this model of family psychoeducation (Anderson, Hogarty, & Reiss, 1980; Anderson, Reiss, & Hogarty, 1986) had a positive impact on the client systems. Those clients receiving only medication experienced a one-year relapse of nearly 40%, whereas those receiving the family psychoeducation or the social skills treatment each experienced a relapse rate of approximately 20%. Remarkably, none of the clients receiving the family psychoeducation and social skills training relapsed during the first year. After two years, the family psychoeducation group continued to demonstrate a significant positive effect on relapse rates, whereas the impact of social skills intervention diminished (Anderson & Reiss, 1994).

The family psychoeducational model reported above was developed for schizophrenic clients of all ages, but it is also relevant for psychotic adolescents and their families and is being used with substance-abusing clients (Anderson & Reiss, 1994). For a detailed exposition on this model, readers are referred to other sources (cf. Anderson, Hogarty, & Reiss, 1980; Anderson, Reiss, & Hogarty, 1986).

MULTIFAMILY THERAPY GROUPS

Multifamily therapy groups (MFTGs) require a practitioner skilled in implementing both family intervention and group work. MFTGs are another way to involve the substance abuser's family in the treatment process. They have been used with various populations since the early 1950s (Laquer, 1980).

MFTGs are often used as part of the therapeutic milieu in substance abuse treatment programs. As part of an inpatient program (see chapter 6), for example, clients and their families might voluntarily attend both individual weekly family therapy sessions and a weekly MFTG. Ideally, MFTG sessions last approximately 1 1/2 to 2 hours.

Springer and Orsbon (2002) have described an MFTG that was implemented with substance-abusing adolescents and their families in a community-based setting. In response to the change in group membership from week to week, the group leaders began each session with introductions and a brief review of the group rules (e.g., confidentiality, respect for one another). The adolescents would introduce themselves and the rest of their family members. The adolescents typically stated why they were in treatment (e.g., "I'm here for drinking, using pot, and depression."). The group leaders sometimes began each group with a brief (10- to 15-minute) presentation of psychoeducational material to group members and then asked the group members to apply the material to their own family or situation. However, sometimes the group leaders began sessions by simply inviting families to share how their week had gone, what type of progress they were making on their goals, and so on. This typically led to free-floating member-to-member interaction.

Psychoeducational material is an important component of any substance abuse treatment program. For example, a group leader might present Wegscheider's (1981) depiction of family roles (see chapter 4) and then ask group members to share with the group the role with which they most identify. However, member-to-member interaction in a group setting is also critical. Accordingly, we propose an interpersonal and mutual-aid approach to facilitating MFTGs by which the practitioner is able to strike a balance between providing structure and direction (perhaps through introducing psychoeducational material) and encouraging member-to-member exchanges.

The interpersonal (Shulman, 1992; Yalom, 1995) and mutual-aid (Gitterman & Shulman, 1994; Schwartz, 1961) MFTG potentially offers several benefits to group participants. As group members interact with one another, it does not take long for them to show their "true colors," a phenomenon that Yalom (1995) refers to as the *group as a social microcosm*. By focusing on the interactions between members and families that take place in the here-and-now of the group experience, group members learn how they impact or are perceived by others, get feedback about their behavior, learn from one another, and practice new skills (Springer & Orsbon, 2002). This is accomplished in the context of a supportive helping system.

In addition to this framework of facilitating the group interactions, the group leaders must also integrate techniques from family therapy approaches, such as the structural–strategic approach to attend to the needs of individual family systems (see chapter 4). For illustration purposes, consider the following example of an MFTG with substance-abusing adolescents and their families. One family in the MFTG, Johnny's family, acts out a problem (i.e., an enactment) during group as Johnny and his parents argue about his substance use. Johnny is minimizing the use, and his parents want to "lock him up and throw away the key." After some time passes with little apparent progress being made, the group leader gently interrupts and asks other families if they are able to relate to what Johnny's family is experiencing. Several other families provide feedback to Johnny's family about what they observe taking place and offer suggestions about how to approach the problem from different angles based on their own experiences. This allows the families an opportunity to relate to one another in a way that lets them know they are not the only ones with these types of problems. Yalom (1995) refered to this as *universality*.

Moreover, parents from several families provide feedback directly to Johnny about his behavior (e.g., "If you were my child, I would be strict with you too at this point"), and adolescents provide feedback directly to Johnny's parents about their parenting style (e.g., "If I were your kid, it would be hard for me to listen to you when you're saying that you want to 'lock me up and throw away the key'). The former is known as *objective parenting* and the latter as *objective childrening*. This type of interaction across generations allows family members the opportunity to hear confirming or challenging perspectives from group members that can serve as a reality check (Springer & Orsbon, 2002). Notice that most of the real work in the above interactions is being done by the group members and not by the group leaders. This is a key feature of an interactional, mutual-aid MFTG.

Depending on the norms of the agency or setting in which the group takes place, more structure may be needed than is illustrated above. For example, in many therapeutic communities (see chapter 6), clients are expected to behave in a certain way during any group activity on the unit. Nevertheless, clients and their family members can still experience the benefits of the interactional and mutual-aid nature of the MFTG experience.

MFTGs have been found effective with a variety of populations (Meezan & O'Keefe, 1998; O'Shea & Phelps, 1985) and have been used successfully with substance-abusing adolescents and their families (Malekoff, 1997; Polcin, 1992; Singh, 1982; Springer & Orsbon, 2002). When possible, practitioners should explore with families how their work in the individual sessions can translate into their participation in the weekly MFTG. This likely will enhance the level of participation and self-disclosure among MFTG members.

SELF-HELP GROUPS

The modern self-help (or more accurately, *mutual*-help) group originated with AA (Gibbs, Potter, & Goldstein, 1995). The esprit de corps evident across self-help groups such as AA epitomizes the mutual-aid approach to group work, and such self-help groups are used widely with substance-abusing offenders. Self-help groups such as AA and Narcotics Anonymous (NA) are the most commonly used (64%) substance abuse programs provided in jails (BJS, 2000).

Founded in 1935 by William Wilson and Robert Holbrook Smith ("Bill W." and "Dr. Bob"), AA is an abstinence-based 12-step program that maintains that alcoholism is a disease that can be coped with but not cured. Thus, according to the AA philosophy, there are recovering alcoholics but not cured or ex-alcoholics. Other self-help 12-step programs, such as NA, follow the same conceptual framework as AA. AA and NA meetings are held in both adult and juvenile secured correctional settings.

There are three parts of these 12-step programs: surrender steps, integrity steps, and serenity steps (Brundage, 1985). The surrender steps require an acknowledgment of a substance dependence problem (whether alcohol or drugs) and that such a problem is destructive to the member's life. The member surrenders to a "higher power," which is not necessarily synonymous with God or any similar deity. Integrity steps allow members to apologize for difficulties caused to others as a result of their drug or alcohol use. The last 3 steps in 12-step programs collectively form the serenity steps and are concerned with the member maintaining a drug-free life.

There are many derivative groups of the 12-step approach to recovery, including Rational Recovery, Secular Organization for Sobriety, and Women for Sobriety. Rational Recovery groups were started in 1985 by Jack Trimpey, a clinical social worker. Trimpey (1989) had difficulty making sense of AA and based RR on Albert Ellis's (1962) rational–emotive therapy, which Trimpey used to overcome his drinking (Hovarth, 1997, as cited in Miller, 1999). Secular Organization for Sobriety, founded by James Christopher, is open to anyone struggling with any type of addiction. Based on six principles (Christopher, 1988), this approach may be useful for clients who do not feel the need for a spiritual or religious focus to their recovery (G. A. Miller, 1999).

Women for Sobriety was introduced in 1976 by Jean Kirkpatrick, a doctor of sociology (1978). Women for Sobriety can be successfully used alone or as a compliment to AA or other programs (Davis & DiNitto, 1998). Rather than the 12 steps of AA, the program uses 13 statements of acceptance, such as "I am a competent woman and have much to give life" (Women for Sobriety, 1989). Kaskutas (1989) has identified four major themes of the program: (a) no drinking, (b) positive thinking, (c) believing one is competent, and (d) growing spiritually and emotionally. Kaskutas describes the Women for Sobriety program as less directive than AA and more accepting than AA with much more "cross talk" taking place during meetings. Members are discouraged from telling stories of their drinking or from introducing themselves as alcoholics or addicts because these are considered negative thinking. A survey of 600 program members revealed that approximately one third are also current members of AA, primarily for "insurance" against relapse; for wider availability of meetings; and for sharing, support, and fellowship (Kaskutas, 1994, as cited in Davis & DiNitto, 1998).

A critical point to consider for practitioners and administrators working with substance-abusing offenders is the prisoners' First Amendment rights to refuse treatment, which includes AA and NA treatment. The First Amendment contains the Establishment Clause. The U.S. Supreme Court in 1947 explained the Establishment Clause in *Everson v. Board of Education* (1947, as cited in R. Alexander, 2000).

> Neither a state nor the federal government can set up a church. Neither can pass laws that aid one religion, aid all religions, or prefer one religion over another. Neither can force nor influence a person to go to or to remain away from church against his [or her] will or force him [or her] to profess a belief or disbelief in any religion. No person can be punished for entertaining or professing religious beliefs or disbelief, for church attendance or nonattendance. No tax in any amount, large or small, can be levied to support any religious activities or institutions, whatever they may be called, or whatever form they may adopt to teach or practice religion. Neither a state nor the federal government can, openly or secretly, participate in the affairs of any religious organizations or groups and vice versa. (*Everson v. Board of Education*, 1947, pp. 15–16).

Nearly five decades later, a Wisconsin prisoner named Kerr stated that he was told by a corrections social worker that attendance at NA was mandatory. Both AA and NA, however, place a heavy emphasis on God. Accordingly, in *Kerr v. Farrey* (1996), the Seventh Circuit of Appeals ruled that Kerr's First Amendment rights were violated when he was coerced into attending the NA program by the social worker. (Apparently, the penalty for not attending the NA meeting would have been a transfer from the minimum-security prison in which Kerr was housed to a medium-security prison and a note in Kerr's records regarding his refusal to participate in drug treatment.) It is interesting to note that "the Judges granted the prison superintendent and social worker qualified immunity because the right to be free from coercion involving NA was not an established right that a reasonable person would know (*Kerr v. Farrey*, 1996)" (Alexander, 2000, p. 52). Since then, other district courts have ruled on this matter. A prison system that has only one option (AA or NA) violates prisoners' rights (*Scarpino v. Grossheim*, 1994; *Warner v. Orange County Dept. of Probation*, 1994); a prison that has treatment options available in addition to AA or NA does not violate prisoners' First Amendment rights (*O'Connor v. California*, 1994, as cited in Alexander, 2000).

The Chemical Abuse/Addiction Treatment Outcome Registry is one of the most extensive longitudinal databases on adolescent drug treatment outcomes to date (Harrison & Hoffman, 1989). Results derived from interviews with 493 youths at 6- and 12-month follow-ups revealed that adolescents who remained in self-help groups (e.g., AA) for one year following treatment had better outcomes than did youths who attended occasionally or not at all (cited in Jenson, 1997). Alford, Koehler, and Leonard (1991) found that AA benefited adolescents who were able to understand and accept AA principles and traditions. However, the lack of a comparison group in the study requires that these findings be interpreted with caution and not generalized to all adolescents. Inpatient substance abuse treatment programs throughout the United States continue to be based on a disease model that utilizes the 12-step approach. However, there is a significant lacuna in the research literature on the effectiveness of such programs (Abadinsky, 1993). Others have criticized AA for its lack of credible research supporting an abstinence-oriented "disease" model (W. R. Miller & Hester, 1980; Ogborne & Glasser, 1985). In general, studies of the effectiveness of AA tend to focus on middle- and upper-class populations with rather stable lives prior to the onset of a drinking problem (B. K. Alexander, 1990), and much of the evidence regarding the effectiveness of self-help groups is based on anecdotal reports (W. R. Miller & Hester, 1986).

We question the blanket prescription of AA and NA programs to all substance-abusing offenders. Recall the discussion from chapter 3 regarding research on the stages-of-change construct that emphasizes the importance of delivering certain types of treatment for clients at different points in the stages-of-change process. Should the offender who is a substance *user* (i.e., has engaged in "experimental" use of one drug) be told that he or she has a disease and has to attend 90 meetings in 90 days, or would this approach better serve those who meet criteria for substance or polysubstance *dependence*? This question is particularly salient for juvenile offenders, as it is our experience that adolescents often express difficulty "buying into" the disease model. Indeed, the majority of adolescents who experiment with hard drugs do not become addicted (Shedler & Block, 1990), and most adolescents appear to "mature out" of problem use as they grow up (Kouzis & Labouvie, 1992, as cited in Waldron, 1997). This issue needs to be explored further by helping professionals and researchers working with this population.

SUMMARY

This chapter has reviewed group treatment with substance-abusing offenders. Guidelines for and illustrations of conducting group therapy were presented. Group workers should be aware of how the group process benefits its members, remaining mindful of the therapeutic factors, stages of group development, and the special needs of offenders in group settings.

We examined structured group-oriented approaches—namely, PPC, EQUIP, and ART—commonly used with juvenile delinquents. EQUIP incorporates into the PPC approach a multicomponent skills training (ART) to provide a more structured format for developing a positive youth group culture. Cognitive-based group interventions such as EQUIP and ART appear promising. Indeed, Pearson, Lipton, Cleland, and Yee (2002) have encouraged policymakers to consider adopting cognitive skills training programs such as ART and the Substance Abuse and Mental Health Services Administration (2002) has issued a 12-week cognitive–behavioral anger management group treatment manual, entitled Anger Management for Substance Abuse *and Mental Health Clients: A Cognitive Behavioral Therapy Manual*, that is available at no cost from the National Clearinghouse on Alcohol and Drug Information (NCADI) (www.samhsa.gov). Nevertheless, further research is needed on these approaches, as "continued favorable findings would suggest that a certain synergy may result from the integration of peer-helping with skills-training approaches" (Gibbs et al., 1996, p. 300).

Additionally, the use of psychoeducational and MFTG approaches with substance-abusing offenders was explored. Based on the available outcome literature, it appears that the impact on change of psychoeducational approaches is maximized when this approach is paired with an interactional, mutual-aid model of group work. Thus, rather than implement psychoeducational approaches as an isolated activity, we encourage group workers to integrate psychoeducational material into peer-helping groups and MFTGs. As this occurs, further research will be needed to determine the efficacy of such efforts.

Finally, self-help programs such as AA, NA, and Women for Sobriety were covered. Although self-help programs are used widely across treatment programs for substance-abusing offenders, the research on these programs has been criticized. To date, studies have been methodologically weak and have focused primarily on middle- and upper-class clients at the exclusion of those from more disenfranchised backgrounds commonly found among offenders. Until further research is able to fill this lacuna, we caution against the blanket use of self-help groups, especially with juvenile offenders.

In sum, group treatment will likely remain one of the most commonly used modalities in treating substance-abusing offenders. Although additional research is called for, it appears that overall structured, cognitive-based, peer-helping group interventions have a positive impact on substance-abusing clients. We now move to a discussion on traditional (chapter 6) and innovative (chapter 7) treatment settings, where many such groups are facilitated.

6

TRADITIONAL TREATMENT
SETTINGS AND APPROACHES

Beginning in the 1950s, treatment for alcoholism took a turn toward the conceptualization of alcoholism as a disease. This was due to the impact of self-help movements such as Alcoholics Anonymous (AA) and the incorporation of AA principles into the Minnesota model, which became the standard for private treatment in the United States (Van Wormer & Davis, 2003). Traditional treatment settings as reviewed in this chapter continue to use the disease model for the treatment of alcoholism and other drug addictions, whereas some of the newer treatment approaches have sought a different paradigm for providing treatment (see chapter 7). Traditional programs use various forms of individual, family, and group therapy in combination with a specific treatment setting (e.g., residential treatment center, therapeutic community), whereas innovative programs tend to target cognitive–behavioral approaches, pharmacotherapies, acupuncture, and the therapeutic influence of the legal system as a major component in treatment. Nevertheless, traditional approaches are still commonly and effectively used to treat substance-abusing offenders.

INPATIENT AND RESIDENTIAL PROGRAMS

Substance abusers involved in the justice system can be referred to inpatient or residential treatment programs for their substance abuse problems in several ways. A judge can court order a person to treatment, a worker at a juvenile assessment center or juvenile addiction receiving facility (see chapter 7) can refer a youth to such a program, or inpatient treatment can be mandated as part of probation.

A DSM Axis I (American Psychiatric Association, 2000) diagnosis for the client is typically needed to justify admission into an inpatient or residential facility. The client should exhibit a high degree of medical risk, suicidal or homicidal threat, or a high likelihood of injury by neglect to warrant inpatient admission. Current health care policy and the fragmentation of community-based service networks make inpatient treatment an expensive and overused form of care (I. Schwartz, 1989).

Inpatient treatment has changed drastically over recent years. The era of 28-day treatment programs is almost gone. The cost of such programs is too high for most people to pay for out-of-pocket, and the great majority of third-party payers no longer reimburse for such services without extensive documentation. Inpatient programs typically provide respite for family, drug education, group encounters with peers, and individual treatment that may include a pharmacological component.

Longer inpatient (residential) programs for offenders, such as therapeutic communities, also exist. Once admitted into such facilities, residents are encouraged to form close emotional ties with other residents. When successful, adolescents will perceive themselves as part of a group of peers who act as a support network (Obermeier & Henry, 1989). If third-party payers are involved, a dual diagnosis of the child or adolescent is required to warrant payment for such treatment.

There is little doubt that extended residential communities are necessary for seriously disturbed children and adolescents. When children or adolescents are chronically endangering themselves with their drug or alcohol use, extended residential treatment may be the desired alternative because of its ability to provide 24-hour monitoring of behavior (Downey, 1991). The same holds true for adults.

One residential model that has been implemented throughout the country is restitution centers, which control and provide support for residents who must pay victim restitution out of earnings from community work. One such program is the Griffin Diversion Center in Georgia, established in the early 1970s. Residents typically work 8 hours a day, maintain the center's operations, complete community service on weekends, attend classes or counseling sessions in the evenings, submit to routine drug testing, participate in sports tournaments, and organize food and clothing drives (DiMascio, 1995).

OUTPATIENT PROGRAMS

An alternative to the more expensive and restrictive inpatient and residential care described above is outpatient treatment. Third-party payers typically demand dual diagnoses to reimburse for inpatient or residential treatment. For example, in addition to demonstrating that a diagnosis of a substance abuse problem (e.g., polysubstance dependence) is warranted, the practitioner or agency must also be able to identify and justify a *DSM* Axis I diagnosis. This practice has resulted in an increased use of intensive outpatient programs (IOPs) and partial hospitalization programs (PHPs) in the field, both of which allow the client to return home each night with his or her family. Generally, a PHP, also referred to as day treatment, is more intense than an IOP. One distinct difference between the two approaches is that a PHP client typically attends treatment Monday through Friday during the day (e.g., from 8 a.m. to 4 p.m.), whereas a client in an IOP might attend only three days a week for 3 hours each day. Otherwise, IOPs and PHPs provide the same services as inpatient or residential treatment at lower costs. These approaches have gained popularity in recent years as goal-oriented and planned short-term treatment is being favored over longer-term treatment approaches (cf. R. A. Wells, 1994).

INPATIENT VERSUS OUTPATIENT TREATMENT

There is no evidence to suggest that inpatient treatment is any more effective with most children and adolescents than outpatient treatment (Gerstein & Harwood, 1990). However, for many parents who avail themselves of extended inpatient treatment for their children, the treatment period acts as a respite. For improvements to be maintained, critics of this approach suggest that children and adolescents need changes to occur while in their home setting (as is done with multisystemic therapy; see chapter 4). Changes that occur in a facility frequently occur within a vacuum; the typical frustrations and challenges that might encourage alcohol and drug use and abuse are absent in an inpatient setting. Thus, improvements seen in the hospital do not necessarily extend to home settings (Joaning, Gawinski, Morris, & Quinn, 1986). One study (A. S. Friedman & Utada, 1983) found that outpatient settings devoted more staff time to individual and family counseling than residential programs, which had a heavier emphasis on art therapy, group counseling, vocational training, and medical services.

Regarding the treatment of cocaine (and crack) dependence, a condition that practitioners are likely to encounter among juvenile and adult offenders, Gold (1997) provided guidelines to use in determining whether inpatient or outpatient treatment is warranted. Gold argued that outpatient treatment is the preferred modality for cocaine abusers for some of the following reasons: Cocaine use can typically be stopped abruptly without medical risk; life is more "normal" in an outpatient setting than inpatient, and returning the client to a "normal" life is a key goal of treatment; the cost of outpatient care is lower; there is less stigma and disruption to one's life in outpatient care than with inpatient; and it is certain that outpatient care will be needed anyway due to the risk of relapse. However, Gold went on to state that "When drug use is severe, or if outpatient care is not possible or has failed in the past, hospitalization is called for. While not a complete listing, indications for inpatient care include

1. Chronic crack, freebase, or intravenous use
2. Concurrent dependency on other addictive drugs or alcohol
3. Serious concurrent medical or psychiatric problems
4. Severe impairment of psychological or neurological functioning
5. Insufficient motivation for outpatient treatment
6. Lack of family and social supports
7. Failure in outpatient treatment." (p. 191)

We have chosen cocaine use to illustrate the issues that must be addressed in the inpatient versus outpatient debate because the use of this drug is common among offenders. However, the above guidelines can be applied to most substances when considering whether inpatient or outpatient treatment is warranted for an offender.

The Forever Free Substance Abuse Program, a 120-bed drug treatment program at the California Institution for Women, was studied to determine how effective it was at reducing drug use and improving behavior among women prisoners and parolees (Prendergast, Wellisch, & Wong, 1996). The program entailed 4 months of treatment during a woman's last 6 months of confinement, followed by 6 months of voluntary (but strongly encouraged) treatment during parole. The program consisted of several components, including individual substance abuse counseling, workshops, psychoeducational services, 12-step programs, parole planning, family treatment, vocational or rehabilitation counseling, recreational and social activities, and monitoring (i.e., urine testing; Prendergast et al., 1996).

Three groups of women were examined: (a) women who completed the program and stayed in the community-based residential program for a minimum of 30 days, (b) women who completed the program but did not continue in the community-based residential treatment program, and (c) women who volunteered for the program but who did not get into the program. There were statistically significant differences between the groups. Over two-thirds (68.4%) of the women in the first group had favorable parole outcomes, compared to about half (52.2%) of the women in the second group and approximately one-quarter (27.2%) of the women who did not get into the treatment program (the third group; Prendergast et al., 1996). Additionally, Prendergast and colleagues found that, when women returned to prison, those women from the first group had a lower rate for new criminal offenses (33.3%) compared to the rates for those women from the second and third groups (45.5% and 50%, respectively). This study lends support to the notion that a comprehensive substance abuse treatment program, combined with community support during parole, contributes to more favorable outcomes for female substance-abusing offenders.

Garrett (1985) conducted a meta-analysis of 111 residential programs for adjudicated delinquents. The findings revealed that programs using behavioral and life skills approaches produced the greatest degree of positive results. A second meta-analysis of 90 community and residential programs for juvenile delinquents (Davidson, Redner, Blakely, Mitchell, & Emshoff, 1987) supported this conclusion, finding that behavioral approaches had the largest effect on recidivism rates. Anglin and Hser (1990, as cited in Deschenes & Greenwood, 1994) reviewed data from two large-scale studies, the Drug Abuse Reporting Program (conducted during the late 1960s and early 1970s) and the Treatment Outcome Prospective Study (conducted from 1979 to 1981), as well as other treatment studies, and concluded that the length of time in treatment was related to posttreatment outcomes for residential programs but not necessarily for outpatient programs. In a comparison of inpatient versus outpatient treatment programs, the U.S. Congress's Office of Technology Assessment review found no clear evidence that either setting produced more effective outcomes in reducing adolescent substance abuse (McBride, VanderWaal, Terry, & VanBuren, 1999).

THERAPEUTIC COMMUNITIES

The therapeutic community (TC) is a highly specialized type of residential treatment program that provides an around-the-clock learning experience in which the drug user's changes in conduct, attitudes, values, and emotions are implemented, monitored, and reinforced daily (De Leon, 1994). Although there is no generally recognized model of the TC, typically it is a highly structured program, lasting 1 to 3 years and occasionally longer. On the other hand, due to the confrontational nature of the community, it is common for residents to leave within the first three months of the program. High dropout rates are normally expected in most TCs: 30 to 40% drop out in the first month, and only 15 to 25% eventually graduate (De Leon, 1994). Research has been done to identify the reasons for dropping out and to improve retention rates (cf. Goldapple, 1990).

The primary "clinical" staff in TCs are former substance abusers (recovering addicts) who were also rehabilitated in TCs. Ancillary staff consist of mental health professionals. Traditionally, about three-fourths of the residents in TCs have been male, with half in their mid-20s. More than three-fourths have an arrest record (De Leon, 1986). In recent years there has been a dramatic increase in women and adolescents in TCs. In the 1960s, most TC residents were heroin addicts; today, the majority of TC residents have abused crack cocaine (W. O'Brien & Devlin, 1997).

Background

TCs emerged in psychiatric settings in the United Kingdom at the end of Word War II, about 20 years before they came to be used for substance abusers (De Leon, 1986). It was an attempt to democratize a traditional hierarchical system in which the domination of medical doctors was replaced by open communication, information sharing, decision making by consensus, and group problem solving. TCs for substance abuse emerged in 1958 with the founding of Synanon by Charles E. Dederich, who was a participant in and advocate of the 12-step model of AA (De Leon, 1986). Synanon is often regarded as the prototypical model of a TC, although most modern TCs have modified or abandoned some of its principles such as the insistence on a *lifetime* commitment to the TC.[1]

The treatment philosophy of a TC is based on the idea that substance abuse is a disorder of the whole person, that the problem lies in the person and not the drug, and that the addiction is simply a symptom and not the essence of the disorder (Pan, Scarpitti, Inciardi, & Lockwood, 1993). The primary goal of the TC approach is to lead the client to a responsible, substance-free life. Although individual, family, and group treatment may be components of the TC, the cornerstone of the program is the peer encounter that takes place in the group process. Rules of the community are specific and enforced by the residents themselves. Generally, the TC staff are themselves recovering substance abusers who have successfully completed treatment in a TC (McNeece, Springer, & Arnold, 2001). S. Cohen (1985) summarized 12 characteristics commonly shared by TCs:

- An arduous admission policy
- Charismatic leadership
- Emphasis on personal responsibility
- Mutual assistance
- Self-examination and confession
- Structure and discipline
- A system of rewards and punishments
- Status as an extended family
- Separation from society
- Staff members who are not seen as authority figures
- Fostering of such characteristics as nonviolence and honesty
- Emphasis on work.

---

[1]According to Abandinsky (2001), "Dederich eventually transformed Synanon into a cultlike phenomenon. In 1980 he pled guilty to plotting the murder of one of his Synanon critics, a lawyer representing former Synanon members who maintained they were held against their will" (p. 213). Dederich received 5 years probation and was banned from further participation in Synanon. He died at age 83 of a heart attack in 1997.

The Therapeutic Community Program

Once admitted to a TC, residents find themselves in a highly structured environment that is almost totally isolated from the rest of society. There are strict rules and regulations and strict consequences for deviation from accepted behavior. The TC is largely self-regulating, with veteran residents being responsible for shaping and guiding the behavior of newer residents. All residents are expected to correct the behavior of other residents at any time—a practice called "dropping a ticket." New residents are assigned to the most demeaning, onerous tasks, such as cleaning toilets. As they display increased responsibility and make progress in "working the program," they are given the opportunity to perform tasks that provide more status (Abadinsky, 2001), and they are rewarded with improvements in their overall quality of life.

For example, at the Delancey Street program in San Francisco, newly admitted residents sleep in bunk beds in a "barracks" type of arrangement, clean toilets, and bus tables in the program's restaurant next door. As they make progress in the program, they may share an apartment with two or three roommates, mop floors or do the laundry, and work as a waiter. Toward the end of their stay they may have their own apartment; supervise others in household chores (but do no chores themselves); and hold jobs such as chef, electrician, or store manager.

Some substance abuse and mental health professionals do not believe that the TC is a good model for many residents because of controversial methods such as "ego stripping" and complete submission to the program rules (Ausabel, 1983). Others fault the TC's core values of separating clients from society, long-term isolation, and insistence on unquestioned conformity to the group (Lewis, Dana, & Blevins, 1994). Behavior changes that occur within the TC may not transfer to the real world, in part because the residents have few opportunities to interact with the outside world. While living in the confrontational but supportive environment of the TC, residents may act in a socially acceptable, productive, and drug-free manner. When deprived of the TC's support, however, they may quickly relapse (Benshoff & Janikowski, 2000).

As an Alternative to Incarceration

In 1963, Daytop Village developed one of the first court diversion programs when it established an experimental project in Staten Island, New York, to treat 25 drug-addicted probationers. Since that time Daytop and several other TCs have developed arrangements with judges, defense attorneys, and prosecuting attorneys to arrange for treatment in a TC when the only other likely alternative is incarceration (W. O'Brien & Devlin, 1997). Beginning in 1990, a program in the district attorney's office of Kings County,

New York, began the program Drug Treatment Alternative-to-Prison, offering eligible defendants 15 to 24 months of treatment either in Daytop Village or Samaritan Village. Prosecution is deferred until the defendant completes treatment, at which time the criminal charges may be reduced or dismissed.

Drug courts across the nation are also using TCs as alternatives to incarceration (see chapter 7). Generally, prosecution is deferred for those who complete the treatment program, and in some cases arrest records may even be expunged for those offenders. Treatment Alternatives to Street Crime programs also refer many eligible offenders to treatment in TCs as an alternative to incarceration.

In Correctional Settings

Along with the ideological shift in corrections in recent years, prison systems have increasingly adopted approaches to drug treatment developed in noninstitutional settings. The TC model has become prominent in this trend as a treatment approach that can be imported into correctional settings without undermining discipline and security (Wexler & Williams, 1986). However, TCs in correctional institutions should more properly be referred to as *modified* TCs, because the degree of client control of clinical issues, policies, and so forth that exists outside a prison simply cannot be allowed on the inside. Typically, a prison TC will have much more input and control by paid professional staff than in a traditional TC model (McNeece, 2000).

Modified TCs have been used in correctional settings for several years (Lipton, Falkin, & Wexler, 1992). To develop a sense of community among TC participants and to minimize any negative peer influence from inmates not involved with treatment, many TC programs are arranged so that participants are isolated from the general population. The implementation of TCs in correctional settings has been hindered at times by (a) a reluctance to provide long-term therapeutic services, (b) philosophical opposition to the use of staff who are former offenders and to coercive treatment strategies, and (c) the need for specialized staff training and technical assistance (R. Peters, 1993).

Several TCs known as "Stay'n Out" TCs have been established in New York, California, and other states. Inmates are selected and recruited from state correctional facilities, screened and admitted to the program, and housed in units segregated from the general population, although they eat and participate in some activities with other prisoners. The program lasts 6 to 9 months and is staffed by graduates of other TCs and by ex-offenders who have been successfully rehabilitated. When released, Stay'n Out graduates are encouraged to maintain connections with an extensive community-based TC network (Abadinsky, 2001).

Cornerstone is another modified TC program (a mixture of milieu therapy and TC principles) that was developed at the Oregon State Hospital in Salem. It was designed for inmates in their last year before eligibility for parole. After release, the parolees move to a halfway house for the period of treatment.

The National Institute of Justice recently funded several in-prison treatment programs for inmates with a dual diagnosis of mental illness and substance abuse. All of those programs were based on a modified TC model. For a description of those programs and their treatment outcomes, please refer to the chapter on dual diagnosis (chapter 8).

Effectiveness

Most research indicates that offenders who leave TCs do not fare significantly better with postrelease drug and crime experiences when compared to their counterparts who did not participate in a TC (McNeece & Daly, 1997). Gerstein and Harwood (1990) concluded that TC programs, when closely linked to community-based supervision and treatment programs, can significantly reduce re-arrest rates. However, Gerstein and Harwood were careful to point out the limitations of available research on the effectiveness of TCs.

> Conclusions about the effectiveness of TCs are limited by the difficulties of applying standard clinical trial methodologies to a complex, dynamic treatment milieu and a population resistant to following instructions. . . . Currently, the strongest conclusions on the effectiveness of TCs are based on nonrandomized or nonexperimental but rigorously conducted studies of clients seeking admission to therapeutic communities. (p. 156)

Research on the effectiveness of TC treatment for criminal justice clients has lagged behind the implementation of prison TC models. The two most famous studies, of the Stay'n Out and the Cornerstone programs, followed offenders released from a prison-based treatment program. Outcome data from the first 3 years of the Amity TC program showed steady improvements in postrelease performance as the time in the program increased from 9 to 12 months (Wexler & Williams, 1986). Similar findings were reported from the Cornerstone Study, which showed that 29% of program graduates were reincarcerated within 3 years after release, compared to 74% of the treatment dropouts.

More recently, a TC at Donovan prison in California released findings indicating that 34% of program graduates were reincarcerated within a 3-year follow-up period, compared to 53% of program dropouts (Winett, Mullen, Lowe, & Missakian, 1992). Research on the impact of the Stay'n Out program found that it reduced recidivism among parolees more than 40 percent at 12 months and more than 50 percent at 24 months (Wexler, De Leon, Thomas, Kressel, & Peters, 1999).

Martin, Butzin, and Inciardi (1995) reported the findings of a TC with adult male substance-abusing offenders in the Delaware Correctional Institute. The program studied consisted of two phases. Phase 1, called KEY, was a 12-month TC inside of the prison. Phase 2, called CREST, was a 6-month work release and residential program. The findings lend evidence to the effectiveness of the KEY and CREST programs at reducing relapse and recidivism rates. At an 18-month follow-up, the offenders who participated in both KEY and CREST had better success rates as evidenced by remaining drug free (76%) and arrest free (71%), compared to offenders who participated only in CREST (drug free = 45%, arrest free = 65%), those who participated only in KEY (drug free = 30%, arrest free = 48%), and those who participated in a no-treatment comparison group (drug free = 19%, arrest free = 30%). Additionally, participation in KEY, CREST, or both programs was a significant predictor of being drug and arrest free (Martin et al., 1995).

The research on the effectiveness of TCs for adolescents reveals that the length of stay in treatment is the largest and most consistent predictor of positive outcomes (Catalano, Hawkins, Wells, Miller, & Brewer, 1990/91; De Leon, 1988). Positive outcomes, such as no criminal activity, no use of alcohol or drugs, and employment, are all associated with longer stays in treatment (McBride et al., 1999). "Therefore, while juvenile TCs advocate comparatively shorter treatment times than adult TCs, it is essential that programs allow adequate time for treatment effectiveness" (McBride et al., 1999, p. 48).

SUMMARY

In this chapter we covered traditional settings and approaches to working with substance-abusing offenders, namely inpatient and residential programs, outpatient care, and TCs. We reviewed the effectiveness of each of these approaches; one of the more significant conclusions was that length of stay in treatment is the largest and most consistent predictor of positive outcomes for juveniles in TCs.

However, the evidence regarding the impact of TCs is mixed. Although some demonstrate evidence of reduced recidivism, the research designs used do not permit a conclusion that they are more successful than other treatment approaches in decreasing substance abuse. The rigorous admission process may effectively eliminate people who are the most likely to fail, and there is a very high dropout rate, especially during the first few weeks of the program. One might be tempted to view these factors as skewing the results in a positive manner, because only those people most highly motivated to succeed seem to stay with the program through completion. Nevertheless, when combined with close supervision and monitoring after clients leave the TC, this model does seem to work for certain "hard-core" addicts who have failed in other programs.

7

INNOVATIVE TREATMENT
SETTINGS AND APPROACHES

Recent years have seen exciting developments in treating substance-abusing adult and juvenile offenders. Innovation in treatment programming has been the result of many factors, including the prohibitive costs of residential care; pressure from insurance companies to develop more cost-efficient means of treating addiction; and the antitreatment backlash of the Reagan era (White, 1998), when the emphasis of the War on Drugs was on interdiction and enforcement rather than on treatment (Rosenbaum, 1997).

Chapter 6 addressed traditional treatment settings and approaches used with substance-abusing offenders; this chapter reviews some of the more innovative treatment settings and approaches used with this population, including juvenile assessment centers (JACs), juvenile addiction receiving facilities (JARFs), juvenile boot camps, treatment alternatives to street crime (TASC), drug courts, mental health courts, and acupuncture. The effectiveness of each approach is discussed through a review of the available outcome literature; some appear more promising than others. JACs have grown rapidly over the past decade, and we turn our attention to these "one-stop shops" first.

JUVENILE ASSESSMENT CENTERS AND JUVENILE ADDICTION RECEIVING FACILITIES

Unfortunately, the nation's juvenile justice system is currently strained and faces many difficulties in dealing with serious juvenile offenders. Historically, resources nationwide have been inadequate to provide treatment for youths in the juvenile detention system. Bazemore (1993) commented on this phenomenon, arguing that detention in many instances has come to represent a holding center or dumping ground for offenders and at-risk adolescents who lack appropriate supervision. In response to the rise in juvenile delinquency and truancy and the inability to effectively deal with this population, many states have adopted legislation that mandates the establishment of community assessment centers, also referred to as JACs.

The organizing principle of the JAC is to serve as a one-stop shop marked by collaboration among substance abuse and mental health providers, law enforcement agencies, schools, health services providers, and others. Each JAC has as a similar objective: to serve as a centralized intake system where law enforcement officers can bring youths charged with truancy, felonies, and misdemeanors. Although organization of these centers can vary, they should have as their cornerstone multidisciplinary screening and assessment systems. The centers are designed to help ensure that the youths' service needs are addressed in disposition recommendations, to link at-risk adolescents and their families with needed services, and to track the outcomes of these problem identification and program-linking activities.

Youths are typically brought into a JAC through a secured area and are fingerprinted and photographed, allowing law enforcement officers to drop off a juvenile in custody and return to patrol (often in less than 10 minutes). The JAC staff assess and determine what should be done with the juvenile. Some assessment centers are using the Problem Oriented Screening Instrument for Teenagers (POSIT; see chapter 2), which is designed to identify problems in any functional area (including substance abuse) that require further assessment or treatment. From the initial screening, a determination is made regarding the necessity of an in-depth assessment. Following all assessments, if the youth meets detention criteria, he or she is transported to the juvenile detention center. Otherwise, the juvenile may be placed in nonsecure detention or another suitable facility; be placed on home detention; or released outright to a parent, guardian, or responsible adult. Juveniles are assigned case managers to monitor their progress through the system, including follow-up assessment and disposition. Various services are provided in the centers, including detoxification, physical and mental health screening, referrals, and urinalysis. The centers are typically operated through a collaborative effort among components of the juvenile justice system and other human services agencies.

Typically, if the initial screening and assessment indicate the presence of substance use, the juvenile is referred for a more in-depth substance abuse assessment. Some JACs have a substance abuse assessment team housed in the center, and some JACs conduct HIV risk assessments. Others have complete detoxification units, often called a JARF. The JARF may be in the same building as the JAC or close by in a separate facility. If a young person is brought to a JAC by an arresting officer and appears to be intoxicated, he or she may be transferred to the JARF for detoxification. Whereas the JAC is strictly a juvenile justice enterprise, the JARF has affiliations with juvenile justice but often is a community-based center. Therefore, the JARF also accepts youths for admission who have not been charged with any offense but are in need of detoxification or substance abuse treatment.

At least one pilot study to date (Dembo & Brown, 1994) has indicated that the assessment center concept as implemented in Tampa, Florida, has the ability to identify multiple-problem, high-risk youths. The study involved 110 truant juveniles brought to the Tampa JAC in January 1993. The majority of these youths were male and ranged in age from 9 to 18 years, with an average age of 14. According to the study, just under half (45%) had a history of one or more arrests on a delinquency charge. An analysis of POSIT results revealed that 96% of these adolescents indicated a potential problem in peer relations; 82% indicated a potential problem in "mental health status"; and 33% to 47% had a potential problem involving substance abuse, physical health, family relations, and vocational status.

Springer, Shader, and McNeece (1999) conducted an in-depth study of six JACs/JARFs in Florida. Results indicated that the primary presenting problems among youths involved peer relations, family relations, mental health, substance abuse, physical health, and school or vocational issues. A key finding was that successful JACs had an energetic and hard-working director with good interpersonal and mediation skills. Many of the staff across the JACs and JARFs appeared stressed because of high caseloads or inadequate work settings. JARFs were found to provide short-term stabilization and detoxification when needed. However, assessments were placed in a youth's file but often were not used to help make appropriate referrals, and staff did not have the resources to provide adequate follow-up case management services. One judge referred to this process as "assessment to nowhere." Additionally, "turf wars" between agencies in the JACs sometimes hindered interagency information sharing and collaboration.

JUVENILE BOOT CAMPS

Today's boot camp can be traced back to the United States' first penitentiaries at the turn of the 19th century, which used military-style marches, physical labor, silence, and discipline (Rothman, 1990). Elements of today's juvenile boot camps (also known as *shock incarceration*) are based on a highly-structured military model and vary from state to state but usually handle small groups and last 3–6 months. They stress discipline, physical conditioning, and strict authoritarian control (McNeece, 1997). Most local and state boot camps are designed for the first-time offenders. It is precisely these characteristics that have made these camps popular with both politicians and the general public. The Shock Probation (see chapter 9) and Scared Straight programs are both based on the boot camp approach. The boot camp philosophy is based on breaking down and then building up the juvenile in a quasimilitary setting (Parent, 1989).

Some criminal justice researchers argue that boot camps do not make a long-term impact on juveniles because they do not meet the needs of offenders and that in fact rearrest rates of boot camp graduates are similar to those of other inmates (MacKenzie, 1994). In general, the research to date on juvenile boot camps indicates that they are not effective in reducing recidivism when compared to traditional probation or parole services (M. Peters, Thomas, & Zamberlan, 1997).

The California Youth Authority (1997) conducted an evaluation of their Leadership, Esteem, Ability, and Discipline (LEAD) juvenile boot camp program. The researchers followed boot camp graduates for 12 to 24 months following release from the program. Juveniles who participated in the LEAD boot camp program did not differ from a control group on several factors, including school attendance or number of days worked, the number of positive drug tests, or rearrest rates. Additionally, the boot camp program was found to be more costly than typical services.

Trulson and Triplett (1999) compared a school-based juvenile boot camp with Intensive Supervision Probationers (ISP) in Conroe, Texas. The school-based juvenile boot camp program (Specialized Treatment and Rehabilitation; STAR) maintained a quasimilitary atmosphere, but it was school-based, nonresidential, and mandated parental participation. Recidivism analyses reveal that 12 months following completion of the respective programs, more STAR participants (53%) were arrested than ISP participants (36%), and they were arrested 41 days sooner than ISP participants.

Using funding from the Office of Juvenile Justice and Delinquency Prevention, Peters, Thomas, and Zamberlan (1997) conducted a study of three juvenile boot camp demonstration sites (in Cleveland, Ohio; Mobile, Alabama; and Denver, Colorado). The boot camps were found to be a cost-effective alternative to traditional confinement but cost significantly more than probation. Juveniles who went through boot camp demonstrated higher recidivism rates than the control group in two of the three sites, and juveniles from all three boot camp sites re-offended earlier on average when compared to the control group (Peters et al., 1997).

Lipsey's (1992) well-known meta-analysis of treatment for juvenile offenders revealed that deterrence programs, such as boot camps, actually had negative treatment effects on delinquent youths. Other studies have also noted negative effects. For example, evaluations of the Louisiana shock incarceration program indicate that graduates of this program were more likely to be rearrested than parolees or probationers (MacKenzie, 1991).

Furthermore, Marcus-Mendoza, Klein-Saffran, and Lutze (1997) examined the processes and procedures used in boot camps with female offenders, noting that they are incompatible with a feminist ideology or belief system. Indeed, Marcus-Mendoza and colleagues went on to assert that

> Feminist therapists working in boot camp or other prison settings must aid the clients in identifying and asserting their own needs while their clients are being denied freedom in an environment that demands conformity. In addition, the therapist must find a way to help women identify and express their feelings, including those about their incarceration, in a way that will not be punished. It is incumbent upon the therapist to face these challenges successfully in order to help to counter the negative messages of the boot camp and prison, support the women and foster growth, and help their clients survive the confusion and trauma they are experiencing. (p. 183)

In general, it appears that despite their popularity among politicians and the media, juvenile boot camps are not cost-effective and do not deliver positive treatment effects for juvenile offenders, when compared to traditional services such as probation or parole. This is particularly worrisome given that most juvenile boot camp participants are nonviolent, first-time offenders (MacKenzie, 1990).

Studies of adult boot camps reveal mixed findings, with some studies indicating that adult boot camp participants do as well as comparison groups of probationers or parolees (MacKenzie, Brame, McDowall, & Souryal, 1995). Other studies indicate that adult boot camp participants do better than comparison groups (C. L. Clark, Aziz, & MacKenzie, 1994), and yet other studies indicate that boot camp participants have higher recidivism rates than comparison groups (MacKenzie & Shaw, 1993). However, as is the case for findings on juvenile boot camps, the outcome research to date on adult boot camps is not promising (Zhang, 1998). A thorough review of the adult boot camp literature by MacKenzie and her colleagues revealed that adult boot camp participants fare no better or worse on recidivism rates than offenders in traditional prison or probation programs (MacKenzie, 1991, as cited in Henggeler & Schoenwald, 1994).

TREATMENT ALTERNATIVES TO STREET CRIME

In the attempt to combat substance abuse in communities, alternatives other than incarceration have been tried in recent years. One of the most widely known alternatives is Treatment Alternatives to Street Crime (TASC), a program initially funded in 1972 by federal monies. TASC targets offenders who appear to have the potential to benefit from treatment and do not pose significant safety risks to communities with supervision (Lipton, 1995). The purpose of TASC is to identify, assess, refer for treatment, and conduct follow-up on drug offenders. Initially, many TASC programs were operated independently of the court and treatment systems (McNeece & Daly, 1997). Offenders in TASC programs are not incarcerated but rather are treated outside the court system in community-based programs. Each offender is assigned a case manager who assists in gaining access to treatment, provides linkages to other needed community services, and reports back to the appropriate court officials about the offender's progress.

The monitoring function of the case manager is one of the hallmarks of TASC. Case managers attempt to get to know offenders and generally visit them while in treatment. For offenders who do not comply with the program, TASC does not have its own enforcement team and must rely on the police to arrest those who are noncompliant. TASC case managers may use the threat of incarceration as a tool to enhance compliance, but they are likely to give offenders who do not comply with the program another chance (Young, Dynia, & Belenko, 1996).

The National Institute on Drug Abuse's (NIDA) Treatment Outcome Prospective Study examined the impact of TASC programs on criminal offenders' posttreatment behavior compared to a voluntary control group. In the 6-month period following program completion, TASC participants were comparable to the control group in regard to drug use, criminal involvement, and employment. The most significant predictor of criminal reinvolvement was a history of predatory crime and arrest before beginning treatment. In addition, the case management services were found to encourage continued treatment participation (J. J. Collins & Allison, 1983).

One of the initial funding sources for TASC programs, the Law Enforcement Assistance Administration required that those agencies receiving funding conduct independent evaluations. From 1972 to 1982, more than 40 evaluations were conducted. The majority of independent evaluators found that TASC programs had effectively intervened with clients to reduce drug abuse and criminal activity, linked the criminal justice and treatment systems, and identified previously untreated drug-dependent offenders (Cook & Weinman, 1985).

A more recent study of narcotic-addicted offenders in TASC programs (Hubbard, Collins, Rachal, & Cavanaugh, 1988) found support for two commonly held beliefs regarding offenders and drug treatment: The high level of structure of programs as found in TASC may provide the necessary environment for offenders to discontinue drug use, and offenders mandated for treatment tend to stay in treatment longer, which is believed to enhance treatment outcomes. In Washington State and Oklahoma, TASC was evaluated, and encouraging results were found; recidivism rates were 14% and 19%, respectively.

Direct federal funding for TASC ceased in the 1980s, but this and other similar programs continue to exist (McNeece & Roberts, 1997). One such off-shoot is the Treatment Alternative Programs; in Wisconsin, an evaluation of these programs showed less favorable results than previous studies: 43% of offenders were re-arrested, and 23% of those re-arrested were arrested on alcohol or drug charges (Van Stelle, Mauser, & Moberg, 1994).

DRUG COURTS

Our entire criminal justice system has undergone a radical transformation due to the impact of the substance abuse problem and the increasing number of offenders arrested on drug-related charges. Since the early 1980s, jails and state and federal prisons have become inundated with drug offenders. In many states, prisons have been forced to adopt a "revolving-door" approach to incarceration, with new admissions (primarily for drug offenses) coming in the front door and literally pushing other, sometimes more serious offenders, out the back door.

The federal response to the drug problem was to declare a War on Drugs and to establish mandatory sentencing requirements as a condition of financial assistance to the states' criminal justice agencies. These tactics had at least three repercussions: (a) an escalation in the number of people incarcerated for drug-related offenses, (b) overcrowded prisons, and (c) increases in the number of early releases from prison.

The number of felony drug arrests has skyrocketed, court dockets have burgeoned, and available resources for addressing the problem are severely limited. It has become obvious that arrest and incarceration are not a solution. They do little to break the cycle of illegal drug use and crime. Furthermore, offenders sentenced to jail or prison for drug offenses have a high rate of recidivism after their release. At the same time, drug abuse treatment has been demonstrably effective in reducing both drug abuse and drug-related crime (NIDA, 1999c).

Because treatment for substance abuse addiction is seen as a key component in preventing re-offenses, the need for alternative programs is evident. A new promising and innovative approach to the growing substance abuse problem is the establishment of diversionary programs known as *drug courts*. Two main types of drug courts exist: those organized simply to speed up the processing of drug offenders and those that exist to provide treatment to offenders. Our focus in this chapter is on treatment-oriented drug courts.

The idea of dedicating specified courtrooms solely to drug cases is not new. Special drug case courtrooms were created in Chicago and New York City in the early 1950s. More than two decades ago, when heroin was the primary drug of choice among offenders in New York City, a special "narcotics court" was created as a way of dealing with the impact of the new, harsher drug laws. Other approaches to link offenders to drug treatment at various points of the criminal justice process have also been tried over the past 20 years. Drug courts evolved from existing efforts to engage defendants in treatment, such as TASC, limited diversion programs, pretrial release programs, probation, and intermediate sanctions programs. However, these earlier efforts were frequently fragmented, inconsistently or inappropriately used, or only minimally effective. Consequently, it was difficult to monitor treatment progress or compliance with court-imposed conditions (cf. Belenko, 1990, 1998; Falkin, 1993).

In 1989, Janet Reno, the sitting state attorney for the 11th judicial circuit (Miami, Florida), established the first treatment-focused drug court. The Miami Drug Court has served as a model for the development of many other courts throughout the nation. Drug courts have since proliferated.

By 1998, drug courts had been implemented in about 275 jurisdictions (Cooper, 1997). The drug court model differs in important ways from previous efforts to provide drug treatment to offenders with underlying drug problems. The drug court model creates an interface between the various components of the criminal justice and substance abuse treatment systems to use the coercive power of the court to promote abstinence and prosocial behavior (Belenko, 1996; Finn & Newlyn, 1993; Goldkamp, 1999). While participation is generally voluntary (except in some juvenile drug courts), offenders must adhere to program requirements to successfully complete the program. In addition to receiving treatment at no or little cost to them, offenders may also be inclined to participate in drug court programs because many programs offer possible expunction of the offenders' criminal records on successful completion of the program. For some offenders, the opportunity to have one's record expunged is a strong incentive to participate. In keeping with the Alcoholics Anonymous philosophy (N. S. Miller, 1995), total abstinence from day one of the recovery process is not expected. Most therapeutic drug courts expect that relapse will be a part of a normal recovery process. Clients are generally sanctioned or reprimanded but are not dismissed from the program because of one or two "slips." This is driven by the assumption that relapse is "an unfortunate characteristic of addiction" that should be viewed as an opportunity to evaluate the client's treatment and recovery plan rather than as a sign of treatment failure (p. 269).

Essential Elements

The mission of drug courts is to eliminate substance abuse and the resulting criminal behavior through a "team effort that focuses on sobriety and accountability as the primary goals" (Drug Courts Program Office, 1997, p. 8). The team of professionals generally includes the state attorney, public

EXHIBIT 7.1
Key Components of Drug Courts

1. Drug courts integrate alcohol and other drug treatment services with justice system case processing.
2. Drug courts use a nonadversarial approach; prosecution and defense counsel promote public safety while protecting participants' due process rights.
3. Eligible participants are identified early and promptly placed in the drug court program.
4. Drug courts provide access to a continuum of alcohol, drug, and other related treatment and rehabilitation services.
5. Abstinence is monitored by frequent alcohol and other drug testing.
6. A coordinated strategy governs drug court responses to participants' compliance.
7. Ongoing judicial interaction with each drug court participant is essential.
8. Monitoring and evaluation measure the achievement of program goals and gauge effectiveness.
9. Continuing interdisciplinary education promotes effective drug court planning, implementation, and operation.
10. Forging partnerships among drug courts, public agencies, and community-based organizations generates local support and enhances drug court effectiveness.

Note. From Drug Courts Program Office (1997).

defender, pretrial intervention or probation staff, treatment providers, and the judge, who is considered to be the central figure on the team. The primary goals of drug courts are to reduce drug use and associated criminal behavior by engaging and retaining drug-involved offenders in programmatic and treatment services; to concentrate and coordinate expertise about drug cases in a single courtroom; to address other defendant needs through clinical assessment and case management; and to free judicial, prosecutorial, and public defense resources for adjudicating nondrug cases (Belenko, 1998).

According to the Drug Court Standards Committee, there are 10 key components to a drug court (Drug Courts Program Office, 1997) (see Exhibit 7.1).

According to the National Drug Court Institute, there were 361 drug courts in operation in June 1999, and another 220 drug courts were in the planning process. Approximately 140,000 offenders had been enrolled in drug court programs at that date, and 98,000 had "graduated" or successfully completed treatment. Three-fourths of those people had previously been incarcerated. Drug courts had about a 70% retention rate (at least 20% higher than most other substance abuse treatment programs). Almost three-fourths of the drug court graduates were employed (National Drug Court Institute, 2001).

There have been several studies or evaluations of drug court programs. In a recent meta-analysis of drug court programs, Belenko (1998) concluded that

> Drug courts have been more successful than other forms of community supervision in closely supervising drug offenders in the community

through frequent monitoring and close supervision including mandatory frequent drug testing, placing and retaining drug offenders in treatment programs, providing treatment and related services to offenders who have not received such services in the past, generating actual and potential cost savings and substantially reducing drug use and recidivism while offenders are in the program. Based on more limited data and to a lesser but still significant extent, drug courts reduce recidivism for participants after they leave the program. Perhaps equally important for the future of the criminal courts system, drug courts have demonstrated the feasibility of employing a team-based, problem solving approach to adjudicating offenders with drug problems in a way that appears to reduce system costs and improve public safety. (p. 12)

Program Similarities and Differences

McNeece, Arnold, Valentine, and McInnis (1999) conducted a study of 12 drug courts and examined several structural, process, and outcome variables. For the most part, the drug courts they studied began as diversionary programs, targeting first-time, nonviolent felony drug offenders. Those charged or suspected of selling drugs were generally excluded from participation. However, offenders with previous arrests or convictions (for nonviolent offenses) were allowed to participate in some drug court programs, as well as those with a history of less serious violent offenses.

Each drug court was organized and operated somewhat differently. Offenders arrested on drug charges were referred to drug court in a variety of ways. Offenders learned of the program through the judge, the state attorney, the public defender, or the pretrial release staff—depending on the program. In most programs offenders must volunteer for participation. Some programs allowed offenders to decline participation in lieu of traditional criminal court proceedings. Some offenders chose this option, as sentencing for a first-time felony drug offense tended to be probation. Those not desirous of treatment could elect to go to a regular criminal court for processing to avoid what they perceived to be a less intrusive sentence.

The 12 courts studied had several other important differences. First, the manner in which sanctions were delivered varied dramatically, depending on the presiding judge. When an offender was not compliant with the terms of the program, some courts had specific automatic and progressive sanctions in place, and others sanctioned offenders on an individual basis. The use of sanctions also appeared to be related to the attitude toward relapse of the drug court team, especially the judge. In courts where relapse was not expected or tolerated, sanctions tended to be more stringent, thus affecting the overall number of offenders who were able to successfully complete the program.

Second, the drug courts differed in their method of communication among team members. The majority of the courts had team meetings or meetings before court to discuss the status of cases and make recommendations for offenders. By contrast, other courts appeared to have little formal communication between the drug court team members outside of the courtroom. These courts tended to rely on written notes in an offender's chart or direct communication during the drug court proceedings.

Third, the courts differed in the type of treatment services provided. Two of the 12 courts provided in-house treatment; the remainder contracted with outside treatment providers for substance abuse services. In all but one drug court, outpatient treatment services were provided to program participants at no charge. However, clients who needed residential or inpatient treatment generally had to pay for the treatment themselves or wait for such services to be available through a county-funded facility. The majority of the courts required a substance abuse assessment, outpatient individual counseling, group counseling, and attendance at 12-step meetings such as Alcoholics Anonymous or Narcotics Anonymous. Three of the 12 courts offered acupuncture as part of the drug court program.

Finally, the manner in which urinalysis was conducted and handled varied dramatically by judicial district. All but one program required offenders to submit to urinalysis to test for the presence of drugs. However, the manner in which the urine specimens were collected varied, with some using sophisticated methods for randomizing and others requiring that specimens be provided at set times. The number and types of drugs for which the offenders were screened also differed. Some judges uniformly sanctioned offenders who tested positive for a drug, some required that the offender start the program again from the beginning, and others tolerated occasional relapses as long as the offender was perceived to be making a legitimate effort.

MENTAL HEALTH COURTS

It is worth noting that a new and promising type of diversion program for offenders with a mental illness, the mental health court, is also being developed in some parts of the country. Modeled in part after drug courts and community courts, mental health courts are judicial, problem-solving courts designed to divert lower level misdemeanor offenders from jail and address the "root causes" of criminal involvement of mentally ill offenders. As of April 2000, four specialized mental health courts were in operation in the United States (Bureau of Justice Assistance, 2000). These courts are located in Broward County (Ft. Lauderdale), Florida; King County (Seattle), Washington; San Bernardino, California; and Anchorage, Alaska (Goldkamp & Irons-Guynn, 2000, as cited in Kelly, 2001). At the time of this writing, there were approximately 29 mental health courts across the U.S. and this number is certain to increase with the recent passage of legislation authorizing federal funds for mental health courts (Slate, 2003).

Although the mental health courts that are currently in operation are too new to have been rigorously evaluated for their effectiveness, preliminary findings appears quite promising (Slate, 2003). Mental health courts generally reflect what research indicates is more effective in the treatment of offenders with a mental illness. This includes, first and foremost, diversion to community-based treatment. Other best practices that are generally present in the four mental health courts include early and accurate screening and assessment, crisis intervention and stabilization, proactive case management, and discharge planning. Moreover, mental health courts are based in part on drug diversion courts, which have been demonstrated to be effective with substance-abusing offenders (Kelly, 2001).

For some unexplained reason, acupuncture is one of the common features of a drug court program, perhaps because acupuncture was a component of the Miami Drug Court, and courts adopting the Miami model simply copied all of its features.

ACUPUNCTURE

Acupuncture is a form of ancient Chinese medicine that has been used for more than 20 years in the United States to treat addictions. It can be used at a variety of points during treatment, including detoxification, rehabilitation, and relapse prevention (Moner, 1996). Acupuncture involves inserting four or five needles into an individual's ear for approximately 45 minutes. Acupuncture is believed to reduce the physical signs of withdrawal, and supporters of acupuncture also claim it relieves depression, anxiety, and insomnia (Turnabout ASAP, 1997). The needles are believed to produce a powerful response that helps decrease the desire for drugs or alcohol by helping the brain regain its chemical balance so that the abuser will become more introspective and receptive to therapy (Edwards, 1993).

It is important to note that little agreement exists regarding the physiological mechanisms of acupuncture. Some believe that blocked energy causes an imbalance in the body (Mitchell, 1995), but others relate the effectiveness of acupuncture to the release of endorphins (Lewith & Vincent, 1996). Given that different substances produce different effects on the body, it can be difficult for even acupuncture's supporters to reach consensus on how one procedure can impact a variety of symptoms. Brewington, Smith, and Lipton (1994) asserted "that it is possible that acupuncture affects substance-specific symptoms and/or certain common symptoms experienced by users of different substances" (p. 300).

Acupuncture can be done on an individual basis, but it is usually conducted in a group setting in a peaceful, tranquil environment (Mitchell, 1995). Those receiving treatment are encouraged to remain silent during the treatment so that they may have time for self-reflection. Limiting talking allows the client to maintain an inward, rather than an external, focus and not experience the pressure of "behavioral or cognitive expectations" (Brumbaugh, 1993, p. 38).

The use of acupuncture to treat chemical dependency was discovered by accident by H. L. Wen, a Hong Kong neurosurgeon. He was preparing an opium-addicted patient for surgery using electro-acupuncture as an analgesic when the patient discovered his withdrawal symptoms had subsided (Singer, 1996). Wen and a colleague, S. Y. C. Cheung, went on to treat 40 other individuals addicted to opiates (Mitchell, 1995).

The first U.S. substance abuse facility known to use acupuncture with substance abusers is Lincoln Hospital Substance Abuse Center in South Bronx, New York. Acupuncture is used there to treat many people with addictions: 250 clients a day in 1993 (U.S. General Accounting Office, 1996). In the United States and Europe, it is performed on 5,000 individuals a day (M. Smith, 1994). As of 1995, 300 facilities in 20 states were using a program modeled after the one at Lincoln Hospital (Mitchell, 1995).

As stated earlier, acupuncture has become particularly popular among drug court programs in the United States. The Dade County, Florida, drug court has used acupuncture as part of its approach to treating drug addicts arrested for nonviolent crimes.

Outcome Studies on Acupuncture

Despite anecdotal reports of success, few empirical studies exist that have examined the effectiveness of acupuncture in treating addictions. The literature has primarily examined outcomes for people with particular types of drug use instead of polysubstance abuse or alcohol abuse. The outcome research described below applies only to adults, as the use and efficacy of acupuncture with juveniles has not yet been examined.

Cocaine

Several studies have examined the impact of acupuncture with inner-city, cocaine-dependent clients on a variety of treatment and drug use outcomes. Margolin, Avants, Chang, and Kosten (1993) reported that the majority (90%) of participants in an 8-week course of treatment remained abstinent for more than one month. However, 50% of participants did not complete the program, a problem experienced by others researching this topic. Lipton, Brewington, and Smith (1994) found that, although experimental and control (placebo) groups had similar rates of retention and decreases in cocaine consumption, those who received acupuncture for more than two weeks had lower levels of cocaine metabolites in their urine.

Others have reported similarly optimistic findings about the use of acupuncture to treat cocaine and crack addiction (cf. Avants, Margolin, Chang, Kosten, & Birch, 1993; Avants, Margolin, Holford, & Kosten, 2000), with some reporting no significant treatment effects (cf. Brewington et al., 1994;

Bullock, Kiresuk, Pheley, Culltion, & Lenz, 1999; Otto, Quin, & Sung, 1998; Richard, Montoya, Nelson, & Spence, 1995).

Opiates

Studies have found mixed results about the use of acupuncture to treat those addicted to opiates. One study found only modest, but statistically significant, differences between acupuncture and methadone detoxification by gradually decreasing dosage levels (W. Clark, 1990); Man and Chuang (1980) found neither to be an effective form of detoxification. Newmeyer, Johnson, and Klot (1984) compared opiate-addicted participants who received medication to those who received acupuncture, finding that those who received acupuncture had a lower percentage of positive urine drug screens and fewer self-reports of heroin use.

Other Types of Substance Use

Although most of the research has focused on cocaine use or heroin addiction, a few studies have examined multiple types of drug use and alcohol use. One study (Konefal, Duncan, & Clemence, 1994) examined the impact of acupuncture on people with differing types of substance use who either volunteered or were ordered by the court to receive treatment. In this study all clients received the standard treatment regime, with some receiving no other services, some receiving additional urine drug screening, and others receiving acupuncture. Although retention rates in treatment were low for all groups, those who received acupuncture were able to achieve the same reduction in rates of positive urine drug screens in less than 57% of the time required by those receiving frequent drug testing. Studies examining the effectiveness of acupuncture to treat alcohol abuse have been mixed, with some reporting positive results (Bullock, Umen, Cullton, & Olander, 1987), and others finding no significant differences between point-specific acupuncture, sham transdermal stimulation,[1] or a control condition (Worner, Zeller, Schwartz, Zwas, & Lyon, 1992).

Outcomes for Offenders

Unfortunately, few studies have examined the impact of acupuncture on offenders with substance abuse problems, particularly those who are not in community-based treatment settings. In one of the few existing studies, Brumbaugh (1994) reported that in a small study of female offenders incarcerated in a minimum security annex of a county jail in California, women who received acupuncture treatment had a 17% lower rate of reincarceration after release than the control group. He also found that those in the control group were more than twice as likely to be re-incarcerated within 120 days as

---

[1]Some assert that sham acupuncture, the insertion of needles into non-traditional acupuncture points, is truly a placebo, while others believe that this may simply be "bad acupuncture" and serve as an inadequate control (Moner, 1996).

those who received acupuncture, and there appeared to be a relationship between reincarceration and the number of acupuncture treatments received: the more treatment, the lower the reincarceration rate.

To date, the studies examining the efficacy of acupuncture to treat addictions provide limited reason for optimism. Some researchers (McLellan, Grossman, Blaine, & Haverkos, 1993; Moon & Latessa, 1994) have asserted that the majority of the studies on this topic do not meet commonly accepted empirical standards and overestimate the evidence from well-controlled studies of acupuncture's effectiveness. In 1997, the National Institutes of Health (NIH) convened a consensus panel to examine the effectiveness of acupuncture for various ailments. For addiction and 11 other conditions or problems, the panel asserted that acupuncture "may be useful as an adjunct treatment or an acceptable alternative or be included in a comprehensive management program" (NIH, 1997, p. 12). The NIDA has been involved in technically evaluating the effectiveness of acupuncture as a legitimate form of substance abuse treatment and has recently funded several studies on its effectiveness.

Barriers to Using Acupuncture With Offenders

There are several significant barriers to the use of acupuncture with offenders. Because federal law categorizes acupuncture as an experimental procedure, offenders cannot be mandated to receive this type of intervention (Brumbaugh, 1993). Offenders must voluntarily agree to receive acupuncture treatments. In addition, acupuncture may not be available in all areas where criminal offenders are receiving substance abuse treatment, particularly in rural areas.

One way of obtaining future support is to demonstrate cost effectiveness. "From a pragmatic political point of view, the burden, deficiency, and stagnation of the law and justice system translate directly into fiscal terms" (Brumbaugh, 1994, p. 185). It is important that policy makers and legal experts examine the outcome data on acupuncture and the potential financial benefits of using this method of intervention with offenders. The cost of treating individuals in the program is less than 4% of the cost of incarcerating that same person for one year (Mitchell, 1995). If acupuncture can save the criminal justice system money currently spent on treatment or incarceration of substance-abusing offenders (the majority of individuals in most prison systems), receptivity will likely be a nonissue for those administrators and treatment providers in the criminal justice system who seek to rehabilitate this group of offenders.

SUMMARY

This chapter reviewed some of the innovative treatment settings and approaches that are being used with substance-abusing offenders. Among the approaches discussed were JACs and JARFs. Research findings (Springer, Shader, & McNeese, 1999) have suggested that changes in juvenile justice policy are needed to promote interagency cooperation within JACs, and assessments need to be better utilized to help make timely referrals. Increased funding is needed for additional staff and resources if JACs and JARFs are to operate effectively. JACs and JARFs are key components in the current movement in the juvenile justice system to create multiagency facilities that process delinquents and at-risk youths. A working understanding of these centers will no doubt be a significant tool in the repertoire of the worker who finds him- or herself employed by agencies serving this type of client.

We addressed the apparent ineffectiveness of juvenile boot camps. In light of recent findings, it is somewhat puzzling and troubling that boot camps continue to receive such accolades and support among politicians and the media. We assert that community-based approaches, such as multisystemic therapy (Henggeler & Borduin, 1990; Henggeler, Schoenwald, Borduin, Rowland, & Cunningham, 1998; see chapter 4, this volume), are preferable.

One approach that has been around for some time, TASC, was also explored. Although funding for TASC was discontinued in the 1980s, similar programs (e.g., Treatment Alternative Programs) continue with comparable positive results.

We discussed drug courts and a new but promising type of diversion program for mentally ill offenders, mental health courts. From a policy perspective, drug courts offer an opportunity for a new focus on the needs of offenders with substance abuse problems in the criminal justice system. Although opinion varies about how to best handle first-time drug offenders, drug courts provide one of the few feasible alternatives to incarceration. Their efforts show promise in preventing offenders from coming back into the legal system, which traditionally viewed them as criminals first and individuals in need of treatment secondarily (or not at all). To ignore the substance abuse treatment needs of first-time offenders does nothing but ensure that they will most likely reappear on court dockets in the future with the same or more severe treatment needs. To ensure that these types of programs meet the long-term needs of participants, further evaluation and longitudinal studies of successful program graduates are needed for both drug courts and mental health courts.

Finally, we addressed acupuncture, a common component of drug courts. To ensure its efficacy, acupuncture should be used as part of a comprehensive approach to substance abuse treatment, not as a sole treatment modality (Brumbaugh, 1993; Commonwealth of Virginia, 1992). Acupuncture has yet to be widely accepted. Culliton and Kiresuk (1996) noted that new treatments are generally not immediately well received, acupuncture has not been endorsed by the medical profession, and studies have experienced methodological flaws (e.g., poorly controlled studies, high attrition rates). Konefal and colleagues (1994) found that men responded better to acupuncture treatment than do women but were unsure whether this was caused by other factors such as the absence of gender-specific treatment programs, staff attitudes, or administrative issues related to the treatment program. Perhaps the high attrition rates reported in acupuncture studies could be offset by introducing complementary interventions (e.g., motivational interviewing) appropriate for clients in the precontemplation or contemplation stages (see chapter 3). Before acupuncture is widely accepted, research will need to address some of these gaps, including the impact that gender has on acupuncture outcomes (Konefal et al., 1994) and whether acupuncture works for juvenile offenders.

8

TREATING DUALLY
DIAGNOSED OFFENDERS

One of the most challenging aspects for practitioners working with substance-abusing offenders is the treatment of offenders who also have mental health disorders. Lurigio and Swartz (2000) have documented the inadequacy of most substance abuse treatment programs in addressing psychiatric comorbidity (the incidence of two or more diagnosable conditions at the same time). The priority in treatment of these people appears to be substance abuse and addiction at the expense of psychiatric disorders (Kelly, 2001).

The defining characteristic of the dually diagnosed client is the combination of a chronically severe mental disorder and a history of abuse of alcohol or other drugs (Drake, McLaughlin, & Minkoff, 1996). Using criteria found in the *Diagnostic and Statistical Manual of Mental Disorders* (*DSM–III–R*; American Psychiatric Association, 1987), K. Sciacca (1991) and Ekleberry (1996) distinguished two large groups of clients who have mental illness and substance abuse disorders. People with mental illness and chemical abuse or addiction (MICAA) are those with severe Axis I mental disorders (such as schizophrenia or bipolar disorder) in addition to Axis I substance abuse or dependence disorders. These individuals are different from those with chemical abuse or mental illness (CAMI) who have no separate Axis I disorder of severe mental illness.

According to Sheehan (1993), "dual diagnosis or comorbidity is said to exist when a patient is suffering with more than one disease. Psychiatry and the addictive medicines refer to the co-existence of a psychoactive chemical use disorder with another major psychiatric disorder" (p. 108). This broad descriptive category, however, encompasses many specific combinations of DSM–IV–TR (American Psychiatric Association, 2000) diagnoses of mental disorders and chemical dependence or abuse. The question of which combinations are treatable underlies several practical issues of program design, from screening and recruitment to aftercare planning.

It is widely accepted that people with mental disorders are at greater risk of developing substance abuse problems than those without mental disorders (Mueser, Bennett, & Kushner, 1995). In addition, the problems in social functioning experienced by individuals with mental and substance abuse disorders may exacerbate difficulties in diagnosis and treatment (Cuffel, 1996). These problems pose a special challenge for treating dually diagnosed offenders, especially those who are incarcerated. As state prison populations have increased in recent years, correctional institutions have received a growing number of offenders with comorbid mental and substance abuse disorders.

Mueser and colleagues (1995) offered a typology of four relationships between substance abuse and mental disorders: (a) the secondary substance abuse disorder, (b) the secondary mental disorder, (c) the common factor, and (d) the bidirectional models. The secondary substance abuse disorder model emphasizes how mental disorders increase clients' vulnerability to substance abuse and how the symptoms of mental disorders may mimic those of alcohol and drug use. The secondary mental disorder model suggests that substance abuse precipitates an emerging mental disorder (Weiss, Najavits, & Mirin, 1997). The common factor explanation asserts that dual disorders may be linked to some common third variable. This model, for example, relates genetic factors to comorbid mental and substance abuse disorders. Finally, the bidirectional explanation suggests that pre-existing mental disorders can be worsened by substance abuse.

The War on Drugs inspired an emphasis on using treatment resources within the criminal justice system to break the cycle of addiction and crime (Kelly, 2001). The resulting treatment programs, however, have neglected the clinical needs of drug-dependent people with comorbid psychiatric disorders. Although descriptions of drug treatment programs in criminal justice settings address the presence of comorbid psychiatric disorders, these discussions often present mental illness in the context of such ancillary problems as vocational and educational deficits, medical conditions, and family dysfunction (Kelly, 2001).

For the past two decades, the possibility of integrated approaches to treating comorbid mental illness and substance abuse or dependency has drawn increasing attention among professionals working in the corrections, mental health, and substance abuse treatment fields (Bachrack, 1983; Brown, Ridgely,

Pepper, Levine, & Ryglewicz, 1989). Nearly a decade ago, Minkoff and Drake (1991) observed that, "although there has been fairly extensive research describing and documenting the clinical characteristics of the dual diagnosis population, little controlled research is available so far to guide clinical treatment or program development" (p. 1). These authors highlighted two issues that persist at this convergence of mental health and substance abuse treatment. One is the uncertainty about how these two types of treatment should be joined. The other is the uncertain relationship between treatment and outcome. More recently, R. H. Peters and Hills (1996) have reported advances in both the integration of treatment for dually diagnosed clients and the growing recognition of their extraordinary need for aftercare planning and coordination. Interest in dual diagnosis treatment was also stimulated by the recent provision of funding by the National Institute of Justice for program implementation and evaluation.

INCIDENCE OF DRUG ABUSE AND MENTAL DISORDERS

Two comprehensive studies have analyzed the prevalence of dual diagnoses: the Epidemiologic Catchment Area (ECA) study, which began in 1978, and the National Comorbidity Survey (NCS), which was conducted between 1990 and 1992. According to the ECA study, a mental disorder more than doubles a person's chances of having an alcohol diagnosis, and it increases the chances of a drug abuse diagnosis by more than four times. The NCS revealed rates of substance abuse and dependence exceeding 50% among those with both affective and anxiety disorders (Regier et al., 1990).

Although both studies found dual disorders to be prevalent, the ECA study focused primarily on institutional populations in mental hospitals, prisons, and nursing homes. Among these, mental hospitals had the highest lifetime rate of substance abusers with mental disorders (82.2%), followed by prisons (82.0%), and nursing homes (65.5%; Regier et al., 1990). (As used here, *lifetime rate* represents the percentage of clients who, at some point during their lives, meet the diagnostic criteria for a substance abuser with a mental disorder.) The remarkably high lifetime prevalence of substance abuse (72%) among prisoners, in which more than half have abused alcohol (56.2%) and evidence some other type of drug disorder (53.7%), accentuate and aggravate other mental disorders (Regier et al., 1990).

Approximately half of all adolescents receiving mental health treatment also have co-existing substance abuse problems (McBride, VanderWaal, Terry, & VanBuren, 1999). Conduct disorder is one of the most common diagnostic groups among juvenile offenders. Winters (1988, as cited in McBride et al., 1999) found that substance use disorders are 2 to 5 times more prevalent among youths with a conduct disorder when compared to youths in a control group. Other, less common co-existing disorders among substance-abusing juveniles include bipolar disorder, anxiety disorders, and attention deficit hyperactivity disorder (Thompson, Riggs, Mikulich, & Crowley, 1996). Both conduct disorder and hyperactivity have been associated with substance abuse problems and delinquent behavior (J. D. Hawkins, Catalano, & Miller, 1992).

PREVALENCE OF COMORBIDITY IN INMATES

Many prison inmates have psychiatric disorders. Approximately 283,800 offenders defined as mentally ill were incarcerated in U.S. prisons and jails as of mid-1998. A recent survey by the Bureau of Justice Statistics (BJS) found that 16% of state prison inmates, 7% of federal inmates, and 16% of those in jails reported having a mental condition or staying in a mental facility overnight (Ditton, 1999). Previous research on the prevalence of severe mental illness in prison or jail shows similarly that the mentally ill make up from 8% to 16% of the incarcerated population (Guy, Platt, Zwerling, & Bullock, 1985; Steadman, Fabisiak, Dvoskin, & Holohean, 1989; Teplin, 1990).

A recent 3-year analysis of substance abuse in American prisons revealed that 1.4 million (82%) of the 1.7 million adults in prison were seriously involved in the use of drugs and alcohol (National Center on Addiction and Substance Abuse [NCASA], 1997). This estimate is supported by the 1997 *Survey of Inmates in State and Federal Correctional Facilities*, which reported that 33% of state prisoners and 22% of federal prisoners were under the influence of an illegal drug at the time of their offense (BJS, 1999a). But drug users are not a homogenous group. Some use drugs occasionally; others are compulsive users. Studies indicate that criminal behavior increases with heavy drug use, but infrequent users may also account for a considerable percentage of arrestees testing positive for drugs (BJS, 1999b).

Researchers have estimated that up to 26% of correctional inmates experience alcohol or drug abuse and a mental disorder (Cote & Hogins, 1990). ECA researchers also found that in prisons, mental disorders co-occurred with addictive disorders in a majority (90%) of the cases (Regier et al., 1990). R. H. Peters and Hills (1993) estimated more conservatively that 3% to 11% of prison inmates meet dual diagnostic criteria. There is no consensus on this issue. Different prisons, holding different types of inmates, probably vary greatly in the number of people with both drug and mental health disorders. Adding to the confusion is the use of different diagnostic standards by different researchers.

It is likely that the proportion of dually diagnosed individuals in prison populations may be as much as four times that of the general population (NCASA, 1997). Many offenders with dual diagnoses have done poorly in addiction treatment programs because their psychiatric symptoms have been undetected. Some sign themselves out of treatment against medical advice or are discharged because of treatment resistance. Dually diagnosed individuals rarely receive simultaneous treatment for both problems, as is required for successful treatment (Weiss et al., 1997).

SCREENING, ASSESSMENT, AND DIAGNOSIS

It is difficult to obtain accurate diagnoses of people with comorbidity for several reasons. As we have seen, definitions of the dually diagnosed determine the extent of the problem and the number of people who are diagnosed. There is also a tendency among mental health professionals to overlook substance use and abuse problems because "everyone drinks" (Ryglewicz & Pepper, 1990), and vice versa, substance abuse professionals historically have overlooked mental health disorders. Making accurate diagnoses also can be difficult, especially during emergencies, because the effects produced by some drugs appear very similar to the manifestations of psychoses (W. Turner & Tsuang, 1990). Until recently, professionals who specialized either in mental health or in substance abuse treatment were not expected to know how to diagnose problems in the other area (McNeece & DiNitto, 1998). There is still relatively little cross training of personnel across both problem areas (McNeece, in press).

Mental health professionals can be aided in recognizing substance use, abuse, and dependence by using screening and assessment instruments such as the CAGE (Ewing, 1984), the Michigan Alcoholism Screening Test (Selzer, Vinokur, & Van Rooijen, 1974), the Addiction Severity Index (McLellan et al., 1985), or the Substance Abuse Subtle Screening Inventory (Miller et al., 1997; see chapter 2).

Likewise, practitioners may detect and monitor common mental illnesses such as depression among their clients by using instruments such as the Generalized Contentment Scale (Hudson, 1982) or the Child and Adolescent Functional Assessment Scale (Hodges, 2000). Functional ability can also be assessed by the use of scales such as the Global Assessment of Functioning, which is Axis V of the *DSM–IV–TR* (American Psychiatric Association, 2000), or the Multnomah Community Ability Scale (Barker, Barron, McFarland, & Bigelow, 1993). With some training, substance abuse professionals might also be able to use the Brief Psychiatric Rating Scale, which is used to assess the severity of a client's current psychiatric symptoms (Lukoff, Neuchterlein, & Ventura, 1986; Overall & Gorham, 1962).

TREATMENT

Consensus has not been reached on the optimal psychotherapeutic treatment for dually diagnosed clients. Historically, mental health and substance abuse treatment systems have operated independently. Treatment of comorbidity in these two systems has been either sequential or parallel. A sequential approach treats one disorder before treating the other; parallel treatment consists of the simultaneous treatment in two different settings (Weiss et al., 1997). The essential feature of integrated treatment is that both illnesses are treated concurrently by the same staff in a single setting (Wexler, 1995). Integrated treatment is not simply combined treatment but the integration of treatment approaches for both substance abuse and mental illness. The literature identifies psychoeducational, pharmacological, cognitive–behavioral, and 12-step approaches to treating this population (R. H. Peters & Hills, 1996; Weiss & Najavits, 1997). Pharmacological treatment of substance abusers has been controversial in combination with 12-step approaches because the latter approach has historically regarded abstinence from drugs as a fundamental requirement.

Treatment providers should address differences among persons with CAMI (who have Axis II personality disorders) and those with MICAA (who have Axis I severe mental illnesses). Differences include such important factors as varying sensitivity to confrontation or "denial" about one or both illnesses for those clients in an earlier (precontemplation or contemplation) stage of change; risk of decompensation (greater for MICAA clients); and the possibility of withdrawal, regression, or becoming delusional (McNeece & DiNitto, 1998). Ekleberry (1996) proposed that, for people with CAMI, treatment should differ according to the specific personality disorder and functional ability of each client. Confrontation, for example, may be an appropriate component of treatment for people with antisocial personality disorder or for high-functioning people with histrionic personality disorder. However, she did not recommend it for people with borderline personality disorder or for those with low global assessment of functioning scores.

Services should probably also be specialized for MICAA subgroups. For example, men with schizophrenia who abuse crack cocaine might benefit from different treatment than might women with the same mental health and substance abuse problems. Unfortunately, treatment of dually diagnosed clients often does not allow for much treatment individualization. If psychopathology is noted in a client following detoxification, alcohol and drug treatment may not be recommended for reasons such as "lack of motivation" or "inability to benefit from treatment." Sometimes they are precluded from participating in programs for people with severe mental illnesses due to fears that they will cause disruptions or influence other clients to use psychoactive substances (McNeece & DiNitto, 1998).

Although we cover pharmacotherapy and psychoeducational and self-help approaches in detail in other chapters in this book (see chapters 3 and 5, respectively), we briefly address these and other treatment approaches below as they relate specifically to dually diagnosed clients.

Psychoeducational Groups

Psychoeducation is most useful when it begins with a definition of substance abuse that clients can understand and appreciate. Kofoed and Keys (1988) suggested the following definition of *substance abuse:* "A loss of consistent control over substances" (p. 1209). Another definition (Keller, 1958) suggested that it is the use of substances that results in serious life problems, including family, social, psychological, job, and legal problems. Definitions such as these can be used to help mentally ill clients discover a repeated cycle of substance use before mental illness exacerbations occur.

Several treatment programs are now using psychoeducational groups for MICAA and CAMI clients. Webb's (1995) Good Chemistry Groups, for example, combines 45 minutes of group therapy with 15 minutes of psychoeducation. Instead of requiring clients to be clean and sober in order to participate, Good Chemistry Groups attempt to create a group norm of trying to become clean and sober (DiNitto, Webb, & Rubin, 2002a). The intervention consists of nine structured sessions, each focused on a different topic:

1. Signs and symptoms of mental and substance use disorders
2. How the illnesses overlap and interact
3. Dangers of mixing nonprescribed substances with medications
4. A closer look at mixing medications with alcohol, marijuana, and cocaine
5. Exploring 12-step programs
6. AA's view of medications
7. Recognizing the cues and triggers of relapse and preparing solutions
8. The importance of asking for extra help when needed
9. The importance of staying involved in treatment.

These groups are being used in several states by people with a dual diagnosis as an alternative to 12-step program group attendance.

DiNitto and colleagues (2002b) conducted a randomized experiment testing the effectiveness of adding Good Chemistry Groups to standard inpatient substance abuse treatment for dually diagnosed clients. No significant treatment effects were found on any of the outcome variables. Given that these findings are generally consistent with those of prior controlled studies, practitioners are encouraged to develop and evaluate alternative integrated treatment approaches that may be more effective.

Pharmacotherapy

A major challenge in treating dually diagnosed clients is the negative interactions that psychotropic drugs have with illicit substances (Bentley &

Walsh, 2001). Bentley and Walsh pointed out that polypharmacy (combining different types of psychotropic drugs) is, nevertheless, sometimes indicated to help dually diagnosed clients abstain from the illegal drug; however, they cautioned that polypharmacy is risky and that relevant research findings are based on a few studies (Janicak, Davis, Preskorn, & Ayd, 1997). For clients with schizophrenia, there is some evidence that disulfram (Antabuse) may increase psychotic symptoms but that naltrexone may help the client resist alcohol and also experience fewer hallucinations (Bentley & Walsh, 2001). For clients with depressive disorders, imipramine and the selective serotonin reuptake inhibitors have been shown in a few studies to reduce the client's craving for alcohol, but only initially. The antianxiety medications, however, have been demonstrated as adjunctive drugs for clients with dual disorders and are as effective as short-term treatment for 20% to 50% of clients who go through withdrawal from alcohol dependence (Bentley & Walsh, 2001).

Self-Help Programs

Peer-led Dual Recovery Anonymous meetings are spreading throughout the United States and offer people with dual disorders the freedom and support they need to simultaneously work on both illnesses. All dual-oriented groups and self-help meetings are worthwhile practices and are integral parts of a full continuum of services for people with dual disorders (DiNitto & Webb, 1998).

Kathleen Sciacca, a mental health program specialist for the New York State Office of Mental Health, is the founding executive director of Sciacca Comprehensive Service Development for Mental Illness, Drug Addiction, and Alcoholism (MIDAA). MIDAA is an integrated treatment approach for people with severe mental illness and substance disorders (K. Sciacca, 1991). Proponents of MIDAA support the use of motivational interviewing (discussed in chapter 2), and there are MICAA support programs available. According to K. Sciacca (1991), these are self-led, self-help support programs developed specifically for MICAA clients. These groups serve as adjuncts to other support programs in helping MICAA clients maintain abstinence and have begun to emerge in scattered locations across the country, both within the traditional AA network (referred to as "Double Trouble" meetings) and within the traditional mental health system.

Although Al-Anon programs are helpful, they often fail to address the complexity of dealing with loved ones with coexisting mental disorders (K. Sciacca, 1991). Thus, to meet the needs of family and friends of MICAA clients, MICAA-NON groups (K. Sciacca, 1989) are available. While MICAA-NON groups are typically run by professionals in agencies with MICAA treatment programs, they are open to members of the community. Additional information can be found at the MICAA Web site (http://users.erols.com/ksciacca).

Integrated Treatment

Treatment programs specifically designed and operated to treat psychiatric comorbidity among substance-abusing offenders are severely lacking in prisons and in communities (Kelly, 2001). The GAINS Center, in collaboration with the Open Society Institute's Center on Crime, Communities and Culture, published *The Courage to Change: A Guide for Communities to Create Integrated Services for People With Co-Occurring Disorders in the Justice System* (December, 1999). The guide provides the building blocks for developing community-based treatment services for mentally ill offenders with substance abuse problems. The core of the strategy is the integration of mental health, substance abuse, and criminal justice systems. It is argued that the key is the recognition of the need for a unique, holistic approach to treating co-occurring disorders, and the willingness to share resources, information, and clients across these three systems (Kelly, 2001). Ideally, treatment for dually diagnosed offenders should be provided by people cross trained in mental health and addictions treatment, and it should address mental health and substance abuse concurrently. In the model K. Sciacca (1991) described, clients may be identified either during the intake process or during mental health treatment. Information is provided about a program (such as a MICAA group) in an informative, nonconfrontational manner. When the client begins to attend a group (it may take weeks or months to reach this step), he or she may still be in denial, and the objective is simply to get the client to talk about alcohol and drugs. The next step is to encourage the client to talk about his or her own drug use and then to get the client to recognize that substance abuse is a problem. Finally, the client is motivated to accept abstinence as a goal.

The research supporting integrated treatment is limited and has shown mixed results. Drake, McHugo, and Noorday (1993) reported positive long-term results from an integrated approach. They reported that 60% of clients with chronic mental disorders achieved stable abstinence during a four-year follow-up. K. Sciacca and Thompson (1996) found that integrated treatment had better outcomes for clients than other models of treatment and was more cost-effective. On the other hand, Lehman, Herron, Schwartz, and Myers (1993) found no reduction in substance abuse among dually diagnosed clients who were treated for one year in an integrated program. Forrest (1994) developed a "holistic" treatment for people diagnosed with both substance abuse problems and antisocial personality disorder. Forrest believed that long-term treatment was needed for such clients, and he argued that they "find it easy to placate and 'get over' on counselors and treatment program personnel in brief treatment settings" (p. 164). His model uses a cognitive–behavioral approach with a great deal of structure. The effectiveness of this approach has not been established. Longitudinal, well-controlled research has yet to be conducted on many other combinations of treatment such as pharmacological and psychoeducation approaches (Weiss et al., 1997).

Treatment for Dually Diagnosed Women

Little has been done to design treatment programs specifically for women with both mental health and substance abuse problems. DiNitto and colleagues (2002a) documented the fact that dually diagnosed females face different problems than dually diagnosed men. Arnold, Stewart, and McNeece (2001) reported that in one dual diagnosis treatment study the addition of special treatment components for female offenders led to higher treatment completion rates.

Najavits, Weiss, Shaw, and Muenz (1998) have designed and tested a cognitive–behavioral model for this population—"Seeking Safety." It consisted of 24 structured sessions divided equally among cognitive, behavioral, and interpersonal coping skills. Sessions focused on such practical matters as asking for help, boundary setting, self-care, self-nurturing, resisting triggers, and HIV risks. The program calls for abstaining from all substances, reducing self-destructive behavior, creating support networks, and protecting oneself from dangers such as HIV and domestic violence.

Practitioners in the Seeking Safety program are trained to use inspirational quotes or maxims, illustrations, practice exercises, and simple language. They also repeatedly use a few core principles throughout the treatment, reinforced by memory exercises designed to help clients remember important objectives. Clients are held accountable for their behavior but are frequently praised for appropriate behavior (R. Alexander, 2000).

The research by Najavits and colleagues (1998) relied on a pretest/posttest design that revealed significant improvements in cognitive, behavioral, and interpersonal functioning at a 3-month follow-up. Sixty-three percent of the clients in the study completed the treatment, and 37% dropped out. Surprisingly, a comparison of completers and dropouts showed that completers were more seriously impaired than were dropouts.

Traumatic Incident Reduction (TIR) is a brief (often one session) memory-based intervention developed by Frank Gerbode (1989) to treat trauma-related symptoms. It is a "client-respectful, therapist-directed, memory-based intervention aimed at the reduction of trauma-related symptoms" (Valentine & Smith, 2001, p. 40). TIR is informed by psychodynamic, behavior, and cognitive theories. Memory-based interventions like TIR rest on the assumption that clients experience trauma-related symptoms (e.g., intrusion, avoidance, arousal) related to past traumatic events and that they must target the specific memory to decrease the symptoms.

The effectiveness of TIR was demonstrated with traumatized female inmates at the Federal Correctional Institute in Tallahassee, Florida (Valentine, 1995; Valentine & Smith, 2001). [One of the authors, David Springer, participated as a practitioner–researcher in this study.] Although these women were not substance abusers per se, this study warrants mention for two reasons. It is one of the few experimental research studies conducted with female inmates, and these women experienced symptoms (posttraumatic stress disorder [PTSD], depression, anxiety, and low self-efficacy) likely to be encountered by practitioners working with dually diagnosed female offenders.

In this study, female inmates (N = 148) were randomly assigned to treatment and control groups. Measures were taken at pretest, posttest, and 3 months following the posttest. Female inmates in the TIR group reported significant decreases in depression, anxiety, and PTSD symptoms and had a significant increase in self-efficacy compared to the control group (Valentine & Smith, 2001). (Brief descriptions of two other treatment programs for dually diagnosed female offenders are provided in Exhibit 8.1.)

DUAL DIAGNOSIS TREATMENT PROGRAMS IN PRISONS

The research on dual diagnosis treatment programs in prison populations is confounded by several methodological problems. Rarely are there any controls for pre-existing differences in the populations studied (such as motivation for treatment), attrition rates may be very high in some programs, and randomization is usually not feasible. Nevertheless, several studies have been conducted.

Edens, Peters, and Hills (1997) studied seven state and federal treatment programs for incarcerated dually diagnosed offenders (see Exhibit 8.1). Edens and colleagues found that referrals to dual diagnosis units occurred primarily in three ways: (a) after symptoms developed while the inmate was in the general population, (b) after screening in a reception center, and (c) as a referral from either a substance abuse program or a mental health program. Admissions were based on DSM–IV diagnoses. Treatment approaches were remarkably similar, with all using a modified therapeutic community approach (e.g., less confrontation, smaller staff caseloads, greater individual counseling) with psychoeducational, 12-step, cognitive–behavioral, and relapse prevention components. Research on the outcomes of these dual diagnosis programs is sparse (R. Alexander, 2000).

At the time of this writing, three states (Alabama, Delaware, and Wisconsin) had reported some specialized program services for dually diagnosed prison inmates, but they have not been evaluated. Three other states (Illinois, Maryland, and Oklahoma) indicated that plans were under way to develop a dual diagnosis program, and Wisconsin has formally established a goal of developing services for this population. A five-year evaluation, funded by the National Institute on Drug Abuse, is being conducted of the San Carlos, Texas, therapeutic community, and research results should inform the feasibility and effectiveness of this effort (Kelly, 2001).

EXHIBIT 8.1
State and Federal Treatment Programs for Dually Diagnosed Inmates

1. The Dual Diagnosis Unit at the Ventress Correctional Facility in Alabama is a 62-bed program for male inmates within a prison designed specifically for prisoners with substance abuse problems. Clients had mostly depression (60%–70%), bipolar disorder (15%), and schizophrenia (10%). Treatment included 12-step group counseling sessions, psychoeducational groups, and relapse prevention—in addition to the same substance abuse services received by other inmates at this facility.

2. The Crisis Care Unit of the Sussex Correctional Institute in Delaware is a 40-bed unit located in a maximum-security institution, initially begun as a unit for prisoners with mental illness and mental retardation but later redesigned to treat inmates with mental illness and substance abuse problems. About three-fourths of the inmates had a diagnosis of substance abuse and schizophrenia. A 2- to 3-month treatment program includes individual and group counseling, medication compliance, psychoeducational groups, relapse prevention, recreational therapy, and case management.

3. The Turning Point Alcohol and Drug Program of the Columbia River Correctional Institution in Oregon is a 50-bed therapeutic community for female inmates lasting a total of 6–15 months. It began as a substance abuse program and was redesigned for dually diagnosed inmates after it was discovered that their high dropout rate was due to mental illness among the residents. Treatment includes group counseling regarding substance abuse and sexual and physical abuse, life skills training, and relapse prevention.

4. The Lexington (Kentucky) Federal Medical Center has a 16-bed Dual Diagnosis Track within a 120-bed substance abuse unit. The majority of clients have a mood disorder or psychotic-spectrum disorders. The 9-month treatment program is based on a biopsychosocial model that includes psychoeducational, cognitive, and relapse prevention groups, as well as individual counseling and medication compliance.

5. The Substance Abuse Felony Punishment Facility in the Estelle Unit of the Texas Department of Criminal Justice is a large 130-bed program lasting 9 to 12 months. About 60% of the clients have mental illnesses. Substance abuse and relapse prevention treatment are provided through groups, with the substance abuse component based on 12-step principles.

6. The largest of the programs studied is the Substance Abuse Felony Punishment Facility in the Hackberry Unit of the Texas Department of Criminal Justice. It is a 9- to 12-month modified therapeutic community model serving 288 women. All of the clients have substance abuse problems, and 55% have major mental disorders. This therapeutic community provides psychoeducational programs, Alcoholics Anonymous groups, and treatment.

7. Finally, a modified therapeutic community in the Dual Diagnosis Unit of the San Carlos Correctional Facility in Colorado was studied. It is a 32-bed unit in a 250-bed prison. About half of the men on this unit had a major depressive disorder, and 40% had a psychotic-spectrum disorder. The one-year program provides 8 hours of psychoeducational, life skills, and cognitive–behavioral treatment each day. Medication plays a significant role in getting inmates stabilized.

Note. From "Treating Prison Inmates With Co-Occurring Disorders: An Integrative Review of Existing Programs," by J. F. Edens, R. H. Peters, and H. A. Hills, 1997, *Behavioral Sciences and the Law, 15,* 439–457. Copyright 1997 by Wiley Intersciences. Reprinted with permission.

SUMMARY

We have reviewed the challenges of treating dually diagnosed offenders in the criminal justice system, including integrated treatment approaches, which may include pharmacotherapy as well as psychoeducational and self-help approaches. Several treatment programs are now using psychoeducational and self-help groups for MICAA and CAMI clients. The essential feature of integrated treatment is that both illnesses are treated concurrently by the same staff in a single setting (Wexler, 1995).

We focused on treating dually diagnosed female offenders. It is critical that the field continue to develop and test gender-sensitive treatment approaches for dually diagnosed female offenders. Mental health and substance abuse professionals must continue to cross boundaries so that they can work together to meet the needs of dually diagnosed female offenders using integrated treatment approaches.

Most research on dual diagnoses has been focused on persons with schizophrenia and substance abuse diagnoses. Lately, more research has focused on people with mood disorders and chemical dependence. Treatment providers should address differences among people with CAMI (who have Axis II personality disorders) and those with MICAA (who have Axis I severe mental illnesses).

To best understand, treat, and research MICAA dual diagnoses, it is critical to break out subgroups. Thus, we must recognize that a person who has schizophrenia and is dependent on marijuana presents very differently than a person who has bipolar disorder and is dependent on alcohol. Furthermore, people who are dependent (or "addicted") to any substance may face a more difficult road to recovery than a person who abuses substances. Of course, a person's problem that originally seems like abuse may eventually meet criteria for dependence (DiNitto & Webb, 1998; McNeece & DiNitto, 1998).

Despite the evidence cited in this chapter, many prison-based studies of dually diagnosed people have been methodologically weak (Wexler, 1995). The absence of control groups and random assignment to treatment conditions has precluded assessment of the direct effects of treatment programs (Catalano, Hawkins, Wells, Miller, & Brewer, 1991). Another research practice, pooling clients from many different programs—as was done in the Stay'n Out study (see chapter 6)—obscures program processes that affect outcomes. Generally, statistical controls are not applied to account for pre-existing group differences (Rouse, 1991). Because of the high attrition rates characteristic of many prison drug treatment programs, findings are often based on shrinking sample sizes (Platt, Perry, & Metzger, 1980).

Finally, it is difficult to determine whether the success of treatment is due to the result of the program itself or high levels of motivation (Rouse, 1991). Prisoners' motivation for treatment is confounded when participation in treatment occurs for reasons unrelated to the disorder being treated. Inmates' motivation for treatment may involve relief from undesirable work assignments or access to better living accommodations. Consequently, assessing an offender's readiness for change and matching treatment interventions accordingly (see chapter 3) may be fruitful for treatment and research efforts with dually diagnosed offenders.

In sum, relatively few studies have been conducted on the effectiveness of mental health or substance abuse programs for dually diagnosed inmates. Formative research conducted on programs being developed for these inmates can provide a basis for improvements in implementation processes and for refinements in program design.

9

MONITORING OFFENDERS

Given the overcrowding of prisons and the costs associated with incarceration, policymakers and criminal justice professionals are continually looking for innovative and effective ways of monitoring offenders. Substance-abusing offenders may be monitored in the community as an alternative to prison or jail time or may be monitored as a condition of parole after incarceration. Substance abuse treatment may be a part of the process, or offenders may simply be ordered by the court not to engage in any form of substance use (even alcohol use). The type of monitoring used will vary depending on the state or community, the resources available, and the needs of the offender. Accordingly, in this chapter we address different methods of monitoring substance-abusing offenders. We review the most commonly used methods: probation, including variations thereof (e.g., shock probation, intensive supervision probation [ISP]), electronic monitoring (EM), and urine drug testing. In addition, we attempt to clarify misconceptions that exist about the role of probation and parole professionals in working with offenders and their families.

PROBATION

Probation is a form of monitoring offenders who are released into the community with certain conditions that they must meet to avoid further penalties or incarceration. Probation, in combination with therapy, support, and surveillance, is the most common type of treatment used as an alternative to incarceration (Lipton, 1995). Given the great number of people in state and federal correctional institutions with substance abuse problems, monitoring these people in the community is one alternative to the current problem of overcrowding in U.S. prisons. At the end of 1997, 1,176,807 persons were incarcerated in state or federal prisons, and more than 3.9 million adults were on probation or parole (U.S. Department of Justice, 1999). In the first national study of adult offenders on probation conducted in 1995, 67.7% of female and 69.9% of male offenders reported that they had used drugs in the past (U.S. Department of Justice, 1998). The main focus of the probation officer's work in the office and out in the field is dealing with offenders and their addictions (Read, 1995). Probation officers must also keep in mind that drug offenders are more likely than other offenders to fail to meet probation requirements (Johnson & Jones, 1998).

Blevins, Morton, and McCabe (1996) studied alcohol use among offenders under federal supervision and reported that approximately half (49%) of participants exhibited problem drinking. They asserted that probation officers should be aware of the impact of these phenomena on supervision and made the following recommendations:

1. Focus on identification of alcohol use, not just drug use;
2. Identify those using alcohol early in the supervisory process so that treatment plans can be made that will address the use; and
3. Use self-report measures to screen all offenders and verify the information reported.

Among juveniles on probation, it is important to consider that the types of drugs used and risk factors for criminal behavior may be somewhat different than for adult offenders. Jenson (1993, as cited in Jenson, 1997) examined drug and alcohol use among youths (N = 475) placed on probation in Utah and found that the most commonly used substances were tobacco (92%), alcohol (90%), and marijuana (70%). Jenson and Howard (1999) reported that, in a sample of juvenile probationers, more than one third (37%) reported using hallucinogens in the last year. Of that group, more than three quarters (76.8%) had used this type of drug one or more times a month. Urban juveniles were more likely to have used hallucinogens than those living in rural areas. Juvenile probationers who used these drugs had significantly lower levels of perceived parent involvement and support and were more likely to have considered suicide as compared to nonusers.

A key component to effective supervision of substance-abusing offenders is to set limits with consequences for noncompliance that the probation officer is prepared to enforce if necessary (Torres, 1997). Some probation offices, such as the Central District in California, maintain a mandatory abstinence policy that is based on the belief that substance use is a choice and any incident of drug use must have a consequence. Regardless of the manner in which violations of the conditions of one's probation are handled, the policies should be known and communicated to the offender.

Probation officers must verify information provided by offenders and let them know at the onset of the relationship what the consequences of noncompliance will be (Boswell, 1996). In most instances, probation officers must live by the question, "How do you know?" (Wooten & Hoelter, 1998), when dealing with substance-abusing offenders. Officers cannot be sure that offenders are giving them reliable information and must not take information at face value. Juvenile offenders in particular must be made aware of the parameters of acceptable behavior and then be allowed to make choices so that they can learn from the positive or negative outcome (U.S. Probation/ Pretrial Services Office, 1997). With juveniles, probation officers must remember that these youths may have come from homes where the rules and consequences for inappropriate behavior were not clearly stated or reinforced.

VARIATIONS IN PROBATION

Efforts aimed at finding the most effective model of probation services are continually under way but, despite these initiatives aimed at innovation, the result is little consistency and coherence (Evans, 1999). Currently, probation services for offenders with substance abuse problems vary dramatically by program. "The administration of probation programs differs across and even within states, with some agencies being highly centralized (state agency based), others localized (county agency based), and still others under the judicial or executive branches of government" (Lucken, 1997, p. 245). The type of monitoring or treatment an offender receives in different counties or states may vary greatly, depending on the applicable laws, rules and regulations, types of services available, amount of individual probation officer discretion, and agency philosophy. Even the amount of contact between the probation officer and offender will vary based on the program and the type of offense. In 1995, 91.4% of substance-abusing offenders on probation reported that they had contact with their probation officer in the past 30 days, with 83.7% reporting a personal contact with their probation officer at the probation office (U.S. Department of Justice, 1998). More limited contact between other officers and offenders may be the result of the offender's behavior (e.g., not maintaining contact with the probation officer as ordered by the court) or the probation officer having a caseload so large that it is difficult to initiate contact regularly. In some instances, the amount of contact may be reduced because the offender has demonstrated stability in his or her life, such as obtaining employment and not engaging in criminal activity, and is meeting the mandated conditions of probation.

SHOCK PROBATION

Shock probation is a type of sanction in which offenders are briefly confined so that they understand the seriousness of their criminal behavior and then receive a period of intensive probation in which they are closely monitored (McNeece, Bullington, Arnold, & Springer, 2002). In addition to causing offenders to experience firsthand the negative consequences associated with substance abuse and criminal behavior, such programs are also intended to save money by reducing the burden on the state prison systems.

Clark, Aziz, and MacKenzie (1994) described one example of a program that utilizes this form of intervention: New York State's Shock Incarceration program for young offenders (see Exhibit 9.1). Positive results for program graduates are noted by Clark and colleagues. Among program graduates, educational improvements are promising: 45% increased their reading scores, 61% increased their math scores, and 70.5% of those tested for the GED passed. At 1 year follow-up, 10% of offenders returned to prison as compared to 16% of offenders prior to the development of the program. The New York Department of Corrections estimated that for every inmate involved in the program, it saves about $20,000 compared to incarceration. Furthermore, in a multisite evaluation of five states where these programs are used, the intensity of the supervision was found to impact the positive adjustment of the offender (Brane & MacKenzie, 1996).

INTENSIVE SUPERVISION PROBATION

Many offenders with substance abuse problems are sentenced to ISP, a more restrictive type of probation than traditional probation. ISP is a method of monitoring that can be used as an alternative to incarceration. It is considered to be a type of intermediate sanction that is not as punitive as incarceration but still conforms to the corrections philosophy of deterrence and surveillance (Chandler & Kassebaum, 1997). ISP requires that the offender and probation officer keep in close contact, which generally includes random home visits to ensure compliance with the requirements of the program. In addition, the offender may have to perform community service, maintain employment, adhere to a curfew, and submit to urine drug testing. Compared to basic probation, ISP is generally more expensive and requires that probation officers have smaller caseloads to accommodate the increased supervision of the offender. Regular probation and parole costs on average $1,110 per year per inmate, as compared to ISP, which averaged $3,470 per year (Camp & Camp, 1998, as cited in Office of National Drug Control Policy [ONDCP], 1999).

One example of an ISP program is the Intensive Case Management Program in Multnomah County, Oregon, for offenders who have violated

EXHIBIT 9.1
Program Example: New York State's Shock Incarceration Program

---

With a total bed capacity of 1,570 offenders, New York State's Shock Incarceration Program serves offenders younger than age 35 whose release after completing the incarceration phase will not endanger the public safety. The program is based on the theoretical foundation of the control theory of delinquency that "assumes that inmates entering the [Department of Corrections] are individuals whose bonds to society are either weakened or broken and that exposure to the philosophies and practices of this program will help restore these bonds" (C. L. Clark & Aziz, 1996, p. 44).

The program consists of two phases (as described by Clark, Aziz, & MacKenzie, 1994):

- *Phase I: Intensive Incarceration*—Program includes physical training, drills, and ceremonial formations of offender platoons; substance abuse treatment (based on 12-step model) and education; academic education (minimum of 260 hours); and hard labor. Daily and weekly evaluations of offender performance are conducted. Violation of rules can lead to dismissal depending on the nature of the violation.
- *Phase II: Intensive Community Supervision ("AfterShock")*—Program includes intensive supervision by a parole officer (size of caseload is 38 offenders to every 2 officers), home visits, monitoring of curfew rules, drug testing, educational and vocational services, and relapse prevention services.

---

the conditions of their parole or probation. The cost of this program is about $3,646 annually per offender, compared to about $1,495 for general supervision in the county (Multnomah County Auditor's Office, 1997). Local officials have estimated that this intensive form of supervision adds at least $470,000 annually in supervision costs. Auditors of this program could not find measurable improvements in offenders who participated in this program as compared to high-risk offenders on general caseloads, nor has the program reduced the number of offenders returning to prison for technical violations (Multnomah County Auditor's Office, 1997). Based on recorded outcomes, the county's auditors did not recommend its expansion.

PROBATION OFFICER–OFFENDER RELATIONSHIP

The nature of the probation officer–offender relationship is the subject of much debate. The relationship will vary by the agency philosophy, as well as the individual officer's view about the most appropriate interactional style. Unfortunately, some officers fall into "nagging or disapproving" interaction that excludes the possibility of meaningful conversations, especially for offenders with antisocial characteristics (Wooten & Hoelter, 1998, p. 30). Many practitioners believe that the relationship should not be approached from a punitive perspective but instead should focus on providing support and surveillance (L. R. Singer, 1991). Boswell (1996) studied probation officers and found that communicating and engaging clients to bring about change are important components of effective probation work. She also reported that probation officers talked about "'starting where the client is' in probation work, and the need to show genuine interest in clients" (p. 36).

Probation officers must try to connect with their juvenile clients to build trust so that the juvenile cares about how the probation officer perceives his or her actions (U.S. Probation/Pretrial Services Office, 1997). In some ways, the probation officer may take on the role of a "substitute parent" by providing discipline and direction along with guidance and support. If the probation officer can build rapport with a juvenile offender, the strong relationship that ensues may have a positive impact on the offender's behavior, particularly for those who may not have other positive supports in their lives. Even with juveniles who have involved parents, the relationships may be strained or tainted by past abuse. Previous research has documented that probationers who come from chemically dependent families have experienced significantly higher levels of violence and abuse in their families compared to probationers not raised in such environments (McGaha, 1993).

Similar relationship issues are present with adults on probation, but the officer–offender relationship can be compared, in some aspects, to the therapist–client relationship in counseling. Probationers or parolees may need someone who they can talk to who understands the variety of challenges that they face in maintaining a drug-free lifestyle in the community. For instance, parolees who are sentenced to remain in their county of commitment may have difficulty avoiding areas known for drug activity, thus making it difficult to distance themselves from past associations and behavior—generally an important component of relapse prevention (Hall, Baldwin, & Prendergast, 2001). Having someone to talk with who understands these challenges but who also holds the offender accountable for his or her actions can be a useful aspect of probation.

FAMILIES AND PROBATION

Family members, although not under the jurisdiction and authority of the probation officer, may have a significant impact on the substance-abusing offender's behavior. Walker (1992) asserted that many family members of those who are on probation have codependent relationships that impact the effectiveness of the probation officer's attempts to intervene with the offender. He noted that family members may lie about the probationer's behavior, make or cancel appointments for the probationer, conceal information about the whereabouts of the probationer, or even make suggestions to the probation officer about how to handle the situation.

Walker (1992) suggested identifying the treatment needs of the family and including these in the offender's treatment plan to enhance the quality of the supervision (see chapter 4 for more on involving family members in treatment). Given that offenders on community supervision may be living with substance-abusing family members, it is critical to acknowledge the impact of those members' behavior on the offender trying to achieve and maintain abstinence. "A nonsupportive or nonrecovering family system will sabotage the best laid intentions of the probation officer who hopes to push an offender to the brink of change" (Read, 1995, p. 19). Family members may benefit from self-help programs such as Alcoholics Anonymous or Narcotics Anonymous if they are using or Al-Anon if they want to enhance their ability to cope with the offender's addiction (see chapter 5). Without examining all aspects of the offender's life that may contribute to future substance abuse or criminal behavior, the likelihood that the offender will return to previous patterns is increased. However, inclusion of the family in probation services is generally not required, and thus, the decision about addressing family issues is typically left up to the individual probation officer.

One increasingly popular approach for working with juvenile offenders is strength-based practice. Based on the strengths perspective of Weick, Rapp, Sullivan, and Kisthardt (1989) and techniques from solution-focused therapy (see Berg, 1994; Berg & Miller, 1992; see also chapter 3, this volume), M. D. Clark (1998), a probation officer, recommended this approach for working with resistant adolescent offenders and their families. His model is based on the following principles: accountability for making needed behavior changes, taking action on the problems that exist, belief in the individual's ability to change, brief interventions that focus on the present, cooperation between the worker and the youth, and belief in the youth's competence. The approach emphasizes culturally sensitive intervention that is not focused solely on problems but instead on strengths and past successes that can be used to address the situation at hand (M. D. Clark, 1998).

Another approach to working with substance-abusing youths and their families is the American Probation and Parole Association's (APPA) five-module skills development curriculum and training for juvenile probation and parole officers. This program also uses a strength-based perspective that involves understanding the youth's perspective on the world and involving the family in case planning (Dickinson & Crowe, 1997). The manual includes a variety of strategies for changing behavior, including modeling of appropriate values and behaviors by adults, behavioral contracting, positive structuring of time and activities, and other counseling techniques.

PROBATION OFFICER'S ROLE IN SUBSTANCE ABUSE TREATMENT

In 1995, 38% of U.S. offenders on probation reported that they had received some form of drug treatment during their current sentence; 32% had received treatment for alcohol abuse, and 17% had received treatment for drug abuse (U.S. Department of Justice, 1998). One of the benefits of community-based substance abuse treatment for offenders is that many are court-ordered to receive such services and thus have an incentive to complete treatment. For those in the criminal justice system, behavioral change through "reinforcing and aversive conditions or incentives" (Corbett & Harris, 1995, p. 68) may provide the necessary leverage for offenders to get the help that they need. Unfortunately, obstacles can prevent probationers from getting access to needed services. Duffee and Carlson (1996) asserted that there are four value positions that hinder probationers seeking treatment:

1. the morally deserving should receive services first;
2. the most amenable clients should be given priority;
3. those persons posing the greatest harm or risk should have greatest access to services; and
4. the agencies best able to manage resources effectively should receive a greater share of service resources (p. 577).

Deciding who gets treatment and under what circumstances can be a complex process. In many instances, probation officers supervising offenders with substance-abuse problems may be the ones to make decisions or recommendations about who gets what type of (if any) substance abuse treatment. Although the judge has the authority to make the final determination, he or she is limited by the availability of treatment services in the community. Unless it is under contract with the court or the state department of corrections to provide services for a specific group of offenders, the agency can set its own guidelines about prioritization for treatment slots. For instance, pregnant women or offenders who are HIV positive may be given priority in some treatment centers.

One of the challenges facing probation officers is that sufficient treatment slots are generally not available for all of the offenders who need treatment. Given the evidence that little meaningful work can be done before treatment, and that many offenders engage in criminal activity during this waiting period, officers must advocate for treatment slots and develop relationships with providers (Duffee & Carlson, 1996). In some instances, probation officers have no choice but to have the offender wait, and in other cases, there may be justification for an officer to advocate for certain individuals to be moved ahead on waiting lists. Probation officers may also opt to seek treatment slots outside of the local community. Even when a treatment bed or slot exists, the probation officer may have to use whatever leverage he or she has to get the offender into treatment. Read (1997) noted that it is erroneous for probation officers to think that they cannot help an addict unless he or she wants help. He stated that officers have generally been trained to think that offenders who do not want help will not benefit from treatment, and changing their mindset can be difficult.

In many instances, probationers receive substance abuse treatment from a community treatment center that has a contract to provide such services.

In 2001, 31,365 (or 21% of those under federal supervision in the United States) received substance abuse treatment from community-based providers under contract to federal probation offices (Office of Probation and Pretrial Services, 2002). However, little is known about the privatization of services for offenders in community corrections (Lucken, 1997). Some have argued that the privatization of services to offenders has benefits. Contracting for services for offenders can allow for criminal justice system control over the services, particularly when officers find that services were not delivered as intended or the quality was poor (Marshall & Vito, 1982).

Other researchers have urged criminal justice officials to look closely at the specific aspects of privatizing services to offenders in the community. Lucken (1997) noted that "The experience of private treatment agencies in community corrections does give cause for concern and further investigation" (p. 255). She stated that mandating treatment in the community adds another layer of supervision and conditions to the offender's sanctions. Treatment programs may impose their own rules and restrictions, and violating these terms may result in additional sanctions for the offender. In other instances, offenders may be allowed to remain in treatment based on the provider's review of the situation without involvement from the probation officer, who may feel differently about the disposition.

Rehabilitation for profit brings a variety of other issues into play that impact offender treatment decisions (Lucken, 1997). As agencies are generally paid per offender, there may be added pressures to maintain individuals in treatment. Although possible, this is unlikely in most cities because of the high demand for treatment slots. Another concern is what constitutes "success" in these programs. Although there are demonstrated benefits from retention in treatment (Libety et al., 1998; ONDCP, 1996), other issues related to compliance with treatment are important for offenders.

Given the recent emphasis on privatization of prisons and other services for offenders, this issue is important to examine. As of 1997, overall about 20% of all U.S. correctional facilities that provide treatment were privately owned, but a higher percentage (48%) of juvenile facilities that provide such services were owned by independent companies (Substance Abuse and Mental Health Services Administration, 1997). The APPA has made clear its position that outlines the limits of their support for privatization:

> The APPA recognizes that the availability of specialized private sector services offers community supervision decision makers additional tools and/or options that, when utilized appropriately, can serve to assist an organization in addressing documented needs and achieving its missions. [APPA does not support or promote, however, the wholesale privatization of probation, parole and/or community-based corrections.] APPA believes that at no time should a private entity be able to make the decision to detain or incarcerate. APPA further believes that at no time can a public sector agency contract its primary responsibility for offender

management . . . and community accountability to a private sector agency (APPA, 2001 p. 1).

In addition to contracting for services, one option for getting offenders into treatment is to train probation officers to provide certain types of substance abuse treatment. Duffee and Carlson (1996) suggested training a small subset of officers and having them provide outpatient substance abuse treatment to offenders. One study (Cunningham, Herie, Martin, & Turner, 1998) found that probation officers were receptive to learning and implementing substance abuse treatment strategies, used the tools they learned with many of their clients, and perceived their efforts as helpful to their clients. Research on this issue confirms that the majority of probation officers support the application of substance abuse counseling techniques, but that time constraints can be an obstacle (Herie, Cunningham, & Martin, 2000).

EFFECTIVENESS OF PROBATION

The available outcome research regarding probation has mainly addressed the issue of mandating probationers to treatment and whether doing so affects criminal recidivism or substance abuse. Hiller, Knight, Devereux, and Hathcoat (1996) examined outcomes for probationers mandated to residential treatment and found that those who completed the program had lower rearrest rates at a 6-month follow-up compared to those who were expelled or transferred out of the program. By contrast, Desmond and Maddux (1996) compared treatment outcomes for methadone maintenance participants who were under compulsory supervision with those who participated voluntarily. Although some small pretreatment differences existed between groups, those who were mandated to treatment fared worse on many important outcomes at 12 months, including number of days incarcerated, number of months engaged in productive activity, and number of days worked for pay.

There is a more developed body of outcome research on ISP than on regular probation. In a randomized field experiment funded by the Bureau of Justice Assistance, S. Turner, Petersilia, and Deschenes (1992) reported that compared to those on routine probation, offenders in ISP programs were seen more often, had more drug testing, received more substance abuse counseling, and had higher levels of employment. No differences were found in rearrest rates at one year, but more ISP participants were incarcerated, mainly for technical violations. However, it is important to note that ISP clients had 3 hours of face-to-face contact per month, compared to those on regular probation who received 20 minutes (Petersilia, Turner, & Deschenes, 1992). In light of these findings, Petersilia and colleagues questioned whether making the program tougher and placing more emphasis on treatment might make ISP programs more effective. Although ISP may be more cost-effective than basic probation in the long-run when the alternative for offenders is prison or jail (Edna McConnell Clark Foundation, 1995), many practitioners still have doubts about its cost effectiveness and outcomes.

In addition, Petersilia (1998) reviewed a decade of research on ISPs and drew several conclusions about the impact of these programs as a form of community corrections. She asserted that overall these programs were underfunded and had low rates of participation (at most 10% of adult probationers and parolees participate). However, she noted that the research on ISPs revealed three consistent findings: (a) participants in ISP were high-risk probationers who were not necessarily prison bound, (b) participation in the program did not impact arrest rates (except for technical violations) or criminal justice system costs, and (c) all evaluations of these programs support the importance of combining monitoring and treatment. Few evaluations of intensive juvenile probation exist, but the existing studies reveal no significant impact on recidivism as compared to incarceration, although these programs tend to be less costly (Corbett, 1999).

The existing research on the provision of probation services reveals that there are some very promising models of service delivery throughout the country, but they have not had the overwhelmingly positive results that were anticipated. As Petersilia (1998) noted, no one program or agency can solve the crime problem, and successful programs need community support and backing. However, we should not focus our efforts just at the program level at the expense of doing what is necessary: shifting our focus to the system level, promoting cooperation among agencies, and creating more options for treatment (Corbett & Harris, 1995).

ELECTRONIC MONITORING

Commonly associated with ISPs, EM is a commonly used attempt to confine offenders to the home ("house arrest"). Apparently inspired by a Spiderman cartoon, Judge Jack Love applied EM technology to enforce house arrest for an offender in 1984 (Fox, 1987, as cited in Bonta, Wallace-Capretta, & Rooney, 2000). Ideally, electronic monitors alert officials when offenders have left their residence or when they have traveled beyond allowable limits. Officials are then immediately dispatched to the offender's location to intervene. The original intention of EM was to enforce house arrest. Later, it became a community-based alternative to incarceration. EM programs are quite popular, particularly in the United States, where more than 40,000 offenders were estimated to be under EM supervision in 1997 (Schmidt, 1998). It is also used in several European countries and in provinces in Canada (Bonta et al., 2000). In a 1996 audit of the Bureau of Prisons (Office of the Inspector General, 1996), it was reported that the bureau reimburses the Administrative Office of the U.S. Court $5 a day for EM and $12 per day for personnel costs associated with EM of a federal home-confined offender. The report also estimated that the cost of implementing EM for all federal home-confined offenders in 1996 was $1 million.

In general, research on home confinement/EM programs has been limited by the low-risk nature of most samples, too few experimental evaluations, and lack of program integrity (Bonta, 1993; Bonta et al., 2000). Findings generally indicate that EM is costly and does not affect recidivism (Brown, Borduin, & Henggeler, 2001). Two studies (Austin & Hardyman, 1991; Baumer & Mendelsohn, 1991) reviewed by Cullen, Wright, and Applegate (1996) used an experimental design to compare the effects of EM on rates of recidivism and technical violations compared to manual supervision. No significant differences were found in rearrest or revocation rates after a one-year follow-up in either study. Approximately 42% of both the electronically and manually monitored groups had unauthorized absences from the home. Some studies have found that enforced house arrest actually increased family stress (Doherty, 1995) and that criminal behaviors such as drug trafficking and prostitution continue unabated (R. Rogers & Jolin, 1989). Moreover, the literature (Bonta et al., 2000; Cullen et al., 1996) supports the notion that EM has a net-widening effect. In other words, when offenders are monitored very closely, illegal behaviors are more likely to be detected.

Bonta and colleagues (2000) conducted a study of three EM programs in Canadian provinces. The study examined perceptions of the EM programs by offenders and staff and examined the impact of the programs on offender recidivism. Two control groups (inmates and probationers) were statistically matched to the EM offenders to control for risk level. Bonta and his colleagues concluded from their findings that EM programs may help ensure that offenders complete a specified period of supervision without incident, but that "if the desired outcome is reduced recidivism, EM has questionable merit" (p. 73).

"In sum, the costs associated with establishing electronic monitoring systems seem unnecessary expenditures because electronic monitoring does not appear to be effective, nor does it appear to augment the effectiveness of home confinement programs" (Brown et al., 2001). Offender treatment, not sanctions, is the most promising approach to reducing recidivism (Andrews & Bonta, 1998).

URINE DRUG TESTING

Urine drug testing in the criminal justice system is a surveillance method to detect whether offenders are currently using drugs or alcohol. The offender must provide a urine sample, which is tested for the presence of specific drugs. Two main types of analysis are commonly used: immunoassays and chromatography (Timrots, 1992). Immunoassays use antibodies to detect whether the specimen has higher quantities of the drug being tested than a calibrator with a known quantity of the drug. If the quantity is higher than the calibrator, the test is considered positive for that particular drug.

The second, more expensive, type of testing—chromatography—involves separating and identifying the components of the urine. Gas chromatography/mass spectrometry is believed to be one of the most effective types of drug testing but is very expensive, generally between $25 and $100 per test (Timrots, 1992).

Among offenders on probation who were imprisoned for a technical violation and sentenced to state prison time, 9.6% had tested positive for drug use while under community supervision in the National Study of State Prison Inmates (R. L. Cohen, 1995). In 1998, 71% of local jail jurisdictions in the United States reported that they had a policy to test inmates or staff for drug use; in June alone, one fourth of the jails tested samples from inmates (Bureau of Justice Statistics [BJS], 2000). Approximately 10% of drug tests conducted on jail inmates in June 1998 revealed use of one or more drugs.

Urine drug testing is used in the criminal justice system with offenders in three primary ways: (a) as an adjunct to community supervision, (b) as an assessment (baseline) tool for offenders entering the system, and (c) as an assessment of drug use during mandated drug treatment. Drug testing serves several purposes in the criminal justice system: to inform judges of the offender's current drug use when considering bail-setting or sentencing, to indicate whether the offender is complying with a mandate to be drug-free, and to identify those offenders who need treatment (Timrots, 1992).

Relying on self-report is insufficient in most cases, because offenders have a strong incentive to report that they are drug-free regardless of whether or not they are. Those who continue to use drugs may have any of several sanctions imposed, depending on their legal jurisdiction or corrections facility. Offenders who test negative for drugs may be tested less frequently or may no longer be required to continue testing (Nurco, Hanlan, Bateman, & Kinlock, 1995).

Monitoring offenders on probation or parole for continued drug use is a continual challenge for officers providing community-based supervision to this population. In some cities, a certain number of positive drug screens (e.g., 4 in Baltimore) are considered a violation of parole (Nurco et al., 1995). It is argued that such monitoring nationwide is crucial because it is estimated that more than half of all people on community supervision are involved in the sale or use of drugs (Nurco, Hanlan, & Kinlock, 1990). Because drug use is believed to be associated with an increase in criminal behavior (Anglin, 1988), assisting offenders in maintaining a drug-free lifestyle may reduce the likelihood of further criminal behavior.

One study found no difference in recidivism between a group that received drug monitoring and treatment and a group that received drug monitoring only (Hepburn & Albonetti, 1994). The authors acknowledged that it is unclear, though, whether the failure of treatment to affect recidivism is a reflection of the treatment implementation or intensity or is the result of using probationers for the sample.

Using drug testing as a part of an initial assessment for offenders entering the court or corrections systems is a relatively new phenomenon. Some programs have asked individuals to submit to urine drug screens at the time of arrest. Those who test positive may be released but asked to submit to drug monitoring as a condition of their pretrial release. The aim of this form of monitoring is to increase the likelihood that the individual will abstain from future drug use and appear at the next scheduled court appearance (State of Florida, 1994).

The use of testing in jails may be rare; a recent national study found that only 3% of jails report screening offenders at the time of admission (R. H. Peters, May, & Kearns, 1992). However, this figure is much lower than the recent findings of the National Institute of Justice Drug Use Forecasting (DUF) program. This program calculates the percentage of offenders arrested in certain cities throughout the country who have positive urine drug screens at the time of arrest. Recent DUF data show that the percentage of male inmates testing positive for any drug ranged from 51% to 83% (ONDCP, 1997).

Urine drug screens may be required to ensure compliance with treatment for those offenders mandated to treatment, or for those who agree to treatment, as a part of their court proceedings. Court and corrections officials will generally want to know if the offender is complying with treatment and remaining abstinent from drugs. In programs in which access to treatment may be limited by available space or funding, those who do not comply may be discharged from treatment. Those who do not successfully complete treatment and continue to have positive drug screens may be sent back to court for sanctions.

S. Turner, Petersilia, and Deschenes (1994) noted that anecdotal evidence suggests that many corrections officials are not sold on the benefits of random drug testing as a deterrent or diagnostic technique. Given problems with failure to revoke probationary status and a lack of treatment options when someone does has a positive drug screen, S. Turner and colleagues recommended asking the following questions prior to establishing widespread use of drug testing for those under community supervision:

1. How do probation/parole agencies implement drug testing orders?
2. How many drug-dependent offenders have testing conditions revoked?
3. How many offenders are actually tested, with what frequency and results?

4. How does the justice system respond to positive drug tests?
5. Do such tests result in added probation/parole conditions, referrals to treatment programs, or revocation?
6. What impact do Intensive Supervision Probation/Parole (ISP) programs with drug testing have on offender recidivism, as measured by official records of technical violations and new arrests?
7. How do jurisdictions differ on these dimensions? (p. 233)

Data from the BJS (2000) answer some of these questions. According to BJS, in 1998, 71% of local jails reported that they had a policy regarding testing inmates for drug use. Testing is most commonly done when suspicion of use exists (69%) but can also be random (49%) or conducted according to specified criteria (30%). A few jurisdictions (5%) test all inmates at admission. In addition, BJS provided outlines regarding the types of sanctions. The percentage of jurisdictions that use sanctions when an inmate tests positive for drugs is as follows: taking away of privileges (70%), taking away good time earned (52%) (time earned towards a reduction in one's sentence due to good behavior), reclassifying the offender (49%), charging the offender with a new offense (39%), increasing the frequency of drug testing (25%), and adding time to the offender's sentence (20%).

For urine drug testing to serve a useful purpose, protocols for positive tests must be in place. If no sanctions are established and no treatment is available, the usefulness of drug testing is difficult to determine.

In the Third District Juvenile Court, Central Probation, Salt Lake City, Utah, an Office of Juvenile Justice and Delinquency Prevention (OJJDP) funded project, all juveniles on probation are subject to testing at the discretion of their probation officer. (In fact, all youths on probation in Utah are subject to testing at the discretion of their assigned probation officer.) The purpose of the testing is as follows (Crowe & Sydney, 2000):

- To document whether a substance abuse problem exists, and if so, compel the juvenile to participate in treatment; and
- To hold the juvenile accountable for his or her behavior. For the first positive drug test, the probation officer reviews the rules and places the youth under house arrest; for a second positive drug test, the juvenile may be returned to court and possibly detained; and for continuing positive drug tests, the juvenile may be ordered to participate in inpatient drug treatment or long-term residential placement.

In addition, a sophisticated process for collecting urine specimens must be in place. Chavaria (1992) advocated for a totally randomized system of collection in which the offender can potentially be required to provide a specimen seven days a week. The code-a-phone system is an example of a randomized system for collecting specimens from offenders. Under this system, each offender is assigned a number and must call in and listen to a recording each day to see if his or her number is on the recording. If the number is on the recording, the offender must provide a urine specimen the next day.

Drug testing for inmates at various points in the legal and corrections system is becoming more prevalent. The federal government has encouraged uniform drug testing of incarcerated offenders. Florida is one state that has responded to such requests. In 1993, the Florida legislature passed the Inmate Substance Abuse Testing Program for offenders in state prisons. The purposes of this project are to identify offenders in need of drug treatment, to discourage drug use, and to increase the number of inmates referred and treated for substance abuse (Department of Community Affairs, Division of Housing and Community Development, State of Florida, 1997).

More than 10 years ago, Canada established a urine drug testing program for offenders in correctional settings and on conditional release in the community that involves nonrandom drug testing at regular intervals (Fraser & Zamecnik, 2002). In 2000, among conditional release offenders 27.2% of urine specimens tested positive for drugs, most commonly cannabinoids (43.3% of specimens).

SUMMARY

In this chapter we focused on commonly used methods of monitoring substance-abusing offenders. We reviewed probation, including variations of probation (e.g., shock probation, ISP), EM, and urine drug testing. It appears that probation and urine drug testing, collectively, can be used effectively to monitor clients when combined with drug treatment. In addition to serving a monitoring role, probation officers can be an important resource in accessing treatment and staying clean for offenders who want to achieve and maintain a drug-free lifestyle. On the basis of the available literature regarding monitoring's lack of effectiveness, we do not recommend the use of any one form of monitoring alone without treatment as a method of reducing substance abuse.

A noteworthy benefit of urine testing not mentioned above is the potential for a "bogus pipeline" effect, in which the offender believes that there is an accurate, follow-up check on self-report use (see chapter 2). This, in turn, has the effect of increasing the offender's honesty in describing his or her use (Miller, Westerberg, & Waldron, 1995, as cited in Waldron, 1997). Urine drug testing is believed to be a more reliable measure of continued substance abuse, because most offenders tend to underreport their drug use (Wish, Toborg, & Bellassai, 1988). Other than showing whether an offender is using drugs, drug testing's only purpose seems to be to help monitor substance-abusing offenders. Drug testing alone is not sufficient to keep offenders from using drugs and reoffending. The best approach may be to combine random drug testing with forms of rehabilitative drug treatment to treat the addiction and, it is hoped, minimize the likelihood that the individual will engage in future criminal behavior (Grabowski, 1986).

In sum, offender treatment, not sanctions, is the most promising approach to reducing recidivism (Andrews & Bonta, 1998).

10

FUTURE DIRECTIONS FOR RESEARCH AND PRACTICE

It appears to us that most of the immediate changes that could be made to improve substance abuse treatment with offenders begin with "macrolevel" changes. We would be well advised to pay close attention to the policy changes regarding drug law enforcement and substance abuse treatment suggested by Elliot Currie (1993):

1. *More reasonable sentences for drug offenses*. The long minimum mandatory sentences for minor drug offenses adopted by the federal government and many state governments in the late 1980s and early 1990s should be changed. Under those laws it is possible for a person possessing a small quantity of illicit drugs to be sent to prison, where treatment is least likely to occur, for life without the possibility of parole. "Intermediate" sentences, usually involving some sort of community service, are less expensive, more humane, and at least as effective. Readers may recall that, in chapter 1 we provided some examples of states that are moving their drug sentencing policies in this direction.

2. *Focus criminal penalties on traffickers, not users.* The combination of a sparing use of punishment and the provision of more accessible options for treatment proved effective in the Netherlands and Sweden in the 1980s, despite President George H. W. Bush's assertion that tolerant drug policies in more liberal nations had led to a "social disaster" (Office of National Drug Control Policy, 1990, p. 5). The punitive treatment of drug users and the severity of their sentences clearly distinguish the American approach from other industrialized nations. (We expand on this below.)

3. *Provide serious help for drug abusers within the justice system.* State officials estimate that, of the 70% to 85% of inmates who need substance abuse treatment, only 13% receive it (Blanchard, 1999). In many prisons there is no treatment available except for self-help programs such as Alcoholics Anonymous (AA) and Narcotics Anonymous (NA). Most drugs are readily available in both federal and state prisons, and understaffed prisons often turn a blind eye to narcotics use by inmates because it pacifies them and makes the seriously overcrowded prisons more manageable. Vaillant (1988) demonstrated in a study of adult offenders that treatment in prison, followed by close parole supervision, was effective in rehabilitating offenders.

4. *Shift law enforcement toward community safety.* Throughout the 1990s U.S. drug policy required the police primarily to funnel drug users and dealers into the criminal justice system for punishment. Beginning in the late 1980s, however, several experiments in "community policing" began to focus on crime prevention and on making communities safer (Trojanowicz & Bucqueroux, 1990). (Actually, the driving philosophy behind community policing is improving the quality of life in the community.) Instead of practicing traditional incident-driven law enforcement, the police now more often organize and empower community residents to prevent crime by changing the conditions within the community so that they are not conducive to drug trafficking.

REDEFINING TREATMENT

Treatment professionals should give careful consideration to redefining chemical dependency treatment. One of the problems is that the "disease concept" or the "medical model" of chemical dependency is based on an assumption that four decades of medical and social sciences research has failed to support: that chemical dependency is a disease in the same sense that pneumonia or a kidney infection or arthritis are diseases and that a specific treatment can bring the problem under control. In fact, addiction to drugs is not at all like most other diseases. People with arthritis do not choose to have the disease, and they cannot choose to stop being arthritic. Drug abusers, on the other hand, do choose, at least in the beginning, to use drugs. More often than many of us suspected, they also choose to stop using drugs or to cut down their use to manageable levels. Although the disease model was initially popular because it did help reduce the stigmatization that came with being labeled an *addict*, treatment professionals are beginning to realize that it can be more of a hindrance than a help. It allows the addict to avoid responsibility, and it steers us into blind alleys in our research efforts. Toward the end of redefining treatment, we should work toward the following.

1. *Taking treatment seriously*. In addition to providing adequate funding for treatment, practitioners and researchers have recently begun paying attention to the *quality* of treatment. Much of what has passed for treatment through the end of the 20th century has been unworthy of the name. Methadone maintenance programs infrequently provide any educational or counseling services. "In-jail counseling" very often means only that weekly AA meetings are held for inmates. Family therapy sometimes means only that the spouses of clients are included in the infrequent chats that are called "counseling" in those programs. Vocational development frequently means only that a client was told of a job possibility on the other side of town.

Treatment must be sophisticated enough to meet the complex needs of offenders. Practitioners are encouraged to conduct thorough and meaningful assessments and to use these assessments to inform holistic treatment planning, whereby evidence-based interventions are matched to an offender's readiness for change and needs. "The broader programming challenge now is to help promote the 'technology transfer' so the effective program models (and related staff recruitment, training, and quality-control processes) diffuse throughout the correctional community and become well implemented" (Pearson, Lipton, Cleland, & Yee, 2002, p. 493).

2. *Making treatment "user-friendly."* A major shortcoming of treatment is that most addicts simply don't participate. One of the problems with the early research literature was that almost all of the research was conducted on a tiny minority of drug abusers who were either trapped in the criminal justice system and *forced* into treatment or more highly motivated than the majority to *voluntarily* seek treatment. Treatment is not user-friendly in the sense that those people seeking treatment are

often in danger of being arrested, which produces a domino effect, losing their jobs, or losing custody of their children.

Treatment programs funded with public money have the same type of stigma associated with public welfare programs. Private programs are too expensive for all but the very rich or the well insured. By 1998, most insurance companies and health maintenance organizations had put such severe limits on chemical dependency treatment that clients were paying well more than 50% of total program costs. Drug policy should guarantee amnesty for all classes of drug users seeking treatment and provide funding for all addictions treatment. One impetus for such a paradigm shift in U.S. drug policy might be found in the AIDS epidemic, because it is rapidly becoming obvious that the entire society is threatened by the spread of HIV/AIDS, and HIV is being spread by intravenous drug users. (It is interesting that the first areas of "socialized medicine" in the United States dealt with epidemics such as polio.)

We should also require that treatment be "culturally competent," because one of our major problems in the last century is that treatment models developed by and for middle-class Protestant men do not attract or effectively serve large numbers of Hispanic, Native American, African American, and other racial or ethnic minority drug abusers. Practitioners should be sensitive to "gender-relevant" treatment, getting beyond the simplistic assumption that any given treatment is equally useful for both men and women. In some cases special treatment models for women and racial or ethnic minorities have been developed; in many others, we still need to develop gender or group-specific treatment models. A portion of the funding should be set aside specifically for women in treatment, including ancillary services such as child care. In the U.S., relatively few treatment programs are geared to the special needs of women offenders, fewer still accept women and their children, and even fewer treat pregnant women (Kassebaum, 1999).

3. *Linking treatment with harm reduction.* The harm reduction strategy promotes public health rather than the criminal justice perspective when determining what to do about drug users (McNeece, Bullington, Arnold, & Springer, 2002). Thus, all drug use, whether of "licit" or illicit substances, is seen as potentially problematic. Proponents of this approach have asserted that the distinctions made between legal and illegal substances are totally artificial and have led to a myopic focus solely on illicit chemicals (McNeece et al., 2002). The Netherlands has been the clear leader in this paradigm shift for how to define drug problems, although similar approaches are also being tried in Switzerland, Spain, Italy, and Germany. At the time of this writing, the British government had begun efforts to relax marijuana laws to allow police to focus enforcement activities on harder drugs.

When agencies are forced to precisely define measurable objectives by which their accomplishments would be evaluated, they usually discover that it is much easier to be successful with harm reduction strategies than with curative approaches. Legislators should make the receipt of federal funding contingent on the repeal of several state laws, including those that prohibit the free distribution of needles and syringes to intravenous drug users. The harm reduction approach may also benefit clients in other ways. Alcoholics who previously considered their battle with alcoholism as a zero-sum game may begin to work on cutting down on their drinking, because they no longer feel doomed to "failure" because of their inability to achieve total abstinence.

4. *Making aftercare a priority.* Considering that practitioners have known for decades that most addicts relapse repeatedly after leaving treatment, the lack of programs that make provisions for working with clients after treatment beyond a referral to AA or NA is strange. This shortcoming is even more surprising when one considers that ample evidence has been in existence for years that well-designed aftercare and community support services dramatically increase the probability of success (Currie, 1993). Aftercare should be mandatory, and it should also be required that the aftercare specialist function as an advocate for the offender, interceding in the housing and labor markets, as well as the criminal justice system.

5. *Linking treatment to work.* As early as 1972 the Vera Institute of Justice in New York City developed a "supported work" program for addicts—the Wildcat Service Corporation (WCS; L. Friedman, 1978). During the next four years, WCS put more than 4,000 ex-addicts and ex-offenders to work. They were successfully placed with the Board of Education, the public libraries, youth counseling agencies, the Bronx District Attorney, and Mount Sinai Hospital. They painted schools and Head Start Centers, renovated buildings in the South Bronx, worked as messengers and translators, and did maintenance work for the police department. About one third of the WCS workers graduated to nonsubsidized employment. The most astounding discovery was that, among an experimental and control group, those who worked at least half-time were much more likely to cut down on their drug use. Research also established that the taxpayers got back $1.12 for every dollar put into the program (L. Friedman, 1978). A larger experiment by the Manpower Demonstration Research Corporation (MDRC, 1980), with an even more difficult and harder to place group of addicts, was successful in making them more

productive and less criminal through subsidized employment, saving the taxpayers several thousand dollars per client.

Such successes should be used to convince Congress to provide funding to guarantee subsidized employment, where needed, for every recovering addict. Subsequent research by MDRC on the success of welfare-to-work programs confirmed the efficacy of using work as a component of the intervention process for substance-abusing welfare recipients (A. Brown, 2001). Ferguson, Springer, and Holleran (2002) analyzed longitudinal data from the Young Women's Health Study (from 1992 to 1996), finding that young mothers who received welfare for more than two years had lower reported drug use consequences than did mothers who never used welfare or relied on it for less than two years. These findings indicate that negative social consequences correlated with drug use will not significantly impact the ability of the vast majority of young mothers to comply with program work requirements. The Center for Substance Abuse Treatment recommended that life skills training, vocational training, and employment be included as components of substance abuse treatment services (cited in Legal Action Center, 1999).

RESEARCH

We have made considerable progress from the early days of alcoholism research when most of those efforts studied White men in voluntary programs (McNeece & DiNitto, 1998). However, our research still shows equivocal results with enough frequency to make most observers somewhat skeptical of treatment efficacy. For years we have been urged to match patients to appropriate treatment, but the latest results indicate that matching makes little difference in treatment outcomes (National Institute on Alcohol Abuse and Alcoholism, 1997). An alternative explanation, however, is that we simply have not learned which factors are important to consider in matching clients to treatment. Several research studies on the stages-of-change construct presented in chapter 3 speak to the construct's clinical utility and predictive validity as it relates to a client's readiness for change (Prochaska & Norcross, 1999). Yet, additional research is needed that informs practitioners of specific client characteristics that are predictive of treatment outcomes across modalities and settings.

One could make a good case for further studies of culturally appropriate treatment. Culture and ethnicity were factors not considered in project MATCH (NIAAA, 1997). It seems obvious from looking at the national and international data on substance abuse that the rates of abuse and addiction vary greatly between cultures. Why shouldn't we expect the same cultural variation with treatment results?

A recent review of the cost–benefit literature on drug treatment is encouraging. In the 18 cost–benefit studies that he reviewed, Cartwright (2000) noted that a persistent finding is that benefits exceed costs, even when not all benefits are accounted for in the analysis. Most studies have emphasized that cost savings accrue to society from the reduction in external costs of the consequences of substance abuse—such as crime and health problems. (A striking omission is the complete absence of cost–benefit studies for adolescents; only one study was found for women in treatment.)

Another avenue of research that is being pursued with more vigor is the study of participants who have successfully terminated an addiction, usually without treatment (Stewart, 1998). If we can determine the common characteristics, if any, of "self-quitters," perhaps we can identify those that have the potential for being transferable via education or training, and incorporate that strategy into our treatment approaches.

Medical and biophysical researchers will no doubt continue research into the genetic factors associated with addiction. Whether that research eventually leads to the development of a "magic pill" is highly doubtful. Even if that miracle does happen, it would appear to be years away.

DETERMINING EFFECTIVENESS IN OUTCOME RESEARCH

Throughout this book, we have given considerable attention to a review of available outcome literature relevant to the different intervention approaches and modalities covered. However, how does one judge whether a program is effective or not? Although substance abuse treatment for offenders varies across programs, facilities, and locations, the National Task Force on Correctional Substance Abuse Strategies (1991) noted that "effective programs" have common characteristics:

- Clearly defined missions, goals, admission criteria, and assessment strategies for those seeking treatment
- Support and understanding of key agency administrators and staff
- Consistent intervention strategies supported by links with other agencies as the offender moves through the system
- Well-trained staff who have opportunities for continuing education
- Ongoing evaluation and development based on outcome and process data.

One of the main controversies among researchers and substance abuse providers has been an operational definition of the term *effective treatment*. As discussed in chapter 1, the Treatment Outcome Working Group, a meeting of treatment and evaluation experts sponsored by the Office of National

Drug Control Policy (1996), has established some results and outcomes that define effective treatment:

1. Reduced use of the primary drug
2. Improved functioning of drug users in terms of employment
3. Improved educational status
4. Improved interpersonal relationships
5. Improved medical status and general improvement in health
6. Improved legal status
7. Improved mental health status
8. Improved noncriminal public safety factors.

Although some of these desired outcomes are not pertinent to incarcerated offenders receiving treatment, they are appropriate long-term goals following release. Failure to accomplish several of the above goals will most likely result in an offender's involvement in future drug use and criminal activity and subsequent incarceration.

One controversy in evaluating drug treatment methods and programs for criminal offenders is that recidivism tends to be defined in terms of rearrest rates. Offenders who successfully complete treatment may continue to use drugs but may not be rearrested. If recidivism is defined only as rearrest, an unknown percentage of inmates may continue to have substance abuse problems. Recidivism statistics may underestimate the actual rate of continued substance abuse among offenders. One alternative to gaining a better estimate of continued drug use is to examine the substance use level and productivity after treatment completion (Van Stelle, Mauser, & Moberg, 1994). However, continuing to monitor offender behavior posttreatment is difficult unless the offender is mandated to have follow-up through probation or parole and also urine drug testing.

CONCLUSION

Freeing up most of the resources we spend on drug interdiction, law enforcement, the courts, and incarceration would allow practitioners and researchers in the field of substance abuse to make substantial progress in improving treatment and making treatment available to those who need it. Reducing the number of people arrested and incarcerated for drug possession and other minor drug offenses would also allow the police to concentrate their efforts on more serious crimes, thus making communities safer (McNeece et al., 2002).

The decline of inner cities and the consequent deterioration of the quality of life for poor and minority people are, to a large degree, responsible for the epidemic of drug abuse. It is foolish to believe that either the threat of criminal punishment or the promise of a short-term treatment program will cause teenagers and adults to avoid lives of crime and involvement with drugs. In the long run, stable families, safe neighborhoods, and economically viable cities are the keys to fighting both drug use and crime (McNeece, Bullington, Arnold, & Springer, 2002).

Meanwhile, advances have been made in the treatment of substance abuse, and we encourage practitioners to avail themselves of the most recent knowledge of treatment effectiveness (Cartwright, 2000; National Institute on Drug Abuse, 1999c). As we have stressed throughout this book, using evidence-based practice methods is the most effective way of assisting substance-abusing offenders.

REFERENCES

Abadinsky, H. (1993). *Drug abuse: An introduction* (2nd ed.). Chicago: Nelson-Hall.

Abadinsky, H. (2001). *Drugs: An introduction* (4th ed.). Belmont, CA: Wadsworth/Thompson.

Achenbach, T. M. (1991). *Integrative guide for the 1991 CBCL/4-18, YSR, and TRF profiles*. Burlington: University of Vermont, Department of Psychiatry.

Achenbach, T. M. (1991). *Manual for the Child Behavior Checklist and Revised Child Behavior Profile*. Burlington, VT: Author.

Ackerman, R. (1983). *Children of alcoholics: Bibliography and resource guide*. Pompano Beach, FL: Health Communications Press.

Albert, J. (1994). Talking like "real people": The "Straight Ahead" prison group. In A. Gitterman & L. Shulman (Eds.), *Mutual aid groups, vulnerable populations, and the life cycle* (2nd ed., pp. 199–214). New York: Columbia University Press.

Alexander, B. K. (1990). Alternatives to the war on drugs. *Journal of Drug Issues, 20*, 1–27.

Alexander, F., & French, T. (1946). *Psychoanalytic therapy: Principles and applications*. New York: Ronald Press.

Alexander, J. F., & Parsons, B. V. (1973). Short-term behavioral intervention with delinquents: Impact on family process and recidivism. *Journal of Abnormal Psychology, 81*, 219–225.

Alexander, R. (2000). *Counseling, treatment, and intervention methods with juvenile and adult offenders*. Belmont, CA: Wadsworth.

Alford, G. S., Koehler, R. A., & Leonard, J. (1991). Alcoholics Anonymous–Narcotics Anonymous model inpatient treatment of chemically dependent adolescents: A two-year outcome study. *Journal of Studies on Alcohol, 52,* 118–126.

Allen, M. J., & Yen, W. M. (1979). *Introduction to measurement theory.* Monterey, CA: Brooks/Cole.

American Correctional Association. (1990). *Standards for adult correctional institutions* (3rd ed.). Laurel, MD: Author.

American Correctional Association. (1991). *Standards for adult local detention facilities.* Laurel, MD: Author.

American Probation and Parole Association. (2001). *APPA position statement on privatization.* Lexington, KY: Author. Retrieved Nov. 25, 2002, from http://www.appa-net.org/about&20appa/proposedstatement.htm.

American Psychiatric Association. (1952). *Diagnostic and statistical manual of mental disorders.* Washington, DC: Author.

American Psychiatric Association. (1987). *Diagnostic and statistical manual of mental disorders* (3rd ed., rev.). Washington, DC: Author.

American Psychiatric Association. (2000). *Diagnostic and statistical manual of mental disorders* (4th ed., text rev.). Washington, DC: Author.

American Public Welfare Association. (1995). APWA's 1994 survey of foster care maintenance rates. *W-Memo, 7*(7), 36.

Amrod, J. (1997). The effect of motivational enhancement therapy and coping skills training on the self-efficacy and motivation of incarcerated male alcohol abusers. *Dissertation Abstracts International, 57*(9-B), 5904.

Anderson, A. R., & Henry, C. S. (1994). Family system characteristics and parental behaviors as predictors of adolescent substance use. *Adolescence, 29,* 405–420.

Anderson, C. M., Hogarty, G., & Reiss, D. (1980). Family treatment of adult schizophrenic patients: A psychoeducational approach. *Schizophrenia Bulletin, 6,* 490–505.

Anderson, C. M., & Reiss, D. J. (1994). A psychoeducational model for treating the adolescent who is seriously emotionally disturbed. In W. Snyder & T. Ooms (Eds.), *Empowering families, helping adolescents: Family-centered treatment of adolescents with alcohol, drug abuse, and mental health problems* (Series 6, pp. 111–118). Rockville, MD: U.S. Department of Health and Human Services, Center for Substance Abuse Treatment.

Anderson, C. M., Reiss, D. J., & Hogarty, G. E. (1986). *Schizophrenia and the family: A practitioner's guide to psychoeducation and management.* New York: Guilford Press.

Andreasen, N. C., & Black, D. W. (1991). *Introductory textbook of psychiatry.* Washington, DC: American Psychiatric Press.

Andrews, D. A., & Bonta, J. (1998). *The psychology of criminal conduct* (2nd ed.). Cincinnati, OH: Anderson.

Andrews, D. A., & Kiesling, J. (1980). Program structure and effective correctional practices: A summary of CaVIC research. In R. Ross & P. Gendreau (Eds.), *Effective correctional treatment.* (pp. 441–463). Toronto, Canada: Butterworth Press.

Anglin, M. D. (1988). The efficacy of civil commitment in treating narcotic addiction. In C. G. Leukefeld & F. M. Tims (Eds.), *Compulsory treatment of drug abuse: Research and clinical practice* (NIDA Research Monograph No. 86). (pp. 8–34). Rockville, MD: National Institute on Drug Abuse.

Aponte, H. J., & VanDeusen, J. M. (1981). Structural family therapy. In A. S. Gurman & D. P. Kniskern (Eds.), *Handbook of family therapy* (pp. 310–360). New York: Brunner/Mazel.

Arbuthnot, J., & Faust, A. (1981). *Teaching moral reasoning: Theory and practice.* New York: Harper & Row.

Arnold, E. M., Stewart, J. C., & McNeece, C. A. (2001). Enhancing services for offenders: The impact on treatment completion. *Journal of Psychoactive Drugs, 33,* 255–262.

Asante, M. K. (1988). *Afrocentricity.* Trenton, NJ: Africa World Press.

Ashery, R. (1992). *Progress and issues in case management* (NIDA Research Monograph 127, DHHS Pub. No. ADM 92-1946). Rockville, MD: National Institute on Drug Abuse.

Ausabel, D. (1983). Methadone maintenance treatment: The other side of the coin. *International Journal of the Addictions, 18,* 851–862.

Austin, J., & Hardyman, P. (1991). *The use of early parole with electronic monitoring to control prison crowding: Evaluation of the Oklahoma Department of Corrections pre-parole supervised release with electronic monitoring.* San Francisco: National Council on Crime and Delinquency.

Avants, S. K., Margolin, A., Chang, P., Kosten, T., & Birch, S. (1993). Acupuncture for the treatment of cocaine addiction: Investigation of a needle puncture control. *Journal of Substance Abuse Treatment 12,* 195–205.

Avants, S. K., Margolin, A., Holford, T. R., & Kosten, T. (2000). A randomized controlled trial of auricular acupuncture for cocaine dependence. *Archives of Internal Medicine, 160,* 2305–2312.

Bachrack, L. L. (1983). Young adult chronic patients: An analytical review of the literature. *Hospital and Community Psychiatry, 33,* 189–197.

Barber, J. G. (1995). *Social work with addictions.* London: Macmillan.

Barker, S., Barron, N., McFarland, B., & Bigelow, D. (1993). *Multnomah Community Ability Scale: User's manual.* Portland, OR: Western Mental Health Center, Oregon Health Science University.

Barkley, R. A. (1987). *Defiant children: A clinician's manual for parent training.* New York: Guilford Press.

Baumer, T., & Mendelsohn, R. (1991, November). *Comparing methods of monitoring home detention: The results of a field experiment.* Paper presented at the meeting of the American Society of Criminology, San Francisco.

Bazemore, G. (1993). Formal policy and informal process in the implementation of juvenile justice reform. *Criminal Justice Review, 18,* 26–45.

Beck, A. (2000). *Prison and jail inmates at midyear 1999.* Washington, DC: Bureau of Justice Statistics.

Beck, A., & Mumola, C. (1999). *Prisoners in 1998.* Washington, DC: Bureau of Justice Statistics.

Beck, A. T., Wright, F., Newman, C., & Liese, B. (1993). *Cognitive therapy of substance abuse.* New York: Guilford Press.

Beeder, A. B., & Millman, R. B. (1997). Patients with psychopathology. In J. H. Lowinson, P. Ruiz, R. B. Millman, & J. G. Langrod (Eds.), *Substance abuse: A comprehensive textbook* (3rd ed., pp. 675–690). Baltimore: Williams & Wilkins.

Belenko, S. (1988). Research on drug courts: A critical review. *National Drug Court Institute Review, 1,* 1–26.

Belenko, S. (1990). The impact of drug offenders on the criminal justice system. In R. Weisheit (Ed.), *Drugs, crime, and the criminal justice system* (pp. 27–78). Cincinnati, OH: Anderson.

Belenko, S. (1996). *Comparative models of treatment delivery in drug courts.* Washington, DC: Sentencing Project.

Belenko, S. (1998). Research on drug courts: A critical review. *National Drug Court Institute Review, 1,* 1–26.

Benshoff, J., & Janikowski, T. (2000). *The rehabilitation model of substance abuse counseling.* Belmont, CA: Wadsworth.

Bentley, K. J., & Walsh, J. F. (2001). *The social worker and psychotropic medication: Toward effective collaboration with mental health clients, families, and providers* (2nd ed.). Belmont, CA: Brooks/Cole.

Bepko, C., & Krestan, J. A. (1985). *The responsibility trap: A blueprint for treating the alcoholic family.* New York: Free Press.

Berg, I. K. (1994). *Family-based services: A solution-focused approach.* New York: Norton.

Berg, I. K., & de Shazer, S. (1991). Solution talk. In D. Sollee (Ed.), *Constructing the future* (pp. 15–29). Washington, DC: American Association for Marriage and Family Therapy.

Berg, I. K., & de Shazer, S. (1993). Making numbers talk: Language in therapy. In S. Friedman (Ed.), *The new language of change: Constructive collaboration in psychotherapy* (pp. 5–24). New York: Guilford Press.

Berg, I. K., & Gallagher, D. (1991). Solution-focused brief treatment with adolescent substance abusers. In T. C. Todd & M. D. Selekman (Eds.), *Family therapy approaches with adolescent substance abusers* (pp. 93–111). Needham Heights, MA: Allyn & Bacon.

Berg, I. K., & Miller, S. D. (1992). *Working with the problem drinker: A solution-focused approach.* New York: Norton.

Beutler, L. E., Machado, P. P., & Nuefeldt, S. A. (1994). Therapist variables. In A. E. Bergin & S. L. Garfield (Eds.), *Handbook of psychotherapy and behavior change* (4th ed., pp. 229–269). New York: Wiley.

Bigelow, D. A., & Young, D. J. (1991). Effectiveness of a case management program. *Community Mental Health Journal, 27,* 115–123.

Black, C. (1981). *It will never happen to me.* Denver, CO: MAC.

Blanchard, C. (1999, Winter). Drugs, crime, prison, and treatment. *Spectrum,* pp. 26–37.

Blevins, L. D., Morton, J. B., & McCabe, K. A. (1996). Using the Michigan Alcoholism Screening Test to identify problem drinkers under federal supervision. *Federal Probation, 60*(2), 38–42.

Block, J., & Block, J. H. (1980). *The California Child Q-Set.* Palo Alto, CA: Consulting Psychologists Press.

Bloom, M., Fischer, J., & Orme, J. G. (1999). *Evaluating practice: Guidelines for the accountable professional* (3rd ed.). Englewood Cliffs, NJ: Prentice-Hall.

Bonczar, T., & Glaze, L. (2000). *Bureau of Justice Statistics press release, July 23, 2000.* Retrieved October 17, 2002, from http://www.ojp.usdoj.gov/bjs.

Bonta, J. (1993). *Everything you wanted to know about electronic monitoring and never bothered to ask.* Ottawa: Ministry Secretariat, Solicitor General Canada.

Bonta, J., Wallace-Capretta, S., & Rooney, J. (2000). Can electronic monitoring make a difference? An evaluation of three Canadian programs. *Crime and Delinquency, 46,* 61–75.

Borduin, C. M., Henggeler, S. W., Blaske, D. M., & Stein, R. (1990). Multisystemic treatment of adolescent sexual offenders. *International Journal of Offender Therapy and Comparative Criminology, 35,* 105–114.

Borduin, C. M., Mann, B. J., Cone, L. T., Henggeler, S. W., Fucci, B. R., Blaske, D. M., et al. (1995). Multisystemic treatment of serious juvenile offenders: Long-term prevention of criminality and violence. *Journal of Consulting and Clinical Psychology, 63,* 569–578.

Bostwick, G., & Kyte, N. (1988). Validity and reliability. In R. M. Grinnell, Jr. (Ed.), *Social work research and evaluation* (3rd ed., pp. 111–136). Itasca, IL: F. E. Peacock.

Boswell, G. (1996). The essentials skills of probation work. In T. M. May & A. A. Vass (Eds.), *Working with offenders* (pp. 31–50). London: Sage.

Brandsma, J. M., & Pattison, E. M. (1985). The outcome of group psychotherapy with alcoholics: An empirical review. *American Journal of Drug and Alcohol Abuse, 11,* 151–162.

Brane, R., & MacKenzie, D. L. (1996). Shock incarceration and positive adjustment during community supervision. In D. L. MacKenzie & E. E. Hebert (Eds.), *Correctional boot camps: A tough intermediate sanction* (NCJ Publication No. 157639). Washington, DC: National Institute of Justice.

Brendtro, L. K., & Ness, A. E. (1982). Perspectives on peer group treatment: The use and abuse of Guided Group Interaction/Positive Peer Culture. *Children and Youth Services Review, 4,* 307–324.

Brewington, V., Smith, M., & Lipton, D. (1994). Acupuncture as a detoxification treatment: An analysis of controlled research. *Journal of Substance Abuse Treatment, 11,* 289–307.

Bronfenbrenner, U. (1979). *The ecology of human development: Experiences by nature and design.* Cambridge, MA: Harvard University Press.

Brook, J. S., Whiteman, M., Balka, E. B., Win, P. T., & Gursen, M. D. (1998). Drug use among African-Americans: Ethnic identity as a protective factor. *Psychology Reports, 83,* 1427–1446.

Brown, A. (2001). *Beyond work first: How to help hard-to-employ individuals get jobs and succeed in the workforce.* New York: Manpower Demonstration Research Corporation.

Brown, A., & Caddick, B. (1993). *Groupwork with offenders.* London: Whiting & Birch.

Brown, T. L., Borduin, C. M., & Henggeler, S. W. (2001). Treating juvenile offenders in community settings. In J. B. Ashford, B. D. Sales, & W. H. Reid (Eds.), *Treating adult and juvenile offenders with special needs* (pp. 445–464). Washington, DC: American Psychological Association.

Brown, V., Ridgely, M., Pepper, B., Levine, I., & Ryglewicz, H. (1989). The dual crisis: Mental illness and substance abuse. *American Psychologist, 44,* 565–569.

Brumbaugh, A. G. (1993). Acupuncture: New perspectives in chemical dependency treatment. *Journal of Substance Abuse Treatment, 10,* 35–43.

Brumbaugh, A. G. (1994). *Transformation and recovery: A guide for the design and development of acupuncture-based chemical dependency treatment programs.* Santa Barbara, CA: Stillpoint Press.

Brundage, V. (1985). Gregory Bateson, Alcoholics Anonymous, and stoicism. *Psychiatry, 48,* 40–51.

Brunk, M., Henggeler, S. W., & Whelan, J. P. (1987). A comparison of multisystemic therapy and parent training in the brief treatment of child abuse and neglect. *Journal of Consulting and Clinical Psychology, 55,* 311–318.

Buentello, S. (1992). Combating gangs in Texas. *Corrections Today, 54,* 58–60.

Bullock, M. L., Kiresuk, T. J., Pheley, A. M., Culliton, P. D., & Lenz, S. K. (1999). Auricular acupuncture in the treatment of cocaine abuse: A study of efficacy and dosing. *Journal of Substance Abuse Treatment, 16,* 31–38.

Bullock, M. L., Umen, A. J., Culliton, P. D., & Olander, R. T. (1987). Acupuncture treatment of alcohol recidivism: A pilot study. *American Journal of Acupuncture, 15,* 313–320.

Bureau of Justice Assistance. (2000). *Emerging judicial strategies for the mentally ill in the criminal caseload: Mental health courts.* Washington, DC: U.S. Department of Justice, Author.

Bureau of Justice Statistics. (1995). *The nation's correctional population tops 5 million.* Washington, DC: U.S. Department of Justice, Author.

Bureau of Justice Statistics. (1997, December). *Characteristics of adults on probation, 1995.* Washington, DC: U.S. Department of Justice, Author.

Bureau of Justice Statistics. (1999a). *Substance abuse and treatment: State and federal prisoners, 1997.* Washington, DC: U.S. Department of Justice, Author.

Bureau of Justice Statistics. (1999b). *U.S. Department of Justice: Drugs and crime fact sheet.* Retrieved October 17, 2002, from www.ojp.usdoj.gov/bjs/dcf/duc.htm.

Bureau of Justice Statistics. (2000, May). *Drug use, testing, and treatment in jails.* Washington, DC: U.S. Department of Justice, Author.

Bureau of Justice Statistics. (2002, April). *Prison and jail inmates at midyear 2001* (p. 1) (NCJ191702). Washington, DC: U.S. Department of Justice, Author.

Burke, B. L., Arkowitz, H., & Dunn, C. (2002). The efficacy of motivational interviewing and its adaptations: What we know so far. In W. R. Miller & S. Rollnick (Eds.), *Motivational interviewing: Preparing people for change* (2nd ed., pp. 217–250). New York: Guilford Press.

Bush, D., Hecht, F. R., LaBarbera, M. J., & Peters, R. H. (in press). *Design and implementation issues for drug treatment in the jail setting.* Washington, DC: U.S. Department of Justice, Bureau of Justice Assistance.

California Youth Authority. (1997). *LEAD: A boot camp and intensive parole program: Final impact evaluation.* Sacramento: Author.

Camp, C. G., & Camp, G. M. (1998). *Probation and parole: The corrections yearbook*. South Salem, NY: Criminal Justice Institute.

Cartwright, W. S. (2000). Cost–benefit analysis of drug treatment services: Review of the literature. *Journal of Mental Health Policy and Economics, 3*, 11–26.

Catalano, R., Hawkins, J., Wells, E., Miller, E., & Brewer, D. (1990/91). Evaluation of the effectiveness of adolescent drug abuse treatment, assessment of risks for relapse, and promising approaches for relapse prevention. *International Journal of Addictions, 25*, 1085–1140.

Cavell, T. A. (2000). *Working with parents of aggressive children: A practitioner's guide*. Washington, DC: American Psychological Association.

Cavell, T. A., & Strand, P. S. (in press). Parent-based interventions for aggressive children: Adapting to a bilateral lens. In L. Kuczynski (Ed.), *Handbook of dynamics in parent-child relations*. Thousand Oaks, CA: Sage.

Center for Substance Abuse Treatment. (1995). *Producing results. . . A report to the nation*. Rockville, MD: Author.

Center for Substance Abuse Treatment. (1997). *National Treatment Improvement Evaluation Study (NTIES)*. Rockville, MD: Author. (Information packet available from the National Clearinghouse for Alcohol and Drug Information, 11426-28 Rockville Pike, Rockville, MD 20852, 800-729-6686)

Center for Substance Abuse Treatment. (2000). *Strengthening America's families: Model family programs for substance abuse and delinquency prevention* (N215 HPER). Salt Lake City: University of Utah, Department of Health Promotion and Education.

Center on Addiction and Substance Abuse. (1996). *Substance abuse and the American woman*. New York: Columbia University, Author.

Cermack, T. (1986). *Diagnosing and treating co-dependency*. Minneapolis, MN: Johnson Institute.

Chaiken, M. (1989, October). *Prison programs for drug-involved offenders*. Washington, DC: National Institute of Justice.

Chandler, S. M., & Kassebaum, G. (1997). Meeting the needs of female offenders. In C. A. McNeece & A. R. Roberts (Eds.), *Policy and practice in the justice system* (pp. 159–180). Chicago: Nelson-Hall.

Chapman, T., & Hough, M. (1998). *Evidence-based practice: A guide to effective practice*. London: Her Majesty's Inspectorate of Probation.

Chavaria, F. R. (1992). Successful drug treatment in a criminal justice setting: A case study. *Federal Probation, 56*, 48–52.

Children's Defense Fund. (1995). AFDC maximum monthly benefit for a three-person family, 1970 and 1994. In *The state of America's children yearbook 1995*. Washington, DC: Author.

Christopher, J. (1988). *How to stay sober: Recovery without religion*. Buffalo, NY: Prometheus Books.

Clark, C. L., & Aziz, D. W. (1996, February). Shock incarceration in New York State: Philosophy, results, and limitations. In D. L. MacKenzie & E. E. Hebert (Eds.), *Correctional boot camps: A tough intermediate sanction* (pp. 39–62). Washington, DC: National Institute of Justice.

Clark, C. L., Aziz, D. W., & MacKenzie, D. L. (1994). *Shock incarceration in New York: Focus on treatment* (NCJ Publication No. 148410). Washington, DC: National Institute of Justice.

Clark, M. D. (1998). Strength-based practice: The ABC's of working with adolescents who don't want to work with you. *Federal Probation, 62*, 46–53.

Clark, W. (1990). *Trial of acupuncture detoxification (TRIAD): Final report to California state legislature*. San Francisco, CA: Community Substance Abuse Services.

Clear, T. (1995). Correction beyond prison walls. In J. F. Sheley (Ed.), *Criminology* (pp. 453–471). Belmont, CA: Wadsworth.

Cohen, R. L. (1995). *Bureau of Justice Statistics special report, survey of state prison inmates, 1991, probation and parole in state prison, 1991*. Washington, DC: U.S. Department of Justice, Bureau of Justice Statistics.

Cohen, S. (1985). *The substance abuse problems: Vol. 2. New issues for the 1980s*. New York: Haworth.

Coleman, M., Pfeiffer, S., & Oakland, T. (1992). Aggression replacement training with behaviorally disordered adolescents. *Behavioral Disorders, 18*, 54–66.

Collins, J. J., & Allison, M. (1983). Legal coercion and retention in drug abuse treatment. *Hospital and Community Psychiatry, 34*, 1145–1149.

Collins, L. (1990). Family treatment of alcohol abuse: Behavioral and systems perspectives. In L. Collins, K. Leonard, & J. Searles (Eds.), *Alcohol and the family: Research and clinical perspectives* (pp. 285–308). New York: Guilford Press.

Collins, R. L. (1995). Issues of ethnicity in research on prevention of substance abuse. In G. J. Botvin, S. Schinke, & M. A. Orlandi (Eds.), *Drug abuse prevention with multiethnic youth* (pp. 28–45). Thousand Oaks, CA: Sage.

Commonwealth of Virginia. (1992). *The feasibility of utilizing acupuncture as a treatment for substance abuse*. (VA House Document No. 6). Richmond, VA: Board of Medicine.

Conrad, K. J., Hultman, C. I., Pope, A. R., Lyons, J. S., Baxter, W. C., Daghestani, A., et al. (1998). Case managed residential care for homeless addicted veterans: Results of a true experiment. *Medical Care, 36,* 40–53.

Cook, L. F., & Weinman, B. A. (1985). *TASC program brief.* Washington, DC: U.S. Department of Justice, Bureau of Justice Assistance.

Cooke, D. (1998). Psychopathy across cultures. In D. Cooke, A. Forth, & R. Hare (Eds.), *Psychopathy: Theory, research and implications for society* (NATO ASI Series, pp. 13–45). Dordrecht, The Netherlands: Kluwer Academic.

Cooke, D., Forth, A., & Hare, R. (Eds.). (1998). *Psychopathy: Theory, research and implications for society.* Dordrecht, The Netherlands: Kluwer Academic.

Cooper, C. (1997). *1997 drug court survey report: Executive summary.* Washington, DC: American University, Drug Court Clearinghouse and Technical Assistance Project.

Corbett, R. P. (1999). Juvenile probation on the eve of the next millennium. *Federal Probation, 63,* 78–86.

Corbett, R. P., & Harris, M. K. (1995). A review of research for practitioners: Treatment for drug-abusing offenders under community supervision. *Federal Probation, 59,* 66–75.

Corcoran, K., & Fischer, J. (2000). *Measures for clinical practice: A sourcebook* (Vols. 1 & 2, 3rd ed.). New York: Free Press.

Cote, G., & Hogins, S. (1990). Co-occurring mental disorders among criminal offenders. *Bulletin of the American Academy of Psychiatry and Law, 18,* 271–281.

Cowger, C. (1997). Assessing client strengths: Assessment for client empowerment. In D. Saleebey (Ed.), *The strengths perspective in social work practice* (2nd ed., pp. 59–73). New York: Longman.

Cox, G. B., Walker, R. D., Freng, S. A., Short, B. A., Meijer, L., & Gilchrist, L. (1998). Outcome of a controlled trial of the effectiveness of intensive case management for chronic public inebriates. *Journal of Studies on Alcohol, 59,* 523–532.

Crocker, L., & Algina, J. (1986). *Introduction to classical and modern test theory.* Fort Worth, TX: Holt, Rinehart & Winston.

Cronbach, L. J. (1951). Coefficient alpha and the internal structure of tests. *Psychometrika, 16,* 297–334.

Crowe, A. H., & Sydney, L. (2000, May). Developing a policy for a controlled substance abuse testing of juveniles. In *Juvenile Accountability Incentive Block Grant (JAIBG) program bulletin* (NCJ Publication No. 178896). Washington, DC: Office of Juvenile Justice and Delinqueny Prevention.

Cuffel, B. J. (1996). Comorbidity substance use disorder: Prevalence, patterns of use, and course. In R. E. Drake & K. T. Mueser (Eds.), *Dual diagnosis of major mental illness and substance abuse* (pp. 93–105). San Francisco, CA: Jossey-Bass.

Cullen, F. T., Wright, J. P., & Applegate, B. K. (1996). Control in the community: The limits of reform? In A. T. Harland (Ed.), *Choosing correctional options that work: Defining the demand and evaluating the supply* (pp. 69–116). Thousand Oaks, CA: Sage.

Culliton, P. D., & Kiresuk, T. J. (1996). Overview of substance abuse acupuncture treatment research. *Journal of Alternative and Complementary Medicine, 2,* 149–159.

Cunningham, J. A., Herie, M., Martin, G., & Turner, B. J. (1998). Training probation and parole officers to provide substance abuse treatment: A field test. *Journal of Offender Rehabilitation, 27,* 167–177.

Currie, E. (1993). *Drugs, the cities, and the American future.* New York: Hill & Wang.

Czuchry, M., Dansereau, D. F., Dees, S. M., & Simpson, D. D. (1995). The use of node-link mapping in drug abuse counseling: The role of attentional factors. *Journal of Psychoactive Drugs, 27,* 161–166.

Dansereau, D. F., Joe, G. W., Dees, S. M., & Simpson, D. D. (1996). Ethnicity and the effects of mapping-enhanced drug abuse counseling. *Addictive Behaviors, 21,* 363–376.

Dansereau, D. F., Joe, G. W., & Simpson, D. D. (1993). Node-link mapping: A visual representation strategy for enhancing drug abuse counseling. *Journal of Counseling Psychology, 40,* 385–395.

Dansereau, D. F., Joe, G. W., & Simpson, D. D. (1995). Attentional difficulties and the effectiveness of a visual representation strategy for counseling drug-addicted clients. *International Journal of the Addictions, 30,* 371–386.

Davidson, W. S., II., Redner, R., Blakely, C., Mitchell, C., & Emshoff, J. (1987). Diversion of juvenile offenders: An experimental comparison. *Journal of Consulting and Clinical Psychology, 55,* 68–75.

Davis, D. R., & DiNitto, D. M. (1998). Gender and drugs: Fact, fiction, and unanswered questions. In C. A. McNeece & D. M. DiNitto (Eds.), *Chemical dependency: A systems approach* (2nd ed., pp. 406–442). Boston: Allyn & Bacon.

Davis, J. (2000). Acamprosate helps alcoholics stay on the wagon: Appears to dampen alcohol withdrawal effects. *WebMD Medical News.* Retrieved October 12, 2002, from http://webcenter.health.webmd.aol.com/contents/article/1728.5617

Davis, M. S., & Muscat, J. E. (1993). An epidemiologic study of alcohol and suicide risk in Ohio jails and lockups, 1975–1984. *Journal of Criminal Justice, 21*, 277–283.

Dees, S. M., Dansereau, D. F., & Simpson, D. D. (1997). Mapping-enhanced drug abuse counseling: Urinalysis results in the first year of methadone treatment. *Journal of Substance Abuse Treatment, 14*, 45–54.

De Leon, G. (1986). The therapeutic community for substance abuse: Perspective and approach. In D. De Leon & J. T. Zeigenfuss (Eds.), *Therapeutic communities for addictions: Readings in theory, research and practice* (pp. 5–18). Springfield, IL: Charles C Thomas.

De Leon, G. (1988). Legal pressures in therapeutic communities. In C. G. Leukefeld & F. Tims (Eds.), *Compulsory treatment of drug abuse: Research and clinical practice* (National Institute on Drug Abuse Research Monograph No. 86, DHHS Publication No. ADM 89-1578, pp. 160–177). Rockville, MD: U.S. Department of Health and Human Services, National Institute on Drug Abuse.

De Leon, G. (1994). Therapeutic communities. In M. Gallanter & H. D. Kleber (Eds.), *Textbook of substance abuse treatment*. Washington, DC: American Psychiatric Association.

DeLong, J. (1972). Treatment and rehabilitation. In *Dealing with drug abuse: A report to the Ford Foundation* (pp. 173–254). Praeger, NY: The Drug Abuse Survey Project.

Dembo, R., & Brown, R. (1994). The Hillsborough County juvenile assessment center. *Journal of Child and Adolescent Substance Abuse, 3*, 25–43.

Denton, R. E., & Kampfe, C. M. (1994). The relationship between family variables and adolescent substance abuse: A literature review. *Adolescence, 29*, 475–495.

Department of Community Affairs, Division of Housing and Community Development, State of Florida. (1997). *Drug control and system improvement program: Annual report, state fiscal years 1991 through 1996*. Tallahassee, FL: Author.

Deschenes, E. P., & Greenwood, P. W. (1994). Treating the juvenile drug offender. In D. L. MacKenzie & C. D. Uchida (Eds.), *Drugs and crime: Evaluating public policy initiatives* (pp. 253–280). Thousand Oaks, CA: Sage.

de Shazer, S. (1985). *Keys to solution in brief therapy*. New York: Norton.

de Shazer, S. (1988). *Clues: Investigating solutions in brief therapy*. New York: Norton.

de Shazer, S. (1991). *Putting difference to work*. New York: Norton.

Desmond, D. P., & Maddux, J. F. (1996). Compulsory supervision and methadone maintenance. *Journal of Substance Abuse Treatment, 13,* 79–83.

Dickinson, T., & Crowe, A. (1997, December). *Capacity building for juvenile substance abuse treatment.* Washington, DC: Office of Juvenile Justice and Delinquency Prevention.

DiClemente, C. C. (1999). Motivation for change: Implications for substance abuse. *Psychological Science, 10,* 209–213.

DiClemente, C. C., & Velasquez, M. M. (2002). Motivational interviewing and the stages of change. In W. R. Miller & S. Rollnick (Eds.), *Motivational interviewing: Preparing people for change* (2nd ed., pp. 201–216). New York: Guilford Press.

DiMascio, W. M. (1995). *Seeking justice: Crime and punishment in America.* New York: Edna McConnell Clark Foundation.

DiNitto, D. M., & Webb, D. K. (1998). Compounding the problem: Substance abuse and other disabilities. In C. A. McNeece & D. M. DiNitto (Eds.), *Chemical dependency: A systems approach* (2nd ed., pp. 347–390). Boston: Allyn & Bacon.

DiNitto, D. M., Webb, D. K., & Rubin, A. (2002a). Gender differences in dually diagnosed clients receiving chemical dependency treatment. *Journal of Psychoactive Drugs, 34,* 105–117.

DiNitto, D. M., Webb, D. K., & Rubin, A. (2002b). The effectiveness of an integrated treatment approach for clients with dual diagnosis. *Research on Social Work Practice 12,* 621–641.

Dinkmeyer, D., & McKay, G. D. (1976). *Systematic training for effective parenting (STEP).* Circle Pines, MN: American Guidance Service.

Ditton, P. M. (1999, July). *Mental health and treatment of inmates and probationers* (Bureau of Justice Statistics Special Report NCJ 174463). Washington, DC: U.S. Department of Justice.

Dixon, L. (2000). Punishment and the question of ownership: Groupwork in the criminal justice system. *Groupwork, 12,* 6–25.

Doherty, D. (1995). Impressions of the impact of the electronic monitoring program on the family. In K. Schultz (Ed.), *Electronic monitoring and corrections: The policy, the operation, the research* (pp. 129–139). Burnaby, Canada: Simon Fraser University.

Dole, V. (1980). Addictive behavior. *Scientific American, 243,* 138–154.

Dowden, C., & Andrews, D. A. (1999). What works for female offenders: A meta-analytic review. *Crime and Delinquency, 45,* 438–452.

Doweiko, A. E. (2002). *Concepts of chemical dependency* (5th ed.). Pacific Grove, CA: Brooks/Cole.

Downey, A. M. (1991). The impact of drug abuse upon adolescent suicide. *Omega Journal of Death and Dying, 22,* 261–275.

Downie, N. M., & Heath, R. W. (1967). *Basic statistical methods.* New York: Harper & Row.

Drake, R. E., McHugo, G. J., & Noorday, D. L. (1993). Treatment of alcoholism among schizophrenic outpatients: 4-year outcomes. *American Journal of Psychiatry, 150,* 328–329.

Drake, R. E., McLaughlin, B. P., & Minkoff, K. (1996). Dual diagnosis of major mental illness and substance disorder: An overview. In K. Minkoff & R. E. Drake (Eds.), *Dual diagnosis of major mental illness and substance abuse disorder* (pp. 3–12). San Francisco, CA: Jossey-Bass.

Drug Court Clearinghouse and Technical Assistance Project. (1997, May). *Drug courts: 1997 overview of operational characteristics and implementation issues* (Technical Report). Washington, DC: American University.

Drug Courts Program Office. (1997). *Defining drug courts: The key components.* Washington, DC: U.S. Department of Justice, Office of Justice Programs.

Duffee, D. E., & Carlson, B. E. (1996). Competing value premises for the provision of drug treatment to probationers. *Crime and Delinquency, 42,* 574–592.

Dumas, J. E. (1989). Treating antisocial behavior in children: Child and family approaches. *Clinical Psychology Review, 9,* 197–222.

Dunn, C., DeRoo, L., & Rivara, F. P. (2001). The use of brief interventions adapted from motivational interviewing across behavioral domains: A systematic review. *Addiction, 96,* 1725–1742.

Eddy, J. M., Dishion, T. J., & Stoolmiller, M. (1998). The analysis of intervention change in children and families: Methodological and conceptual issues embedded in intervention studies. *Journal of Abnormal Child Psychology, 26,* 53–69.

Edens, J. F., Peters, R. H., & Hills, H. A. (1997). Treating prison inmates with co-occurring disorders: An integrative review of existing programs. *Behavioral Sciences and the Law, 15,* 439–457.

Edens, J. F., Skeem, J. L., Cruise, K. R., & Cauffman, E. (2001). Assessment of "juvenile psychopathy" and its association with violence: A critical review. *Behavioral Sciences and the Law, 19,* 53–80.

Edna McConnell Clark Foundation. (1995). *Seeking justice: Crime and punishment in America.* New York: Author.

Edwards, B. (1993, June 23). Drug court's success rate outstanding. *Tampa Tribune,* pp. 1–2.

Edwards, M., & Steinglass, P. (1995). Family therapy treatment outcomes for alcoholism. *Journal of Marital and Family Therapy, 21*, 475–509.

Ekleberry, S. (1996, March/April). Dual diagnosis: Addiction and Axis II personality disorder. *The Counselor*, pp. 7–13.

El-Bassel, N., Schilling, R. F., Ivanoff, A., Chen, D., Hanson, M., & Bidassie, B. (1998). Stages of change profiles among incarcerated drug-using women. *Addictive Behavior, 23*, 389–394.

Ellis, A. (1962). *Reason and emotion in psychotherapy*. New York: Lyle Stuart.

Ellis, A., & Dryden, W. (1996). *The practice of rational–emotive behavior therapy*. New York: Springer.

Empey, L., & Erickson, M. L. (1972). *The Provo experiment: Evaluating community control of delinquency*. Lexington, MA: Heath.

Enos, R., & Southern, S. (1996). *Correctional case management*. Cincinnati, OH: Anderson Publishing Co.

Erickson, C. (2000). *Drugs, the brain, and behavior*. New York: Haworth Medical Press.

Evans, D. G. (1999). Rethinking probation: Community supervision, community safety. *Corrections Today, 61*, 159.

Evans, M. E., & Dollard, N. (1992). Intensive case management for youth with serious emotional disturbance and chemical abuse. In R. S. Ashery (Ed.), *Progress and Issues in Case Management* (pp. 289–315). NIDA Research Monograph Series (127). Rockville, MD: U.S. Department of Health and Human Services, National Institute on Drug Abuse.

Everson v. Board of Education, 330 U.S. 1 (1947).

Ewing, J. A. (1984). Detecting alcoholism: The CAGE questionnaire. *Journal of the American Medical Association, 252*, 1905–1907.

Eyberg, S. (1988). Parent–child interaction therapy: Integration of traditional and behavioral concerns. *Child and Family Behavior Therapy, 10*, 33–45.

Faul, A. C., & Hudson, W. W. (1997). The Index of Drug Involvement: A partial validation. *Social Work, 42*, 565–572.

Falkin, G. (1993). *Coordinating drug treatment for offenders: A case study*. New York: National Development and Research Institutes.

Falkin, G. P., Wexler, H. K., & Lipton, D. S. (1990). *Establishing drug treatment programs in prisons* (Draft). New York: Narcotic and Drug Research.

Farmer, K. A., Felthous, A. R., & Holtzer, C. E. (1996). Medically serious suicide attempts in a jail with a suicide-prevention program. *Journal of Forensic Sciences, 41*, 240–246.

Feindler, E. L., Marriott, S. A., & Iwata, M. (1984). Group anger control for junior high school delinquents. *Cognitive Therapy and Research, 8*, 299–311.

Ferguson, M. J., Springer, D. W., & Holleran, L. (2002). Shredding the safety net: Young mothers and TANF restrictions in federal and state substance abuse policy. *Social Policy Journal, 1*, 19–36.

Ferguson, R. T. (1998). Motivational interviewing with less motivated driving under the influence of alcohol second offenders with an exploration of the processes related to change (Doctoral dissertation, University of Wyoming, 1998). *Dissertation Abstracts International, 59*(1-B), 0415.

Ferrara, M. L. (1992). *Group counseling with juvenile delinquents.* Newbury Park, CA: Sage.

Festinger, L. (1950). Informal social communication. *Psychological Review, 57*, 271–282.

Finn, P., & Newlyn, A. K. (1993, June). *Miami's "drug court": A different approach.* Washington, DC: U.S. Department of Justice, National Institute of Justice.

Fishman, H. C., Stanton, M. D., & Rosman, B. (1982). Treating families of adolescent drug abusers. In M. D. Stanton, T. C. Todd, & Associates (Eds.), *The family therapy of drug abuse and addiction.* New York: Guilford Press.

Fleuridas, C., Nelson, T. S., & Rosenthal, D. M. (1986). The evolution of circular questions: Training family therapists. *Journal of Marital and Family Therapy, 12*, 113–127.

Flores, P. J. (1988). *Group psychotherapy with addicted populations.* New York: Haworth.

Florida Department of Corrections. (1997–1998). *Annual report* [on-line]. Retrieved October 24, 2002, from www.dc.state.fl.us/search/index.asp.

Forehand, R. L., & McMahon, R. J. (1981). *Helping the noncompliant child: A clinician's guide to present training.* New York: Guilford Press.

Forrest, G. (1994). *Chemical dependency and antisocial personality disorder: Psychotherapy and assessment strategies.* New York: Haworth.

Forth, A. E., & Burke, H. C. (1998). Psychopathy in adolescence: Assessment, violence, and developmental precursors. In D. Cooke, A. Forth, & R. Hare (Eds.), *Psychopathy: Theory, research, and implications for society* (pp. 205–230). Dordrecht, The Netherlands: Kluwer.

Forth, A. E., Hart, S. D., & Hare, R. D. (1990). Assessment of psychopathy in male young offenders. *Psychological Assessment, 2*, 342–344.

Fossom, M., & Mason, M. (1986). *Facing the shame: Families in recovery.* New York: Norton.

Franklin, R. K. (1988). Deliberate self-harm: Self-injurious behavior within correctional mental health population. *Criminal Justice and Behavior, 15*, 210–218.

Fraser, A. D., & Zamecnik, J. (2002). Substance abuse monitoring by the correctional service of Canada. *Therapeutic Drug Monitoring, 24,* 187–191.

Frick, P. J., & Hare, R. D. (in press). *The psychopathy screening device.* Toronto: Multi-Health Systems.

Friedman, A. S., & Utada, A. (1983). High school drug use. *Clinical research notes.* Washington, DC: National Institute on Drug Abuse.

Friedman, L. (1978). *The Wildcat experiment: An early test of supported work in drug abuse rehabilitation.* Washington, DC: National Institute on Drug Abuse.

Fuller, R. K., Branchey, L., Brightwell, D. R., Derman, R. M., Emrick, C. D., Iber, F. L., et al. (1986). Disulfiram treatment of alcoholism: A Veterans Administration cooperative study. *Journal of the American Medical Association, 256,* 1449–1455.

Gabel, S. (1992). Behavioral problems in sons of incarcerated or otherwise absent fathers: The issue of separation. *Family Process, 31,* 303–314.

Gacono, C. B. (Ed.). (2000). *The clinical and forensic assessment of psychopathy: A practitioner's guide.* Mahwah, NJ: Erlbaum.

Gacono, C. B., Nieberding, R. J., Owen, A., Rubel, J., & Bodholdt, R. (2001). Treating conduct disorder, antisocial, and psychopathic personalities. In J. B. Ashford, B. D. Sales, & W. H. Reid (Eds.), *Treating adult and juvenile offenders with special needs* (pp. 99–129). Washington, DC: American Psychological Association.

Garland, J. A., Jones, H. E., & Kolodny, R. L. (1973). A model for stages of development in social work groups. In S. Bernstein (Ed.), *Explorations in group work* (pp. 17–71). Boston: Milford House.

Garrett, C. J. (1985). Effects of residential treatment of adjudicated delinquents. *Journal of Research in Crime and Delinquency, 22,* 287–308.

Garvin, C. D. (1997). *Contemporary group work* (3rd ed.). Boston: Allyn & Bacon.

Gendreau, P., & Ross, R. (1984). Correctional treatment: Some recommendations for successful intervention. *Juvenile and Family Court Journal, 22,* 31–40.

Gendreau, P., & Ross, R. R. (1987). Revivification of rehabilitation: Evidence from the 1980s. *Justice Quarterly, 4,* 349–408.

Gerbode, F. (1989). *Beyond psychology: An introduction to metapsychology.* Palo Alto, CA: IRM Press.

Gerstein, D. R., & Harwood, H. J. (Eds.). (1990). *Treating drug problems* (Vol. 1). Washington, DC: National Academy Press.

Gerstley, L. J., Alterman, A. I., McLellan, A. T., & Woody, G. E. (1990). Antisocial personality disorder in substance abusers: A problematic diagnosis? *American Journal of Psychiatry, 147*, 173–178.

Gibbs, J., Arnold, K., Ahlborn, H., & Cheesman, F. (1984). Facilitation of sociomoral reasoning in delinquents. *Journal of Consulting and Clinical Psychology, 52*, 37–45.

Gibbs, J. C., Potter, G. B., Barriga, A. Q., & Liau, A. K. (1996). Developing the helping skills and prosocial motivation of aggressive adolescents in peer group programs. *Aggression and Violent Behavior, 1*, 283–305.

Gibbs, J. C., Potter, G. B., & Goldstein, A. P. (1995). *The EQUIP program: Teaching youth to think and act responsibly through a peer-helping approach*. Champaign, IL: Research Press.

Gingerich, W. J. (2000). Solution-focused brief therapy: A review of the outcome research. *Family Process, 39*, 477–498.

Ginsburg, J. I. D., Mann, R. E., Rotgers, F., & Weekes, J. R. (2002). Motivational interviewing with criminal justice populations. In W. R. Miller & S. Rollnick (Eds.), *Motivational interviewing: Preparing people for change* (2nd ed., pp. 333–346). New York: Guilford Press.

Ginzburg, H. (1986). *Naltrexone: Its clinical utility*. Rockville, MD: National Institute on Drug Abuse.

Gitterman, A., & Germain, C. B. (1976). Social work practice: A life model. *Social Service Review, 50*, 601–610.

Gitterman, A., & Shulman, L. (Eds.). (1994). *Mutual aid groups, vulnerable populations, and the life cycle* (2nd ed.). New York: Columbia University Press.

Glassman, U., & Kates, L. (1983). Authority themes and worker-group transactions: Additional dimensions to the stages of group development. *Social Work With Groups, 6*, 33–52.

Glassner, B., & Loughlin, J. (1987). *Drugs in adolescent worlds: Burnouts to straight*. New York: St. Martin's Press.

Glick, B. (1996). Aggression Replacement Training in children and adolescents. In *The Hatherleigh guide to child and adolescent therapy* (pp. 191–226). New York: Hatherleigh Press.

Glick, B., & Goldstein, A. P. (1987). Aggression Replacement Training: An intervention for counselors. *Journal of Counseling and Development, 65*, 356–362.

Gold, M. S. (1997). Cocaine (and crack): Clinical aspects. In J. H. Lowinson, P. Ruiz, R. B. Millman, & J. G. Langrod (Eds.), *Substance abuse: A comprehensive textbook* (3rd ed., pp. 181–198). Baltimore: Williams & Wilkins.

Goldapple, G. (1990). *Enhancing retention: A skills-training program for drug dependent therapeutic community clients*. Doctoral dissertation, Florida State University, Tallahassee, FL.

Goldenberg, I., & Goldenberg, H. (1991). *Family therapy: An overview*. Monterey, CA: Brooks/Cole.

Goldkamp, J. S. (1999). Challenges for research and innovation: When is a drug court not a drug court? In W. C. Terry, III (Ed.), *The early drug courts: Case studies in judical innovation* (pp. 166–177). Thousand Oaks, CA: Sage Publications.

Goldkamp, J., & Irons-Guynn, C. (2000). *Emerging judicial strategies for the mentally ill in the criminal caseload: Mental health courts in Fort Lauderdale, Seattle, San Bernardino, and Anchorage*. Washington, DC: U.S. Department of Justice, Bureau of Justice Assistance.

Goldstein, A. P. (1988). *The Prepare curriculum*. Champaign, IL: Research Press.

Goldstein, A. P., & Glick, B. (1987). *Aggression replacement training: A comprehensive intervention for aggressive youth*. Champaign, IL: Research Press.

Goldstein, A. P., & Huff, C. R. (1993). *The gang intervention handbook*. Champaign, IL: Research Press.

Gorey, K. M., Leslie, D. R., Morris, T., Carruthers, W. V., John, L., & Chacko, J. (1998). Effectiveness of case management with severely and persistently mentally ill people. *Community Mental Health Journal, 34,* 241–250.

Grabowki, J. (1986). *Acquisition maintenance cessation and re-acquisition: Overview and behavioral perspective of relapse and tobacco use* (Research Monograph Series). Washington, DC: National Institute on Drug Abuse.

Greenfeld, L. A., & Snell, T. A. (1999). Women offenders. In *Bureau of Justice Statistics special report* (p. 5). Washington, DC: U.S. Department of Justice.

Groom, B. (1999). Handling the triple whammy: Serious mental illness, substance abuse and criminal behavior. *Corrections Today,* 114–119.

Guerney, B. (1964). Filial therapy: Description and rationale. *Journal of Consulting Psychology, 28,* 304–310.

Guerney, L. F. (1983). Introduction to filial therapy: Training parents as therapists. In P. A. Keller & L. G. Ritt (Eds.), *Innovations in clinical practice: A source book* (Vol. 2, pp. 26–39). Sarasota, FL: Professional Resource Exchange.

Gutstein, S. E., Rudd, M. D., Graham, J. C., & Rayha, L. L. (1988). Systemic crisis intervention as a response to adolescent crises: An outcome study. *Family Process, 27,* 201–211.

Guy, E., Platt, J., Zwerling, I., & Bullock, S. (1985). Mental health status of prisoners in an urban jail. *Criminal Justice and Behavior, 12*, 29–53.

Haley, J. (1975). Why a mental health clinic should avoid family therapy. *Journal of Marriage and Family Counseling, 1*, 3–13.

Haley, J. (1976). *Problem solving therapy.* San Francisco, CA: Jossey-Bass.

Hall, E. A., Baldwin, D. M., & Prendergast, M. L. (2001). Women on parole: Barriers to success after substance abuse treatment. *Human Organization, 60*, 225–233.

Hamilton, C. J., & Collins, J. J. (1981). The role of alcohol in wife beating and child abuse: A review of the literature. In J. J. Collins (Ed.), *Drinking and crime: Perspectives on the relationship between alcohol consumption and criminal behavior* (pp. 253–287). New York: Guilford Press.

Hanf, C. (1969, April). *A two-stage program for modifying maternal controlling during mother–child interaction.* Paper presented at the meeting of the Western Psychological Associations, Vancouver, British Columbia, Canada.

Hanson, G., & Venturelli, P. (1995). *Drugs and society* (4th ed.). Boston: Jones & Bartlett.

Hare, R. D. (1980). A research scale for the assessment of psychopathy in criminal populations. *Personality and Individual Differences, 1*, 111–119.

Hare, R. D. (1991). *The Hare Psychopathy Checklist–Revised.* Toronto: Multi-Health Systems.

Hare, R. D. (1998). The Hare PCL-R: Some issues concerning its use and misuse. *Legal and Criminological Psychology, 3*, 99–119.

Hare, R. D., & Herve, H. F. (1999). *Hare P-Scan: Research version manual.* Toronto: Multi-Health Systems.

Harper, R., & Hardy, S. (2000). An evaluation of motivational interviewing as a method of intervention with clients in a probation setting. *British Journal of Social Work, 30*, 393–400.

Harrison, P. A., & Hoffman, N. G. (1989). *CATOR report: Adolescent completers one year later.* St. Paul, MN: Chemical Abuse/Addiction Treatment Outcome Registry, Ramsey Clinic.

Hart, S. D., Cox, D. N., & Hare, R. D. (1995). *Manual for the Screening Version of the Psychopathy Checklist (PCL:SV).* Toronto: Multi-Health Systems.

Hart, S. D., & Hare, R. D. (1989). Discriminant validity of the Psychopathy Checklist in a forensic psychiatric population. *Psychological Assessment: A Journal of Consulting and Clinical Psychology, 1*, 211–218.

Hart, S. D., Hare, R. D., & Harpur, T. J. (1992). The Psychopathy Checklist–Revised (PCL–R): An overview for researchers and clinicians. In J.

C. Rosen & P. McReynolds (Eds.), *Advances in psychological assessment* (Vol. 8, pp. 103–130). New York: Plenum.

Harvey, A. R., & Coleman, A. A. (1997). An Afrocentric program for African American males in the juvenile justice system. *Child Welfare, 76,* 197–211.

Hawkins, C. A. (1998). Family systems and chemical dependency. In C. A. McNeece & D. M. DiNitto (Eds.), *Chemical dependency: A systems approach* (2nd ed., pp. 229–254). Boston: Allyn & Bacon.

Hawkins, J. D., Catalano, R. F., & Miller, J. Y. (1992). Risk and protective factors for alcohol and other drug problems in adolescence and early adulthood: Implications for substance abuse prevention. *Psychological Bulletin, 112,* 64–105.

Haycock, J. (1992). Listening to "attention seekers": The clinical management of people threatening suicide. *Jail Suicide Update, 4,* 8–11.

Hayes, L. M. (1983). And darkness closes in. *Criminal Justice and Behavior, 10,* 461–484.

Hayes, L. M. (1989). National study of jail suicides: Seven years later. *Psychiatric Quarterly, 60,* 7–29.

Hayes, L. M. (1995). Prison suicide: An overview and a guide to prevention. *The Prison Journal, 75,* 431–456.

Hayes, L. M. (1998). Model suicide prevention programs—Part II. Juvenile facilities. *Jail Suicide/Mental Health Update, 7,* 1–8.

Healey, K. M. (1999, February). Case management in the criminal justice system. *National Institute of Justice Research in Action.* Washington, DC: U.S. Department of Justice, Office of Justice Programs.

Health Insurance Association of America. (1994). Cost of maternity care, physicians' fees, and hospital charges, by census regions, based on Consumer Price Index, 1991. In *The sourcebook of insurance data—1993.* Washington, DC: Author.

Heburn, J. R., & Albonetti, C. A. (1994). Recidivism among drug offenders: A survival analysis of the effects of offender characteristics, type of offense, and two types of intervention. *Journal of Quantitative Criminology, 10,* 159–179.

Hecht, M., Trost, M. R., & MacKinnon, D. (1997). Ethnicity and sex similarities and differences in drug resistance. *Journal of Applied Communication Research, 25,* 75–90.

Hemphill, J. F., Hare, R. D., & Wong, S. (1998). Psychopathy and recidivism: A review. *Legal and Criminological Psychology, 3,* 139–170.

Hemphill, J. F., Hart, S. D., & Hare, R. D. (1994). Psychopathy and substance use. *Journal of Personality Disorders, 8,* 169–180.

Henggeler, S. W. (1997). The development of effective drug-abuse services for youth. In J. A. Egertson, D. M. Fox, & A. I. Leshner (Eds.), *Treating drug abusers effectively* (pp. 253–279). New York: Blackwell.

Henggeler, S. W. (1999). Multisystemic therapy: An overview of clinical procedures, outcomes, and policy implications. *Child Psychology and Psychiatry, 4,* 2–10.

Henggeler, S. W., & Borduin, C. M. (1990). *Family therapy and beyond: A multisystemic approach to treating the behavior problems of children and adolescents.* Pacific Grove, CA: Brooks/Cole.

Henggeler, S. W., Borduin, C. M., Melton, G. B., Mann, B. J., Smith, L. A., Hall, J. A., et al. (1991). Effects of multisystemic therapy on drug use and abuse in serious juvenile offenders: A progress report from two outcome studies. *Family Dynamics of Addiction Quarterly, 1,* 40–51.

Henggeler, S. W., Clingempeel, W. G., Brondino, M. J., & Pickrell, S. G. (2002). Four-year follow-up of multisystemic therapy with substance-abusing and substance-dependent juvenile offenders. *Journal of American Academy of Child and Adolescent Psychiatry, 41,* 1–7.

Henggeler, S. W., Melton, G. B., & Smith, L. A. (1992). Family preservation using multisystemic therapy: An effective alternative to incarcerating serious juvenile offenders. *Journal of Consulting and Clinical Psychology, 60,* 953–961.

Henggeler, S. W., Melton, G. B., Smith, L. A., Schoenwald, S. K., & Hanely, J. H. (1993). Family preservation using multisystemic treatment: Long-term follow-up to a clinical trial with serious juvenile offenders. *Journal of Child and Family Studies, 2,* 283–293.

Henggeler, S. W., Rodick, J. D., Borduin, C. M., Hanson, C. L., Watson, S. M., & Urey, J. R. (1986). Multisystemic treatment of juvenile offenders: Effects on adolescent behavior and family interactions. *Developmental Psychology, 22,* 132–141.

Henggeler, S. W., & Schoenwald, S. K. (1994). Boot camps for juvenile offenders: Just say no. *Journal of Child and Family Studies, 3,* 243–248.

Henggeler, S. W., Schoenwald, S. K., Borduin, C. M., Rowland, M. D., & Cunningham, P. B. (1998). *Multisystemic treatment of antisocial behavior in children and adolescents.* New York: Guilford Press.

Hepburn, J. R., & Albonetti, C. A. (1994). Recidivism among drug offenders: A survival analysis of the effects of offenders' characteristics, type of offense, and two types of intervention. *Journal of Quantitative Criminology, 10*(2), 159–179.

Herie, M., Cunningham, J. A., & Martin, G. W. (2000). Attitudes toward substance abuse treatment among probation and parole officers. *Journal of Offender Rehabilitation, 32,* 181–195.

Hiller, M. L., Knight, K., Devereux, J., & Hathcoat, M. (1996). Posttreatment outcomes for substance-abusing probationers mandated to residential treatment. *Journal of Psychoactive Drugs, 28*, 291–296.

Hodges, K. (2000). *The Child and Adolescent Functional Assessment Scale Self Training Manual.* Ypsilanti: Eastern Michigan University, Department of Psychology.

Hodges, K., & Cheong-Seok, K. (2000). Psychometric study of the Child and Adolescent Functional Assessment Scale: Prediction of contact with the law and poor school attendance. *Journal of Abnormal Child Psychology, 28*, 287–297.

Hodges, K., Doucette-Gates, A., & Oinghong, L. (1999). The relationship between the Child and Adolescent Functional Assessment Scale (CAFAS) and indicators of functioning. *Journal of Child and Family Studies, 8*, 109–122.

Hodges, K., & Wong, M. M. (1996). Psychometric characteristics of a multidimensional measure to assess impairment: The Child and Adolescent Functional Assessment Scale. *Journal of Child and Family Studies, 5*, 445–467.

Hodgins, D. C., & El, G. N. (1992). More data on the Addiction Severity Index: Reliability and validity with the mentally ill substance abuser. *Journal of Nervous and Mental Disorders, 180*, 197–201.

Hokanson, J. E. (1983). *Introduction to the therapeutic process.* Reading, MA: Addison-Wesley.

Holleran, L. K., Reeves, L., Dustman, P., & Marsiglia, F. F. (2002). Creating culturally grounded videos for substance abuse prevention. *Journal of Social Work Practice in the Addictions, 2*, 55–78.

Hooker, T., & Bryant, L. (1993). *HIV/AIDS facts to consider.* Washington, DC: National Conference of State Legislators.

Hopps, J. G., & Pinderhughes, E. (1999). *Group work with overwhelmed clients.* New York: The Free Press.

Hoyt, S., & Scherer, D. G. (1998). Female juvenile delinquency: Misunderstood by the juvenile justice system, neglected by social science. *Law and Human Behavior, 22*, 81–107.

Hubbard, R. L., Collins, J. J., Rachal, J. V., & Cavanaugh, E. R. (1988). The criminal justice client in drug abuse treatment. In C. G. Leukefeld & F. M. Tims (Eds.), *Compulsory treatment of drug abuse: Research and clinical practice* (NIDA Research Monograph No. 86, pp. 57–80). Rockville, MD: National Institute on Drug Abuse.

Hudak, J., Krestan, J., & Bepko, C. (1999). Alcohol problems and the family life cycle. In B. Carter & M. McGoldrick (Eds.), *The expanded family life* cycle: Individual, family, and social perspectives (3rd ed., pp. 455–469). Boston: Allyn & Bacon.

Hudson, W. W. (1982). The clinical measurement package: A field manual. Homewood, IL: Dorsey Press.

Hughes, J. N., & Cavell, T. A. (1994). Enhancing competence in aggressive children. In G. Cartledge & J. F. Milburn (Eds.), Teaching social skills to children: Innovative approaches (3rd ed.). New York: Pergamon.

Huizinga, D., Loeber, R., & Thornberry, T. P. (1994). Urban delinquency and substance abuse: Initial findings. Washington, DC: U.S. Department of Justice.

Inciardi, J. A., & McBride, D. C. (1991). Treatment Alternatives to Street Crime (TASC): History, experiences, and issues. Rockville, MD: National Institute on Drug Abuse.

Ivanoff, A. (1989). Identifying psychological correlates of suicidal behavior in jail and detention facilities. Psychiatric Quarterly, 60, 73–84.

Ivanoff, A., & Hayes, L. M. (2001). Preventing, managing, and treating suicidal actions in high-risk offenders. In J. B. Ashford, B. D. Sales, & W. H. Reid (Eds.), Treating adult and juvenile offenders with special needs (pp. 313–331). Washington, DC: American Psychological Association.

Izzo, R. L., & Ross, R. R. (1990). Meta-analysis of rehabilitation programs for juvenile delinquents. Criminal Justice and Behavior, 17, 134–142.

Jackson, M. S. (1995). Afrocentric treatment of African American women and their children in a residential chemical dependency program. Journal of Black Studies, 26, 17–30.

Jackson, M. S., & Springer, D. W. (1997). Social work practice with African-American juvenile gangs: Professional challenge. In C. A. McNeece & A. R. Roberts (Eds.), Policy and practice in the justice system (pp. 231–248). Chicago: Nelson-Hall.

Jacobs, T. (1990). The corrective emotional experience: Its place in current technique. Psychoanalytic Inquiry, 10, 433–545.

Jamieson, Beals, Lalonde, & Associates. (2000). Motivational enhancement treatment (MET) manual: Theoretical foundation and structured curriculum. Individual and group sessions (Developed for the State of Maine, Department of Mental Health, Mental Retardation and Substance Abuse Services, Office of Substance Abuse). Ottawa, Canada: Author.

Janicak, P. G., Davis, J. M., Preskorn, S. H., & Ayd, F. J. (1993). Principles and practice of psychopharmacotherapy. Baltimore: Williams & Wilkins.

Jensen, J. P., Bergin, A. E., & Greaves, D. W. (1990). The meaning of eclecticism: New survey and analysis of components. Professional Psychology: Research and Practice, 21, 124–130.

Jenson, J. M. (1997). Juvenile delinquency and drug abuse: Implications for social work practice in the justice system. In C. A. McNeece & A. R. Roberts (Eds.), *Policy and practice in the justice system* (pp. 107–123). Chicago: Nelson-Hall.

Jenson, J. M., & Howard, M. O. (1999). Hallucinogen use among juvenile probationers: Prevalence and characteristics. *Criminal Justice and Behavior, 26,* 357–372.

Joaning, H., Gawinski, B., Morris, J., & Quinn, W. (1986). Organizing a social ecology to treat adolescent drug abuse. *Journal of Strategic and Systemic Therapies, 5,* 55–66.

Joaning, H., Quinn, W., Thomas, F., & Mullen, R. (1992). Treating adolescent drug abuse: A comparison of family systems therapy, group therapy, and family drug education. *Journal of Marital and Family Therapy, 18,* 345–356.

Joe, G. W., Dansereau, D. F., & Simpson, D. D. (1994). Node-link mapping for counseling cocaine users in methadone treatment. *Journal of Substance Abuse, 6,* 393–406.

Johnson, V. (1986). *Intervention: How to help someone who doesn't want help.* Minneapolis, MN: Johnson Institute.

Johnson, W. W., & Jones, M. (1998). Probation, race, and the war on drugs: An empirical analysis of drug and non-drug felony probation outcomes. *Journal of Drug Issues, 28,* 985–1003.

Johnston, D. (1995). Effects of parental incarceration. In K. Gabel & D. Johnston (Eds.), *Children of incarcerated parents* (pp. 59–88). New York: Lexington Books.

Jordan, C., & Franklin, C. (1995). *Clinical assessment for social workers: Quantitative and qualitative methods.* Chicago: Lyceum Books.

Jordan, C., & Franklin, C. (1999). Mental Research Institute (MRI), Strategic, and Milan family therapy. In C. Franklin & C. Jordan (Eds.), *Family practice: Brief systems methods for social work* (pp. 45–72). Pacific Grove, CA: Brooks/Cole.

Kaskutas, L. A. (1989). Women for sobriety: A qualitative analysis. *Contemporary Drug Problems, 16,* 177–200.

Kaskutas, L. A. (1994). What do women get out of self-help? Their reasons for attending Women for Sobriety and Alcoholics Anonymous. *Journal of Substance Abuse Treatment, 11,* 184–195.

Kassebaum, P. A. (1999). *Substance abuse treatment for women offenders: Guide to promising practices* (DHHS Publication No. SMA 99-3303). Rockville, MD: U.S. Department of Health and Human Services, Substance Abuse and Mental Health Services Administration, Center for Substance Abuse Treatment.

Kazdin, A. E. (1987). Treatment of antisocial behavior in children: Current status and future directions. *Psychology Bulletin, 102*, 187–203.

Kazdin, A. E. (1997). Parent management training: Evidence, outcomes, and issues. *Journal of the American Academy of Child and Adolescent Psychiatry, 36*, 1349–1356.

Keller, M. (1958). Alcoholism: Nature and extent of the problem. In S. Bacon (Ed.), *Understanding alcoholism* (pp. 1–11). Philadelphia: Annals of the American Academy of Political and Social Science.

Kelly, W. R. (2001). *Criminal justice and mental illness: Prevalence and treatment.* Unpublished manuscript, University of Texas at Austin.

Kendall, P. C., & Braswell, L. (1993). *Cognitive–behavioral therapy for impulsive children* (2nd ed.). New York: Guilford Press.

Kerr v. Farrey, 95 F.3d 472 (7th Cir. 1996).

Khantzian, E. J. (1997). The self-medication hypothesis of substance use disorders: A reconsideration and recent applications. *Harvard Review of Psychiatry, 4*, 231–244.

King, A. E. O. (1994). An Afrocentric cultural awareness program for incarcerated African-American males. *Journal of Multicultural Social Work, 3*, 17–28.

King, A. E. O. (1997). Understanding violence among young African American males: An Afrocentric perspective. *Journal of Black Studies, 28*, 79–96.

Kirkpatrick, J. (1978). *Turnabout: Help for a new life.* Garden City, NY: Doubleday.

Klein, N. C., Alexander, J. F., & Parsons, B. V. (1976). Impact of family systems intervention on recidivism and sibling delinquency: A model of primary prevention and program evaluation. *Journal of Consulting and Clinical Psychology, 45*, 469–474.

Ko, S. J., & Wasserman, G. A. (2002). Seeking best practices for mental health assessment in juvenile justice settings. *Report on emotional and behavioral disorders in youth, 2*(4), 88–99. Kingston, NJ: Civic Research Institute.

Kofoed, L., & Keys, A. (1988). Using group therapy to persuade dual-diagnosis patients to seek substance abuse treatment. *Hospital and Community Psychiatry, 39*, 1209–1211.

Koefoed, L., Tolson, R., Atkinson, R., Toth, R., & Turner, J. (1986). Outpatient treatment of patients with substance abuse and coexisting psychiatric disorders. *American Journal of Psychiatry, 143*, 867–872.

Konefal, J., Duncan, R., & Clemence, C. (1994). The impact of the addition of an acupuncture treatment program to an existing Metro-Dade County outpatient substance abuse treatment facility. *Journal of Addictive Diseases, 13,* 71–99.

Koons, B. A., Burrow, J. D., Morash, M., & Bynum, T. (1997). Expert and offender perceptions of program elements linked to successful outcomes for incarcerated women. *Crime and Delinquency, 43,* 512–532.

Korzenny, F., & McClure, J. (1990). Ethnicity, communication, and drugs. *Journal of Drug Issues, 20,* 87–98.

Kosten, T. (1993). Clinical and research perspectives on cocaine abuse: The pharmacology of cocaine abuse. In F. Tims & C. Leukefeld (Eds.), *Cocaine treatment: Research and clinical perspectives* (pp. 48–56). Rockville, MD: National Institute on Drug Abuse.

Kouzis, A. C., & Labouvie, E. W. (1992). Use intensity, functional elaboration, and contextual constraint as facets of adolescent alcohol and marijuana use. *Psychology of Addictive Behaviors, 6,* 188–195.

Kyte, N. S., & Bostick, G. J., Jr. (1997). Measuring variables. In R. M. Grinnell, Jr. (Ed.), *Social work research and evaluation: Quantitative and qualitative approaches* (5th ed., pp. 161–183). Itasca, IL: F. E. Peacock.

Laken, M. P., & Ager, J. W. (1996). Effects of case management or retention in prenatal substance abuse treatment. *American Journal of Alcohol Abuse, 22,* 439–448.

Laken, M. P., McComish, J. F., & Ager, J. (1997). Predictors of prenatal substance use and birth weigh during outpatient treatment. *Journal of Substance Abuse Treatment, 14,* 359–366.

Lambert, M. J., & Bergin, A. E. (1983). Therapist characteristics and their contribution to psychotherapy outcome. In C. E. Walker (Ed.), *The handbook of clinical psychology* (Vol. 1, pp. 205–241). Homewood, IL: Dow Jones-Irwin.

Laqueur, H. P. (1980). The theory and practice of multiple family therapy. In L. R. Wolberg & M. L. Aronson (Eds.). *Group and family therapy* (pp. 15–23). New York: Brunner/Mazel.

Leccese, M., & Waldron, H. B. (1994). Assessing adolescent substance abuse: A critique of current measurement instruments. *Journal of Substance Abuse Treatment, 11,* 553–563.

Leeman, L. W., Gibbs, J. C., & Fuller, D. (1993). Evaluation of a multicomponent group treatment program for juvenile delinquents. *Aggressive Behavior, 19,* 281–292.

Legal Action Center. (1999). *Steps to success: Helping women with alcohol and drug problems move from welfare to work.* New York: Legal Action Center.

Lehman, A., Herron, J., Schwartz, R., & Myers, P. (1993). Rehabilitation for young adults with severe mental illness and substance use disorders: A clinical trial. *Journal of Nervous and Mental Disease, 181,* 86–90.

Leukefeld, C. G., & Tims, F. M. (Eds.). (1992). *Drug abuse treatment in prisons and jails* (NIDA Research Monograph Series No. 188). Washington, DC: National Institute on Drug Abuse.

Leukefeld, C. G., & Walker, R. (1998). Substance use disorders. In J. B. W. Williams & K. Ell (Eds.), *Advances in mental health research: Implications for practice* (pp. 182–202). Washington, DC: NASW Press.

Levitt, J., & Reid, W. (1981). Rapid-assessment instruments for practice. *Social Work Research and Abstracts, 17,* 13–19.

Levy, J., Gallmeier, C., & Wiebel, W. (1995). The outreach assisted peer-support model for controlling drug dependency. *Journal of Drug Issues, 25,* 507–529.

Lewis, J., Dana, R., & Blevins, G. (1994). *Substance abuse counseling* (2nd ed.). Pacific Grove, CA: Brooks/Cole.

Lewith, G. T., & Vincent, C. (1996). On the evaluation of the clinical effects of acupuncture: A problem reassessed and a framework for future research. *Journal of Alternative and Complementary Medicine, 2,* 79–90.

Libety, H. H., Johnson, B. D., Jainchill, N., Ryder, J., Messina, M., Reynolds, S., et al. (1998). Dynamic recovery: Comparative study of therapeutic communities in homeless shelters for men. *Journal of Substance Abuse Treatment 15,* 401–423.

Liddle, H. A., & Dakof, G. A. (1995). Efficacy of family therapy for drug abuse: Promising but not definitive. *Journal of Marital and Family Therapy, 21,* 511–544.

Liddle, H. A., Dakof, G. A., Parker, K., Diamond, G. S., Barrett, K., & Tejeda, M. (2001). Multidimensional family therapy for adolescent drug abuse: Results of a randomized clinical trial. *American Journal of Drug and Alcohol Abuse, 27,* 651–688.

Lieberman, M., Yalom, I., & Miles, M. (1973). *Encounter groups: First facts.* New York: Basic Books.

Lindforss, L., & Magnusson, D. (1997). Solution-focused therapy in prison. *Contemporary Family Therapy, 19,* 89–103.

Ling, W., Rawson, R., & Compton, M. (1994). Substituting pharmacotherapies for opioid addiction: From methadone to LAAM and buprenorphine. *Journal of Psychoactive Drugs, 26,* 119–128.

Lipsey, M. W. (1992). Juvenile delinquency treatment: A meta-analytic inquiry into the variability of effects. In T. D. Cook, H. Cooper, D. S. Corday, H. Hartman, L. V. Hedges, R. J. Light, et al. (Eds.), *Meta-analysis for explanation: A casebook* (pp. 83–127). New York: Russell Sage Foundation.

Lipsey, M. W., & Wilson, D. B. (1998). Effective intervention for serious juvenile offenders: A synthesis of research. In R. Loever & D. Farrington

(Eds.), *Serious and violent juvenile offenders: Risk factors and successful interventions* (pp. 313–344). London: Sage.

Lipton, D. S. (1995). *The effectiveness of treatment for drug abusers under criminal justice supervision.* Washington, DC: U.S. Department of Justice, National Institute of Justice Research Report.

Lipton, D. S., Brewington, V., & Smith, M. (1994). Acupuncture for crack-cocaine detoxification: Experimental evaluation of efficacy. *Journal of Substance Abuse Treatment, 11,* 205–215.

Lipton, D. S., Falkin, G. P., & Wexler, H. K. (1992). Correctional drug abuse treatment in the United States: An overview. In C. Leukefeld & F. Tims (Eds.), *Drug abuse treatment in prisons and jails* (National Institute on Drug Abuse, Research Monograph Series No. 118). Washington, DC: U.S. Government Printing Office.

Lipton, D., Martinson, R., & Wilks, J. (1975). *The effectiveness of correctional treatment: A survey of treatment evaluation studies.* New York: Praeger.

Longshore, D., Grills, C., Annon, K., & Grady, R. (1998). Promoting recovery from drug abuse: An Africentric intervention. *Journal of Black Studies, 28,* 319–333.

Losel, F. (1998). Treatment and management of psychopaths. In D. Cooke, A. Forth, & R. Hare (Eds.), *Psychopathy: Theory, research, and implications for society* (pp. 303–354). Dordrecht, The Netherlands: Kluwer Academic.

Lucken, K. (1997). Privatizing discretion: "Rehabilitation" treatment in community corrections. *Crime and Delinquency, 43,* 243–259.

Lukas, S. (1993). *Where to start and what to ask: An assessment handbook.* New York: Norton.

Lukoff, D., Nuechterlein, K. H., & Ventura, J. (1986). Manual for Expanded Brief Psychiatric Rating Scale (BPRS). *Schizophrenia Bulletin, 12,* 594–602.

Lurigio, A., & Swartz, J. (2000). Changing the contours of the criminal justice system to meet the needs of persons with serious mental illness. *Criminal Justice, 3.* Washington, DC: U.S. Department of Justice, National Institute of Justice.

Lyman, D. R. (1997). Pursuing the psychopath: Capturing the fledgling psychopath in a nomological set. *Journal of Abnormal Psychology, 106,* 425–438.

MacKenzie, D. L. (1990). Boot camp prisons: Components, evaluations, and empirical issues. *Federal Probation, 54(3),* 44–52.

MacKenzie, D. L. (1991). The parole performance of offenders released from shock incarceration (boot camp prisons): A survival time analysis. *Journal of Quantitative Criminology, 7,* 213–236.

MacKenzie, D. L. (1994). Boot camps: A national assessment. *Overcrowded Times, 5*(4), pp. 1, 14–18.

MacKenzie, D. L., Brame, R., McDowall, D., & Souryal, C. (1995). Boot camp prisons and recidivism in eight states. *Criminology, 33,* 327–357.

MacKenzie, D. L., & Shaw, J. (1993). The impact of shock incarceration on technical violations and new criminal activities. *Justice Quarterly, 10,* 463–486.

Madanes, C. (1981). *Strategic family therapy.* San Francisco: Jossey-Bass.

Malekoff, A. (1997). *Group work with adolescents: Principles and practice.* New York: Guilford Press.

Man, P., & Chuang, M. (1980). Acupuncture in methadone withdrawal. *International Journal of the Addictions, 15,* 921–926.

Manpower Demonstration Research Corporation. (1980). *Summary and findings of the Supported Work Demonstration Project.* Cambridge, MA: Bollinger Publishing Company.

Marcus, P., & Alcabes, P. (1993). Characteristics of suicides by inmates in an urban jail. *Hospital and Community Psychiatry, 44,* 256–261.

Marcus-Mendoza, S. T., Klein-Saffran, J., & Lutze, E. (1997). A feminist examination of boot camp prison programs for women. *Women and Therapy, 21,* 173–185.

Margolin, A., Avants, S. K., Chang, P., & Kosten, T. (1993). Acupuncture for the treatment of cocaine dependence in methadone-maintained patients. *American Journal on Addictions, 2,* 194–201.

Marlow, H., Marlowe, J., & Willetts, R. (1983). The mental health counselor as case manager: Implications for working with the chronically mentally ill. *AMHCA Journal, 5,* 184–191.

Marshall, F. M., & Vito, G. F. (1982). Not without the tools: The task of probation in the eighties. *Federal Probation, 46,* 37–39.

Marsiglia, F. F., Cross, S., & Mitchell, V. (1998). Culturally grounded group work with adolescent American Indian students. *Social Work with Groups, 21,* 89–102.

Martin, S. S., Butzin, C. A., & Inciardi, J. A. (1995). Assessment of a multistage therapeutic community for drug-involved offenders. *Journal of Psychoactive Drugs, 27,* 109–116.

Martin, S. S., & Inciardi, J. A. (1993). Case management approaches for criminal justice clients. In J. A. Inciardi (Ed.), *Drug treatment and criminal justice, 27* (pp. 81–96). Newbury Park, CA: Sage.

Martinson, R. (1974). What works? Questions and answers about prison reform. *The Public Interest, 35,* 22–54.

Mason, B., Salvato, F., Williams, L., Lauren, D., Ritro, E., & Cutler, R. (1999). A double-blind, placebo-controlled study of oral nalmefene for alcohol dependence. *Archives of General Psychiatry, 56,* 719–724.

McBride, D. C., VanderWaal, C. J., Terry, Y. M., & VanBuren, H. (1999). *Breaking the cycle of drug use among juvenile offenders* [On-line]. Retrieved October 24, 2002, from http://www.ncjrs.org/pdffiles1/179273.pdf

McCance, E. (1997). Overview of potential treatment medications for cocaine dependence. In B. Tai, N. Chiang, & P. Bridge (Eds.), *Medication development for the treatment of cocaine dependence: Issues in clinical efficacy trials* (pp. 36–72). Rockville, MD: National Institute on Drug Abuse.

McCorkle, L., Elias, A., & Bixby, F. L. (1958). *The Highfields story.* New York: Holt.

McGaha, J. E. (1993). Alcoholism and the chemically dependent family: A study of adult felons on probation. *Journal of Offender Rehabilitation, 9,* 57–69.

McGuire, J. (1995). *What works: Reducing re-offending.* Chichester, England: Wiley.

McKinney, F., Miller, D. J., Beier, L., & Bohannon, S. R. (1978). Self-concept, delinquency, and positive peer culture. *Criminology, 15,* 529–538.

McLellan, A. T., Grossman, D. S., Blaine, J. D., & Haverkos, H. W. (1993). Acupuncture treatment for drug abuse: A technical review. *Journal of Substance Abuse Treatment, 10,* 568–576.

McLellan, A. T., Hagan, T. A., Levine, M., Meyers, K., Gould, F., Bencivengo, M., et al. (1999). Does clinical case management improve outpatient addiction treatment? *Drug and Alcohol Dependence, 55,* 91–103.

McLellan, A. T., Luborsky, L., Cacciola, J., Griffith, J., Evans, F., Barr, H. L., et al. (1985). New data from the Addiction Severity Index: Reliability and validity in three centers. *Journal of Nervous and Mental Disease, 173,* 412–423.

McLellan, A. T., Luborsky, L., Woody, G. E., & O'Brien, C. P. (1980). An improved diagnostic instrument for substance abuse patients: The addiction severity index. *Journal of Nervous and Mental Disorders, 168(1),* 151–159.

McNeece, C. A. (1997). Future directions in justice system policy and practice. In C. A. McNeece & A. R. Roberts (Eds.), *Policy and practice in the justice system* (pp. 263–269). Chicago: Nelson-Hall.

McNeece, C. A. (in press). Implications of the end of the "War on Drugs" for social work education. *Journal of Social Work Education.*

McNeece, C., Arnold, E., Valentine, P., & McInnis, M. (1999). Evaluating drug courts. In G. Mays & P. Gregware (Eds.), *Courts and justice: A reader* (pp. 419–431). Prospect Heights, IL: Waveland Press.

McNeece, C. A., Bullington, B., Mayfield, E. L., & Springer, D. W. (1999). The war on drugs: Treatment, research, and substance abuse intervention in the twenty-first century. In R. Muraskin & A. R. Roberts (Eds.), *Visions for change: Crime and justice in the twenty-first century* (2nd ed., pp. 9–30). Upper Saddle River, NJ: Prentice-Hall.

McNeece, C. A., Bullington, B., Mayfield Arnold, E. L., & Springer, D. W. (2002). The war on drugs: Treatment, research, and substance abuse intervention in the twenty-first century. In R. Muraskin & A. R. Roberts (Eds.), *Visions for change: Crime and justice in the twenty-first century* (3rd ed., pp. 11–36). Upper Saddle River, NJ: Prentice-Hall.

McNeece, C. A., & Daly, C. M. (1997). Treatment and intervention with chemically involved adult offenders. In C. A. McNeece & A. R. Roberts (Eds.), *Policy and practice in the justice system* (pp. 69–86). Chicago: Nelson-Hall.

McNeece, C. A., & DiNitto, D. M. (1994). *Chemical dependency: A systems approach*. Englewood Cliffs, NJ: Prentice-Hall.

McNeece, C. A., & DiNitto, D. M. (1998). *Chemical dependency: A systems approach* (2nd ed.). Boston: Allyn & Bacon.

McNeece, C. A., & Roberts, A. R. (Eds.). (1997). *Policy and practice in the justice system*. Chicago: Nelson-Hall.

McNeece, C. A., Springer, D. W., & Arnold, E. M. (2001). Treating substance abuse disorders. In J. Ashford, B. D. Sales, & W. H. Reid (Eds.), *Treating adult and juvenile offenders with special needs* (pp. 131–169). Washington, DC: American Psychological Association.

McNichol, R. W., & Logsdon, S. A. (1988). Disulfiram: An evaluation research model. *Alcohol Health and Research World, 12*, 202–209.

Medieros, M., & Prochaska, J. O. (1993) *Predicting premature termination from psychotherapy*. Unpublished manuscript, University of Rhode Island, Kingston.

Meezan, W., & O'Keefe, M. (1998). Evaluating the effectiveness of multifamily group therapy in child abuse and neglect. *Research on Social Work Practice, 8*, 330–353.

Meichenbaum, D. H. (1977). *Cognitive–behavioral modification: An integrative approach*. New York: Plenum.

Mejta, C. L., Bokos, P. J., Mickenberg, J., Maslar, M. E., & Senay, E. (1997). Improving substance abuse treatment access and retention using a case management approach. *Journal of Drug Issues, 27*, 329–340.

Mercer, J. R. (1979). *System of multicultural pluralistic assessment technical manual*. San Antonio, TX: The Psychological Corporation.

Meyers, L. (1988). *Understanding an Afrocentric world view: Introduction to an optimal psychology*. Dubuque, IA: Kendall/Hunt.

Michigan Department of Social Services. (1983). *The institution centers: Objectives and progress*. Lansing, MI: Institutional Services Division, Office of Children and Youth Services.

Miller, G. A. (1985). *The substance abuse subtle screening inventory manual*. Bloomington, IN: SASSI Institute.

Miller, G. A. (1999). *Learning the language of addiction counseling*. Boston: Allyn & Bacon.

Miller, G. A., Miller, F. G., Roberts, J., Brooks, M. K., & Lazowski, L. G. (1997). *The SASSI-3*. Bloomington, IN: Baugh Enterprises.

Miller, N. S. (1995). *Addiction psychiatry: Current diagnosis and treatment*. New York: Wiley.

Miller, W. R. (1976). Alcoholism scales and objective measures. *Psychological Bulletin, 83*, 649–674.

Miller, W. R., & Hester, R. K. (1980). Treating the problem drinker: Modern approaches. In W. R. Miller (Ed.), *The addictive behaviors* (pp. 11–141). New York: Pergamon.

Miller, W. R., & Hester, R. K. (1986). The effectiveness of alcoholism research: What research reveals. In W. R. Miller & N. Heather (Eds.), *Treating addictive behaviors: Processes of change* (pp. 175–204). New York: Plenum.

Miller, W. R., & Rollnick, S. (2002). *Motivational interviewing* (2nd ed.). New York: Guilford Press.

Miller, W. R., Westerberg, V., & Waldron, H. B. (1995). Evaluating alcohol problems in adults and adolescents. In R. K. Hester & W. R. Miller (Eds.), *Handbook of alcoholism treatment approaches: Effective alternatives* (2nd ed., pp. 17–53). Boston: Allyn & Bacon.

Minkoff, K., & Drake, R. (1991). *Dual diagnosis of major mental illness and substance disorder*. San Francisco, CA: Jossey-Bass.

Minnesota Department of Corrections. (1973). *The Red Wing Training School follow-up study*. Minneapolis: Author, Research Division.

Minuchin, S. (1974). *Families and family therapy*. Cambridge, MA: Harvard University Press.

Minuchin, S., & Fishman, H. C. (1981). *Family therapy techniques*. Cambridge, MA: Harvard University Press.

Mitchell, E. R. (1995). *Fighting drug abuse with acupuncture: The treatment that works*. Berkeley, CA: Pacific View Press.

Moner, S. E. (1996). Acupuncture and addiction treatment. *Journal of Addictive Diseases, 15*, 79–100.

Moon, M. M., & Latessa, E. J. (1994). Drug treatment in adult probation: An evaluation of an outpatient and acupuncture program. *Journal of Evaluation and Program Planning, 17*, 217–226.

Moore, R. A. (1972). The diagnosis of alcoholism in a psychiatric hospital: A trial of the Michigan Alcohol Screening Test (MAST). *American Journal of Psychiatry, 128,* 115–119.

Morash, M., Bynum, T. S., & Koons, B. A. (1995). *Findings from the national study of innovative and promising programs for women offenders.* East Lansing: Michigan State University, School of Criminal Justice.

Morash, M., Bynum, T. S., & Koons, B. A. (1998). Women offenders: Programming needs and promising approaches. In *National Institute of Justice research in brief* (August 1998, NCJ171668). Washington, DC: U.S. Department of Justice, National Institute of Justice.

Morash, M., & Rucker, L. (1990). A critical look at the idea of the boot camp as a correctional reform. *Crime and Delinquency, 36,* 204–222.

Morris, R. E., Harrison, E. A., Knox, G. W., Tromanhauser, E., Marquis, M. A., & Watts, L. L. (1995). Health risk behavioral survey from 39 juvenile correctional facilities in the United States. *Journal of Adolescent Health, 17,* 334–344.

Morrison, J. (1995). *DSM-IV made easy: The clinician's guide to diagnosis.* New York: Guildford Press.

Morton, L. A. (1978). *The Risk Prediction Scales.* Indianapolis, IN: Department of Mental Health, Division of Addiction Services.

Mueser, K., Bennett, M., & Kushner, M. (1995). Epidemiology of substance use disorders among persons with chronic mental illnesses. In A. F. Lehman & L. F. Dixon (Eds.), *Double jeopardy: Chronic mental illness and substance use disorders* (pp. 9–25). Chur, Switzerland: Harwood.

Multnomah County Auditor's Office. (1997, January). *Community corrections: Mixed results from new supervision programs.* Portland, OR: Author. Retrieved October 24, 2002, from http://www.co.multnomah.or.us/auditor/ccsum.html

Mumola, C. (1998). *Substance abuse and treatment: State and federal prisoners, 1997.* Washington, DC: Bureau of Justice Statistics.

Mumola, C. (2000). Incarcerated parents and their children. *Bureau of Justice Statistics special report.* Washington, DC: Department of Justice, Office of Justice Programs.

Munger, R. L. (1993). *Changing children's behavior quickly.* Lanham, MD: Madison Books.

Najavits, L., Weiss, R., Shaw, S., & Muenz, L. (1998). Seeking safety: Outcome of a new cognitive–behavioral psychotherapy for women with posttraumatic stress disorder and substance dependence. *Journal of Traumatic Stress, 11,* 437–456.

National Center on Addiction and Substance Abuse. (1997, December). *Behind bars: Substance abuse and America's prison population.* New York:

Columbia University, National Court Appointed Special Advocate Association.

National Commission on Correctional Health Care. (1995). *Standards for health services in juvenile detention and confinement facilities*. Chicago: Author.

National Commission on Correctional Health Care. (1996). *Standards for health services in jails*. Chicago: Author.

National Commission on Correctional Health Care. (1997). *Standards for health services in prisons*. Chicago: Author.

National Council on Crime and Delinquency. (1995). *Reducing crime in America: A programmatic approach*. San Francisco, CA: Author.

National Drug Control Strategy. (1990). National drug control strategy 1990. Washington, DC: U.S. Government Printing Office.

National Drug Court Institute. (2001). *Drug court today*. Retrieved October 24, 2002, from http://www.ndci.org/courtfacts.htm.

National Institute of Justice. (1999). *ADAM: 1998 Annual report on adult and juvenile arrestees*. Washington, DC: U.S. Department of Justice.

National Institute of Justice. (2001). *ADAM preliminary 2000 findings on drug use and drug markets* (NCJ 189101). Washington, DC: U.S. Department of Justice, Office of Justice Programs.

National Institute on Alcohol Abuse and Alcoholism. (1990). *Seventh special report to the U.S. Congress on alcohol and health*. Rockville, MD: U.S. Department of Health and Human Services.

National Institute on Alcohol Abuse and Alcoholism. (1997). Patient-treatment matching,. *Alcohol Alert, 36*, 1–4.

National Institute on Drug Abuse. (1991). The adolescent assessment/referral system manual. (DHHS Publication No. ADM 91–1735). Rockville, MD: U.S. Department of Health and Human Services, National Institutes of Health, National Institute on Drug Abuse.

National Institute on Drug Abuse. (1994). *Mental health assessment and diagnosis of substance abusers: Clinical report series* (NIH Publication No. 94 3846). Washington, DC: U.S. Department of Health and Human Services, National Institutes of Health, National Institute on Drug Abuse.

National Institute on Drug Abuse. (1997). Medication for treating heroin dependence proven safe and effective if used in high enough doses. Press release, June 24. Rockville, MD: U.S. Department of Health and Human Services.

National Institute on Drug Abuse. (1998). *The economic costs of alcohol and drug abuse in the United States*. Rockville, MD: U.S. Department of Health and Human Services.

National Institute on Drug Abuse. (1999a). *Drug Abuse and addiction research [on-line]. Section: NIDA research priorities and highlights: Role of research: Minority population studies.* Retrieved October 24, 2002, from www.nida.nih.gov/STRC/Role7.html.

National Institute on Drug Abuse. (1999b). *NIDA strategic plan: Bringing the power of science to bear on drug abuse and addiction.* (Draft) [on-line]. Retrieved October 24, 2002, from http://www.drugabuse.gov/StrategicPlan/Index.html.

National Institute on Drug Abuse. (1999c, October). *Principles of drug addiction treatment: A research-based guide* (NIH Publication No. 99-4180). Washington, DC: Author.

National Institutes of Health. (1997). *Acupuncture NIH Consensus Statement Online, 15*(5), 1–34.

National Task Force on Correctional Substance Abuse Strategies. (1991). *Intervening with substance abusing offenders: A framework for action.* Washington, DC: U.S. Department of Justice, National Institute of Corrections.

Newmeyer, T., Johnson, G., & Klot, S. (1984). Acupuncture as a detoxification modality. *Journal of Psychoactive Drugs, 16,* 241–261.

Niles, W. (1986). Effects of a moral development discussion group on delinquent and predelinquent boys. *Journal of Counseling Psychology, 33,* 45–51.

Noonan, W. C., & Moyers, T. B. (1997). Motivational interviewing: A review. *Journal of Substance Misuse, 2,* 8–16.

Norcross, J. C., Karg, R. S., & Prochaska, J. O. (1997). Clinical psychologist in the 1990s. *The Clinical Psychologist, 50,* 4–9.

Norcross, J. C., & Newman, C. F. (1992). Psychotherapy integration: Setting the context. In J. C. Norcross & M. R. Goldfried (Eds.), *Handbook of psychotherapy integration* (pp. 3–45). New York: Basic Books.

Northen, H. (1988). *Social work with groups* (2nd ed.). New York: Columbia University Press.

Novaco, R. W. (1975). *Anger control: The development and evaluation of an experimental treatment.* Lexington, MA: Heath.

Nowinski, J., & Baker, S. (1992). *The twelve-step facilitation handbook: A systematic approach to early recovery from alcoholism and addiction.* New York: Lexington Books.

Nugent, W. R., Bruley, C., & Allen, P. (1999). The effects of aggression replacement training on male and female antisocial behavior in a runaway shelter. *Research on Social Work Practice, 9,* 466–482.

Nunnally, J. C., & Bernstein, I. H. (1994). *Psychometric theory* (3rd ed.). New York: McGraw-Hill.

Nurco, D. N., Hanlan, T. E., Bateman, R. W., & Kinlock, T. W. (1995). Drug abuse treatment in the context of correctional surveillance. *Journal of Substance Abuse Treatment, 12*, 19–27.

Nurco, D. N., Hanlan, T. E., & Kinlock, T. W. (1990). *Offenders, drugs, crime and treatment* (Draft). Washington, DC: U.S. Department of Justice, Bureau of Justice Assistance.

Obermeier, G. E., & Henry, P. B. (1989). Adolescent inpatient treatment. *Journal of Chemical Dependency, 2*, 163–182.

O'Brien, C., & Bruggen, P. (1985). Our personal and professional lives: Learning positive connotations and circular questioning. *Family Process, 24*, 311–322.

O'Brien, W., & Devlin, C. (1997). The therapeutic community. In J. Lowinson, P. Ruiz, R. Millman, & J. Langrod (Eds.), *Substance abuse: A comprehensive textbook* (pp. 400–405). Baltimore: Williams & Wilkins.

O'Connor v. California, 855 F. Supp. 303 (C.D. Cal. 1994).

Oetting, E. R., Beauvias, F., & Goldstein, G. S. (1982). *Drug abuse among Native American youth: Summary of findings (1975–1981)*. Fort Collins: Colorado State University.

Office of National Drug Control Policy. (1990). *National drug control strategy: 2000 annual report*. Washington, DC: U.S. Government Printing Office.

Office of National Drug Control Policy. (1996, March). *Treatment protocol effectiveness study*. Washington, DC: U.S. Government Printing Office.

Office of National Drug Control Policy. (1997, February). *The national drug control strategy: 1997* (NCJ Publication No. 163915). Washington, DC: U.S. Government Printing Office.

Office of National Drug Control Policy. (1999). *ONDCP policy discussion paper, drugs, alcohol abuse, and adult and juvenile offenders: Breaking the cycle—breaking free of the cycle: Policy for community and institutional interventions to safeguard public safety and restore public health*. Washington, DC: Author.

Office of National Drug Control Policy. (2000). *National drug control strategy: 2000 annual report*. Washington, DC: U.S. Government Printing Office.

Office of National Drug Control Policy. (2001). *Drug treatment in the criminal justice system*. Retrieved October 24, 2002, from *www.whitehousedrugpolicy.gov*.

Office of Probation and Pretrial Services, Administrative Office of the United States Courts. (2002, May). *United States probation and pretrial services system: Year-in-review report, fiscal year 2001*. Washington, DC: Author.

Office of the Inspector General, U.S. Department of Justice. (1996, March). *The home confinement program in the Bureau of Prisons: Audit report 96-09*. Washington, DC: Author.

Ogborne, A. C., & Glaser, F. B. (1985). Evaluating Alcoholics Anonymous. In T. E. Bratter & G. G. Forrest (Eds.), *Alcoholism and substance abuse* (pp. 176–192). New York: Free Press.

O'Shea, M. D., & Phelps, R. (1985). Multiple family therapy: Current status and critical appraisal. *Family Process, 24,* 555–582.

Otto, K. C., Quinn, C., & Sung, Y. F. (1998). Auricular acupuncture as an adjunctive treatment for cocaine addiction: A pilot study. *American Journal on Addictions, 7,* 164–170.

Overall, J. E., & Gorham, D. R. (1962). The Brief Psychiatric Rating Scale. *Psychological Reports, 10,* 799–812.

Palmer, T. (1992). *The re-emergence of correctional intervention*. Newbury Park, CA: Sage.

Pan, H., Scarpitti, F. R., Inciardi, J. A., & Lockwood, D. (1993). Some considerations on therapeutic communities in corrections. In J. A. Inciardi (Ed.), *Drug treatment and criminal justice* (No. 27, pp. 30–43). Newbury Park, CA: Sage.

Parent, D. (1989). *Shock incarceration: An overview of existing programs*. Washington, DC: U.S. Department of Justice, National Institute of Justice.

Patterson, G. R. (1985). Beyond technology: The next stage in developing an empirical base for parent training. In L. L'Abate (Ed.), *Handbook of family psychology* (Vol. 2, pp. 1344–1379). Homewood, IL: Dorsey.

Patterson, G. R., Reid, J. B., Jones, R. R., & Conger, R. E. (1975). *A social learning approach to family intervention: Vol. 1. Families with aggressive children*. Eugene, OR: Castalia.

Pearson, F. S., Lipton, D. S., Cleland, C. M., & Yee, D. S. (2002). The effects of behavioral/cognitive–behavioral programs on recidivism. *Crime and Delinquency, 48*(3), 476–496.

Pernanen, K. (1991). *Alcohol in human violence*. New York: Guilford Press.

Peters, M., Thomas, D., & Zamberlan, C. (1997). *Boot camps for juvenile offenders*. Washington, DC: U.S. Department of Justice.

Peters, R. H. (1993). Drug treatment in jails and detention settings. In J. A. Inciardi (Ed.), *Drug treatment and criminal justice* (No. 27, pp. 44–80). Thousand Oaks, CA: Sage.

Peters, R. H., & Hills, H. A. (1993). Inmates with co-occurring substance abuse and mental health disorders. In H. J. Steadman & J. J. Cocozzo (Eds.), *Mental illness in America's prisons* (pp. 159–211). Washington DC: National Coalition for the Mentally Ill in the Criminal Justice System.

Peters, R. H., & Hills, H. (1996). *Dual diagnosis treatment program manual.* Tampa, FL: University of South Florida, Florida Mental Health Institute.

Peters, R. H., May, R. L., & Kearns, W. D. (1992). Drug treatment in jails: Results of a nationwide survey. *Journal of Criminal Justice, 20,* 283–295.

Petersilia, J. (1990). Conditions that permit intensive supervision program. *Crime and Delinquency, 36,* 126–145.

Petersilia, J. (1998). A decade of experimenting with intermediate sanctions: What have we learned? *Federal Probation, 62*(2), 3–9.

Petersilia, J., Turner, S., & Deschenes, E. P. (1992). The costs and effects of intensive supervision for drug offenders. *Federal Probation, LVI,* 12–17.

Pitre, U., Dansereau, D. F., & Joe, G. W. (1996). Client education levels and the effectiveness of node-link maps. *Journal of Addictive Disorders, 15,* 27–44.

Pitre, U., Dansereau, D. F., Newbern, D., & Simpson, D. D. (1998). Residential drug abuse treatment for probationers: Use of node-link mapping to enhance participation and progress. *Journal of Substance Abuse Treatment, 15,* 535–543.

Pitre, U., Dansereau, D. F., & Simpson, D. D. (1997). The role of node-link maps in enhancing counseling efficiency. *Journal of Addictive Diseases, 16,* 39–49.

Platt, J. J., Perry, G. M., & Metzger, D. S. (1980). The evaluation of a heroin addiction treatment program within a correctional environment. In R. Ross & P. Gendreau (Eds.), *Effective correctional treatment* (pp. 419–437). Toronto: Butterworths.

Platt, J. J., Widman, M., Lidz, V., Rubenstein, D., & Thompson, R. (1998). The case for support services in substance abuse treatment. *American Behavioral Scientist, 41,* 1050–1062.

Pokornoy, A. D., Miller, B. A., & Kaplan, H. B. (1972). The Brief MAST: A shortened version of the Michigan Alcoholism Screening Test (MAST). *American Journal of Psychiatry, 129,* 342–345.

Polcin, D. (1992). A comprehensive model for adolescent chemical dependency treatment. *Journal of Counseling and Development, 70,* 376–382.

Pomeroy, E. C., Kiam, R., & Green, D. L. (2000). Reducing depression, anxiety, and trauma of male inmates: An HIV/AIDS psychoeducational group intervention. *Social Work Research, 24,* 156–167.

Potter-Efron, R. (1989). *Shame, guilt, and alcoholism*. New York: Haworth Press.

Prendergast, M. L., Grella, C., Perry, S. M., & Anglin, M. D. (1995). Levo-alpha-acetylmethodal (LAAM): Clinical, research, and policy issues of a new pharmacotherapy for opioid addiction. *Journal of Psychoactive Drugs, 27,* 239–247.

Prendergast, M. L., Wellisch, J., & Wong, M. M. (1996). Residential treatment for women parolees following prison-based drug treatment: Treatment experiences, needs and services, outcomes. *The Prison Journal, 76,* 253–274.

Pressman, J. L., & Wildavsky, A. (1984). *Implementation* (3rd ed., exp.). Berkeley: University of California Press.

Prochaska, J. O. (1999). How do people change and how can we change to help many more people? In M. A. Hubble, B. L. Duncan , & S. D. Miller (Eds.), *The heart and soul of change: What works in therapy* (pp. 227–255). Washington, DC: American Psychological Association.

Prochaska, J. O., & DiClemente, C. C. (1984). *The transtheoretical approach: Crossing the traditional boundaries of therapy*. Homewood, IL: Dow Jones/ Irwin.

Prochaska, J. O., & DiClemente, C. C. (1992). Stages of change in the modification of problem behaviors. In M. Hersen, R. M. Eisler, & P. M. Miller (Eds.), *Progress in behavior modification* (pp. 183–218). Sycamore, IL: Sycamore.

Prochaska, J. O., DiClemente, C. C., & Norcross, J. C. (1992). In search of how people change: Applications to addictive behaviors. *American Psychologist, 47,* 1102–1114.

Prochaska, J. O., & Norcross, J. C. (1999). *Systems of psychotherapy: A transtheoretical analysis* (4th ed.). Pacific Grove, CA: Brooks/Cole.

Prochaska, J. O., Norcross, J. C., Fowler, J. L., Follick, M. J., & Abrams, D. B. (1992). Attendance and outcome in a work site weight control program: Processes and stages of change as process and predictor variables. *Addictive Behaviors, 17,* 35–45.

Prochaska, J. O., Velicer, W. F., Rossi, J. S., Goldstein, M. G., Marcus, B. H., Rakowski, W., et al. (1994). Stages of change and decisional balance for twelve problem behaviors. *Health Psychology, 13,* 39–46.

Project MATCH Research Group. (1997). Project MATCH secondary a priori hypotheses. *Addiction, 92,* 1671–1698.

Quigley, R., & Steiner, M. E. (1996). Unleashing the power of young women through peer helping groups. *Reclaiming Children and Youth, 5,* 102–106.

Quinney, R. (1977). *Class, state and crime: On the theory and practice of criminal justice*. New York: David McKay.

Quinney, R. (2000). Socialist humanism and the problem of crime: Thinking about Erich Fromm in the development of critical/peacemaking criminology. In K. Anderson & R. Quinney (Eds.), *Erich Fromm and critical criminology: Beyond the punitive society* (pp. 147–156). Urbana: University of Illinois.

Radosh, P. F. (2002). Reflections on women's crime and mothers in prison: A peacemaking approach. *Crime and Delinquency, 48,* 300–315.

Rahdert, E. R. (1991). *The Adolescent Assessment/Referral System Manual* (DHHS Publication No. ADM 91-1735). Rockville, MD: U.S. Department of Health and Human Services, National Institute on Drug Abuse.

RAND Corporation. (1994). *Projecting future cocaine use and evaluating control strategies* (RB-6002). Santa Monica, CA: Author.

Rasmussen, D., & Benson, B. (1994). *The economic anatomy of a drug war.* Lanham, MD: Rowman & Littlefield.

Read, E. M. (1995). Posttreatment supervision challenges: Introducing Al-Anon, Narc-Anon, and Oxford House, Inc. *Federal Probation, 59,* 18–26.

Read, E. M. (1997). Variety on the job: Special skills, special duties in federal probation. *Federal Probation, 61,* 25–26.

Regier, D. A., Farmer, M. E., Rae, D. S., Locke, B. Z., Keith, S. J., Judd, L. L., et al. (1990). Comorbidity of mental disorders with alcohol and other drug abuse. *Journal of the American Medical Association, 264,* 2511–2518.

Rettig, R. A., & Yarmolinsky, A. (Eds.). (1995). *Federal regulation of methadone treatment.* Washington, DC: National Academy Press.

Richard, A. J., Montoya, I. D., Nelson, R., & Spence, R. T. (1995). Effectiveness of adjunct therapies in crack addiction. *Journal of Substance Abuse Treatment, 12,* 401–413.

Ridgely, M. S., Morrissey, J. P., Paulson, R. I. & Goldman, H. H. (1996). Characteristics and activities of case managers in the RWJ foundation program on chronic mental illness. *Psychiatric Services, 47(7),* 737–743.

Rogers, C. R. (1959). A theory of therapy, personality, and interpersonal relationships as developed in the client-centered approach. In S. Koch (Ed.), *Psychology: The study of a science: Volume 3. Formulations of the person and the social context* (pp. 184–256). New York: McGraw-Hill.

Rogers, R., & Jolin, A. (1989). Electronic monitoring: A review of the empirical literature. *Journal of Contemporary Criminal Justice, 5,* 141–153.

Rogers, R., & Jolin, A. (1991). Electronically monitored house arrest: Development and critique. *Indiana Journal of Criminology, 19,* 2–8.

Rogers Wiese, M. R. (1992). A critical review of parent training research. *Psychology in the Schools, 29,* 229–236.

Rollnick, S., Mason, P., & Butler, C. (1999). *Health behavior change: A guide for practitioners*. London: Churchill Livingstone.

Rooney, R. H. (1992). *Strategies for working with involuntary clients*. New York: Columbia University Press.

Rosecan, J., & Nunes, E. (1987). Pharmacological management of cocaine abuse. In H. Spitz & J. Rosecan (Eds.), *Cocaine abuse: New directions in treatment and research* (pp. 299–323). New York: Brunner/Mazel.

Rosenbaum, M. (1997). Women: Research and policy. In J. H. Lowinson, P. Ruiz, R. B. Millman & J. G. Langrod (Eds.), *Substance abuse: A comprehensive textbook* (3rd ed., pp. 654–665). Baltimore: Williams & Wilkins.

Rosenbaum, M., Washburn, A., Knight, K. R., Kelley, M., & Irwin, J. (1995). *Methadone maintenance: Treatment as harm reduction, policy as harm maximization* (Final report to the National Institute on Drug Abuse R01DA08982). Washington, DC: NIDA.

Rothman, D. (1990). *The discovery of the asylum: Social order and disorder in the new republic*. Boston: Little, Brown.

Rouse, J. J. (1991). Evaluation research on prison-based drug treatment programs and some policy implications. *International Journal of the Addictions, 26*, 29–44.

Ryglewicz, H., & Pepper, B. (1990). *Alcohol, drugs, and mental/emotional problems: What you need to know to help your dual-disorder client*. New York: Information Exchange.

Sack, W. H., Seidler, T., & Thomas, S. (1976). Children of imprisoned parents: A psychosocial exploration. *American Journal of Orthopsychiatry, 46*, 618–628.

Saleebey, D. (Ed.). (1997). *The strengths perspective in social work practice* (2nd ed.). New York: Longman.

Santisteban, D. A., Szapocznik, J., Perez-Vidal, A., Kurtines, W. M., Murray, E. J., & LaPerriere, A. (1996). Efficacy of interventions for engaging youth/families into treatment and the factors that contribute to differential effectiveness. *Journal of Family Psychology, 10*, 35–44.

Sarrazin, M. S. V., Hall, J. A., Richards, C., & Carswell, C. (2002). A comparison of computer-based versus pencil-and-paper assessment of drug use. *Research on Social Work Practice, 12*, 669–683.

Sarri, R., & Selo, E. (1974). Evaluation process and outcome in juvenile corrections: A grim tale. In P. O. Davidson, F. W. Clark, & L. A. Hamerlynch (Eds.), *Evaluation of community programs*. Champaign, IL: Research Press.

Scahill, M. (2000). *OJJDP Fact Sheet: Juvenile delinquency probation caseload, 1988–1997*. Washington, DC: U.S. Department of Justice, Office of Justice Programs, Office of Juvenile Justice and Delinquency Prevention.

Scarpino v. Grosshiem, 852 F. Supp. 798 (S.D. Iowa 1994).

Schaler, J. A. (1994). Alcoholism is not a disease. In B. Leone (Ed.), *Alcoholism* (pp. 34–44). San Diego, CA: Greenhaven Press.

Schmidt, A. K. (1998). Electronic monitoring in Europe: What does the literature tell us? *Federal Probation, 62,* 10–19.

Schoenwald, S. K., Borduin, C. M., & Henggeler, S. W. (1998). Multisystemic therapy: Changing the natural and service ecologies of adolescents and families. In M. H. Epstein, K. Kutash, & A. Duchnowski (Eds.), *Outcomes for children and youth with emotional and behavioral disorders and their families: Programs and evaluation best practice* (pp. 485–511). Austin, TX: Pro-Ed.

Schoenwald, S. K., & Rowland, M. D. (2002). Multisystemic therapy. In B. J. Burns & K. Hoagwood (Eds.), *Community treatment for youth: Evidence-based interventions for severe emotional and behavioral disorders* (pp. 91–116). New York: Oxford University Press.

Schoenwald, S. K., Ward, D. M., Henggeler, S. W., Pickrel, S. G., & Patel, H. (1996). Multisystemic therapy treatment of substance abusing or dependent adolescent offenders: Costs of reducing incarceration, inpatient, and residential placement. *Journal of Child and Family Studies, 5,* 431–444.

Schwartz, I. (1989). Hospitalization of adolescents for psychiatric and substance abuse treatment: Legal and ethical issues. *Journal of Adolescent Health Care, 10,* 473–478.

Schwartz, W. (1961). The social worker in the group. In *New perspectives on services to groups: Theory, organization, and practice* (pp. 7–34). New York: National Association of Social Workers.

Sciacca, K. (1989). MICAA-NON, working with families, friends, and advocates of Mentally Ill Chemical Abusers and Addicted (MICAA). *Tielines, 6*(3), 6–7.

Sciacca, K. (1991). An integrated approach for severely mentally ill offenders with substance abuse disorders. In K. Minkoff & R. E. Drake (Eds.), *Dual diagnosis of major mental illness and substance abuse disorder* (pp. 69–84). San Francisco, CA: Jossey-Bass.

Sciacca, K., & Thompson, C. M. (1996). Program development and integrated treatment across systems for dual diagnosis: Mental illness, drug addiction and alcoholism, MIDAA. Journal of Mental Health Administration, 23, 288–297.

Scott, E. M. (1993). Prison group therapy with mentally and emotionally disturbed offenders. *International Journal of Offender Therapy and Comparative Criminology, 37,* 131–145.

Seagram, B. C. (1997). The efficacy of solution-focused therapy with young offenders. Unpublished doctoral dissertation, York University, New York, Ontario, Canada.

Sederer, L. I., & Dickey, B. (Eds.). (1996). *Outcomes assessment in clinical practice*. Baltimore: Williams & Wilkins.

Selekman, M. D. (1991). "With a little help from my friends": The use of peers in the family therapy of adolescent substance abusers. *Family Dynamics of Addiction Quarterly, 1,* 69–77.

Selekman, M. D. (1993). *Pathways to change: Brief therapy solutions with difficult adolescents*. New York: Guilford Press.

Selekman, M. D. (1997). *Solution-focused therapy with children: Harnessing family strengths for systemic change*. New York: Guilford Press.

Selzer, M. L. (1971). The Michigan Alcoholism Screening Test: The quest for a new diagnostic instrument. *American Journal of Psychiatry, 127,* 1653–1658.

Selzer, M. L., Vinokur, A., & Van Rooijen, L. A. (1974). Self-administered Short Michigan Alcoholism Screening Test (SMAST). *Journal of Studies on Alcohol, 15,* 276–280.

Serketich, W. J., & Dumas, J. E. (1996). The effectiveness of behavioral parent training to modify antisocial behavior in children: A meta-analysis. *Behavior Therapy, 27,* 493–518.

Shaffer, D., Fisher, P. W., & Lucas, C. P. (1999). Respondent-based interviews. In D. Shaffer, C. P. Lucas, & J. E. Richters (Eds.), *Diagnostic assessment in child and adolescent psychopathology* (pp. 3–33). New York: Guilford Press.

Shaffer, D., Fisher, P., Lucas, C. P., Dulcan, M., & Schwab-Stone, M. E. (2000). NIMH Diagnostic Interview Schedule for Children, Version IV (NIMH DISC–IV): Description, differences from previous versions, and reliability of some common diagnoses. *Journal of the American Academy of Child and Adolescent Psychiatry, 39,* 28–38.

Shaffer, D., Lucas, C. P., & Richters, J. E. (Eds.). (1999). *Diagnostic assessment in child and adolescent psychopathology*. New York: Guilford Press.

Shedler, J., & Block, J. (1990). Adolescent drug use and psychological health: A longitudinal inquiry. *American Psychologist, 45,* 612–630.

Sheehan, M. F. (1993). Dual diagnosis. *Psychiatric Quarterly, 64,* 107–134.

Sheridan, M. J. (1996, June). Comparison of the life experiences and personal functioning of men and women in prison. *Families in Society,* pp. 423–434.

Showers, J. (1993). Assessing and remedying parenting knowledge among women inmates. *Journal of Offender Rehabilitation, 20(1–2),* 35–46.

Shulman, L. (1992). *The skills of helping: Individuals, families, and groups* (3rd ed.). Itasca, IL: F. E. Peacock.

Siegal, H. A., Fisher, J. H., Rapp, R. C., Kelliher, C. W., Wagner, J. H., O'Brien, W. F., et al. (1996). Enhancing substance abuse treatment with case management: Its impact on employment. *Journal of Substance Abuse Treatment, 13,* 93–98.

Siegal, H. A., Rapp, R. C., Li, L., Saha, P., & Kirk, K. D. (1997). The role of case management in retaining clients in substance abuse treatment: An exploratory analysis. *Journal of Drug Issues, 27,* 821–831.

Simpson, D. D., Chatham, L. R., & Joe, G. W. (1993). Cognitive enhancements to treatment in DATAR: Drug abuse treatment for AIDS risk-reduction. In J. Inciardi, F. Tims, & B. Fletcher (Eds.), *Innovative approaches to the treatment of drug abuse: Program models and strategies* (pp. 161–177). Westport, CT: Greenwood Press.

Simpson, D. D., Dansereau, D. F., & Joe, G. W. (1997). The DATAR project: Cognitive and behavioral enhancements to community-based treatments. In F. M. Tims, J. A. Inciardi, B. W. Fletcher, & A. M. Horton, Jr. (Eds.), *The effectiveness of innovative approaches in the treatment of drug abuse* (pp. 182–203). Westport, CT: Greenwood Press.

Singer, J. A. (1996, Spring). *An analysis of acupuncture therapy for the treatment of chemical dependency and its struggle for legitimacy.* Stony Brook: State University of New York.

Singer, L. R. (1991). A non-punitive paradigm of probation practice: Some sobering thoughts. *British Journal of Social Work, 21,* 611–626.

Singh, N. (1982). Notes and observations on the practice of multiple family therapy in an adolescent unit. *Journal of Adolescence, 5,* 319–332.

Slate, R. N. (2003). From the jailhouse to Capitol Hill: Impacting mental health court legislation and defining what constitutes a mental health court. *Crime and Deliquency, 49*(1), 6–29.

Smith, J. (1990). *Cognitive–behavioral relaxation training: A new system of strategies for treatment and assessment.* New York: Springer.

Smith, M. (1994). [Letter to the Editor]. *Journal of Substance Abuse Treatment, 11,* 587.

Smith, S. S., & Newman, J. P. (1990). Alcohol and drug abuse/dependence disorders in psychopathic and nonpsychopathic criminal offenders. *Journal of Abnormal Psychology, 99,* 430–439.

Snair, J. R. (1989). *Report on evaluation research review conducted for the Governor's study commission on crime prevention and law enforcement.* Tallahassee: Florida State University.

Snyder, H. (2000). *Juvenile arrests 1999.* Washington, DC: U.S. Department of Justice, Office of Juvenile Justice and Delinquency Prevention.

Snyder, W. (1994). Seeing the troubled adolescent in context: Family systems theory and practice. In W. Snyder & T. Ooms (Eds.), *Empowering families, helping adolescents: Family-centered treatment of adolescents with alcohol, drug abuse, and mental health problems* (Publication series 6, pp. 13–37). Rockville, MD: U.S. Department of Health and Human Services, Center for Substance Abuse Treatment.

Sobell, L. C., & Sobell, M. B. (1992). Timeline follow-back: A technique for assessing self-reported alcohol consumption. In R. Z. Litten & J. P. Allen (Eds.), *Measuring alcohol consumption: Psychosocial and biochemical methods* (pp. 41–72). Totowa, NJ: Humana Press.

Solomon, S. D. (1982). Individual versus group therapy: Current status in the treatment of alcoholism. *Advances in Alcohol and Substance Abuse, 2,* 69–86.

Spitz, H., & Rosecan, J. (1987). Overview of cocaine abuse treatment. In H. Spitz & J. Rosecan (Eds.), *Cocaine abuse: New directions in treatment and research* (pp. 97–118). New York: Brunner/Mazel.

Springer, D. W. (2002). Assessment protocols and rapid assessment instruments with troubled adolescents. In A. R. Roberts & G. J. Greene (Eds.), *Social workers' desk reference* (pp. 217–221). New York: Oxford University Press.

Springer, D. W. (in press-a). Standardized assessment measures and computer-assisted technologies. In C. J. Jordan & C. Franklin (Eds.), *Clinical assessment for social workers: Quantitative and qualitative methods* (2nd ed.). Chicago: Lyceum Books.

Springer, D. W. (in press-b). Treating substance-abusing youth. In C. A. McNeece & D. M. DiNitto (Eds.), *Chemical dependency: A systems approach* (3rd ed.). Boston: Allyn & Bacon.

Springer, D. W., Abell, N., & Hudson, W. W. (2002). Creating and validating rapid assessment instruments for practice and research: Part 1. *Research on Social Work Practice, 12,* 408–439.

Springer, D. W., Abell, N., & Nugent, W. R. (2002). Creating and validating rapid assessment instruments for practice and research: Part 2. *Research on Social Work Practice, 12,* 805–832.

Springer, D. W., Lynch, C., & Rubin, A. (2000). Effects of a solution-focused mutual aid group for Hispanic children of incarcerated parents. *Child and Adolescent Social Work Journal, 17,* 431–442.

Springer, D. W., & Orsbon, S. H. (2002). Families helping families: Implementing a multi-family therapy group with substance-abusing adolescents. *Health and Social Work, 27(3),* 161–240.

Springer, D. W., Pomeroy, E. C., & Johnson, T. (1999). A group intervention for children of incarcerated parents: Initial blunders and subsequent solutions. *Groupwork, 11,* 54–70.

Springer, D. W., Shader, M. A., & McNeece, C. A. (1999). Operation of juvenile assessment centers: Trends and issues. *Journal for Juvenile Justice and Detention Services, 14,* 45–62.

Stahl, A. (1998). *OJJDP fact sheet* (No. 81). Washington, DC: U.S. Department of Justice, Office of Juvenile Justice and Delinquency Prevention.

Stanton, M. D., & Shadish, W. R. (1997). Outcome, attrition, and family/marital treatment for drug abuse: A meta-analysis and review of the controlled, comparative studies. *Psychological Bulletin, 122,* 170–191.

Stanton, M. D., & Todd, T. C. (1979). Structural family therapy with drug addicts. In E. Kaufman, & P. Kaufmann (Eds.), *The family therapy of drug and alcohol abuse* (pp. 55–69). New York: Gardner Press.

Stanton, M. D., & Todd, T. C. (1982). The therapy model. In M. D. Stanton, T. C. Todd, & Associates (Eds.), *The family therapy of drug abuse and addiction.* New York: Guilford Press.

Stanton, M. D., & Todd, T. C., & Associates. (1982). *The family therapy of drug abuse and addiction.* New York: Guilford Press.

Stanton, M. D., Todd, T. C., Heard, D. B., Kirschner, S., Kleiman, J. I., Mowatt, D. T., et al. (1978). Heroin addiction as a family phenomenon: A new conceptual model. *American Journal of Drug and Alcohol Abuse, 5,* 125–150.

State of Florida, Advisory Council on Intergovernmental Relations. (1994). *Community corrections: A review of current policy and programs* (Monograph). Tallahassee: Author.

Steadman, H., Fabisiak, S., Dvoskin, J., & Holohean, E. (1989). A survey of mental disability among state prison inmates. *Hospital and Community Psychiatry, 38,* 1086–1090.

Stewart, J. C. (1998). A qualitative investigation of informants who quit cigarette smoking without treatment (Doctoral dissertation, Florida State University, 1998). *Dissertation Abstracts International, AAT 9824611.*

Strain, E., Stitzer, M., Liebson, I., & Bigelow, G. (1994). Comparison of buprenorphine and methadone in the treatment of opiod dependence. *American Journal of Psychiatry, 151,* 1025–1030.

Substance Abuse and Mental Health Services Administration, Center for Substance Abuse Treatment. (2002). *Anger management for substance abuse and mental health clients: A cognitive behavioral therapy.* Washington, DC: Author.

Substance Abuse and Mental Health Services Administration, Office of Applied Studies. (1997). *Uniform Facility Data Set (UFDS) 1997 survey of correctional facilities.* Washington, DC: Author.

Sullivan, H. (1953). *The interpersonal theory of psychiatry.* New York: Norton.

Swarthout, D. W. (1988). Enhancing the moral development of behaviorally emotionally handicapped students. *Behavioral Disorders, 14,* 57–68.

Szapocznik, J., Kurtines, W. M., Foote, F. H., Perez-Vidal, A., & Hervis, O. (1983). Conjoint versus one-person family therapy: Some evidence for the effectiveness of conducting family therapy through one person with drug-abusing adolescents. *Journal of Consulting and Clinical Psychology, 51,* 990–999.

Szapocznik, J., Kurtines, W. M., Foote, F. H., Perez-Vidal, A., & Hervis, O. (1986). Conjoint versus one-person family therapy: Further evidence for the effectiveness of conducting family therapy through one person with drug-abusing adolescents. *Journal of Consulting and Clinical Psychology, 54,* 395–397.

Szapocznik, J., Murray, E., Scopetea, M., Hervis, O., Rio, A., Cohen, R., et al. (1989). Structural family versus psychodynamic child therapy for problematic Hispanic boys. *Journal of Consulting and Clinical Psychology, 57,* 571–578.

Tarter, R., & Hegedus, A. (1991). The Drug Use Screening Inventory: Its application in the evaluation and treatment of alcohol and drug abuse. *Alcohol Health Research World, 15,* 65–75.

Teplin, L. A. (1990). The prevalence of severe mental disorder among male urban jail detainees: Comparison with the Epidemiologic Catchment Area Program. *American Journal of Public Health, 80,* 663–669.

Thompson, L. T., Riggs, P. D., Mikulich, S. K., & Crowley, T. J. (1996). Contribution of ADHD symptoms to substance problems and delinquency in conduct-disordered adolescents. *Journal of Abnormal Child Psychology, 24,* 325–334.

Timrots, A. (1992). *Fact sheet: Drug testing in the criminal justice system.* Rockville, MD: Drugs & Crime Data Center and Clearinghouse.

Tobin, S. S., Ellor, J. W., & Anderson-Ray, S. (1986). *Enabling the elderly: Religious institutions within the community service system.* New York: State University of New York Press.

Todd, T. C., & Selekman, M. (Eds.). (1991). *Family therapy approaches with adolescent substance abusers.* Englewood Cliffs, NJ: Prentice-Hall.

Todd, T. C., & Selekman, M. (1994). A structural–strategic model for treating the adolescent who is abusing alcohol and other drugs. In W. Snyder, & T. Ooms (Eds.), *Empowering families, helping adolescents: Family-centered treatment of adolescents with alcohol, drug abuse, and mental health problems* (Publication series 6, pp. 79–89). Rockville, MD: U.S. Department of Health and Human Services, Center for Substance Abuse Treatment.

Toller, W., & Tsagaris, B. (1996). Managing institutional gangs: A practical approach combining security and human services. *Corrections Today*, 58, 110–111.

Toneatto, T. (1995). The regulation of cognitive states: A cognitive model of psychoactive substance abuse. *Journal of Cognitive Psychotherapy*, 9, 93–104.

Torres, S. (1997). An effective supervision strategy for substance-abusing offenders. *Federal Probation*, 61, 38–43.

Toseland, R. W., & Rivas, R. F. (2001). *An introduction to groupwork practice* (4th ed.). Boston: Allyn & Bacon.

Towberman, D. B. (1993). Group vs. individual counseling: Treatment mode and the client's perception of the treatment environment. *Journal of Group Psychotherapy, Psychodrama, and Sociometry*, 45, 163–174.

Trimpey, J. (1989). *Rational recovery from alcoholism: The small book*. New York: Delacorte.

Trojanowicz, R., & Bucqueroux, B. (1990). *Community policing: A contemporary perspective*. Cincinnati, OH: Anderson.

Trulson, C. R., & Triplett, R. (1999). School-based juvenile boot camps: Evaluating specialized treatment and rehabilitation (STAR). *Journal for Juvenile Justice and Detention Services*, 14, 19–44.

Tuckman, B. W. (1965). Developmental sequence in small groups. *Psychological Bulletin*, 63, 384–399.

Turnabout ASAP. (1997). *Acupuncture treatment for substance abuse*. Santa Monica, CA: RAND.

Turner, S., Petersilia, J., & Deschenes, E. P. (1992). Evaluating intensive supervision probation/parole (ISP) for drug offenders. *Crime and Delinquency*, 38, 539–556.

Turner, S., Petersilia, J., & Deschenes, E. P. (1994). The implementation and effectiveness of drug testing in community supervision: Results of an experimental evaluation. In D. L. MacKenzie & C. D. Uchida (Eds.), *Drugs and crime: Evaluating public policy initiatives* (pp. 231–252). Thousand Oaks, CA: Sage.

Turner, W., & Tsuang, M. (1990). Impact of substance abuse on the course and outcome of schizophrenia. *Schizophrenia Bulletin*, 16, 87–95.

The University of Florida College of Medicine. (1992). Naltrexone: Breakthrough treatment for many addictions. *The Fact About Drugs and Alcohol* [Brochure]. Gainesville, FL: Author.

U.S. Department of Justice. (1998). *Substance abuse and treatment of adults on probation, 1995* (NIJ Publication No. NCJ 166611). Washington, DC: Author.

U.S. Department of Justice. (1999). Office of justice programs fiscal year 1999 program plan [On-line]. Retrieved October 24, 2002, from www.ojp.usdoj.gov/99progplan/99prog.pdf.

U.S. General Accounting Office. (1996, June). *Cocaine treatment: Early results from various approaches* (GAO/HEHS-96-80). Washington, DC: Author.

U.S. Probation/Pretrial Services Office, District of South Dakota. (1997). Federal juvenile corrections in South Dakota. *Federal Probation, 61*, 38–46.

Vaillant, G. (1988). What can long-term follow-up teach us about relapse and prevention of relapse in addiction? *British Journal of Addiction, 83*, 1151–1152.

Valentine, P. (1995). Traumatic incident reduction: A review of a new intervention. *Journal of Family Psychotherapy, 6*, 73–78.

Valentine, P., & Smith, T. E. (2001). Evaluating traumatic incident reduction therapy with female inmates: A randomized controlled study. *Research on Social Work Practice, 11*, 40–52.

Van Stelle, K. R., Mauser, E., & Moberg, D. P. (1994). Recidivism to the criminal justice system of substance-abusing offenders diverted into treatment. *Crime and Delinquency, 40*, 175–196.

Van Wormer, K., & Davis, D. R. (2003). *Addiction treatment: A strengths perspective*. Pacific Grove, CA: Brooks/Cole.

Velicer, W. F., Norman, G. J., Fava, J. L., & Prochaska, J. O. (1999). Testing 40 predictions from the transtheoretical model. *Addictive Behaviors, 24*, 455–469.

Vito, G. F. (1989). The Kentucky substance abuse program: A private program to treat probationers and parolees. *Federal Probation, 53*, 65–72.

Volkow, N., Wang, G., Fowler, J., Logan, J., Gatley, S., Hitzemann, R., et al. (1999). Reinforcing effects of psychostimulants in humans are associated with increases in brain dopamine and occupancy of D_2 Receptors. *Journal of Pharmacology and Experimental Therapeutics, 29*, 409–415.

Volpicelli, J. R., Markman, M. A., Monterosso, J., Filing, J., & O'Brien, C. P. (2000). Psychosocially enhanced treatment for cocaine-dependent mothers: Evidence of efficacy. *Journal of Substance Abuse Treatment, 18*, 41–49.

von Bertalanaffy, L. (1968). *General systems theory*. New York: George Brazillier.

Vorrath, H. H., & Brendtro, L. K. (1985). *Positive peer culture* (2nd ed.). New York: Aldine de Gruyter.

Waldinger, R. J. (1990). *Psychiatry for medical students* (2nd ed.). Washington, DC: American Psychiatric Press.

Waldron, H. B. (1997). Adolescent substance abuse and family therapy outcome: A review of randomized trials. *Advances in Clinical Child Psychology, 19*, 199–234.

Walker, M. C. (1992). Co-dependency and probation. *Federal Probation, 6*, 16–18.

Warner v. Orange County Dept. of Probation, 870 F. Supp. 69 (S.D.N.Y. 1994).

Washington State Institute for Public Policy. (1998). *Watching the bottom line: Cost-effective interventions for reducing crime in Washington*. Olympia, WA: The Evergreen State College.

Wasserman, G. A., McReynolds, L. S., Lucas, C. P., Fisher, P., & Santos, L. (2002). The Voice DISC-IV with incarcerated male youths: Prevalence of disorder. *Journal of the American Academy of Child and Adolescent Psychiatry, 41*, 314–321.

Webb, D. (1995). *Good chemistry co-leader's manual*. Unpublished manuscript.

Webb, D. K. (1990). *Mottos*. Austin, TX: Author.

Webster-Stratton, C. (1987). *The parents and children series*. Eugene, OR: Castalia.

Webster-Stratton, C., & Herbert, M. (1994). *Troubled families—Problem children*. New York: Wiley.

Wegscheider, S. (1981). *Another chance: Hope and health for the alcoholic family*. Palo Alto, CA: Science & Behavior Books.

Weick, A., Rapp, C., Sullivan, W. P., & Kisthardt, S. (1989). A strengths perspective for social work. *Social Work, 34*, 350–354.

Weil, M., & Karls, J. (1985). *Case management in human service practice*. San Francisco, CA: Jossey-Bass.

Weiss, R. D., & Najavits, L. M. (1997). Overview of treatment modalities for dual diagnosis patients: Pharmacotherapy, psychotherapy, and twelve-step programs. In H. R. Kranzler & B. J. Rounsaville (Eds.), *Substance abuse and comorbid medical and psychiatric disorders* (pp. 1–19). New York: Marcel Dekker.

Weiss, R. D., Najavits, L. M., & Mirin, S. M. (1997). Substance abuse and psychiatric disorders. In R. J. Francis & S. I. Miller (Eds.), *Clinical textbook of addictive disorders* (pp. 3–43). New York: Guilford Press.

Wells, L. E., & Rankin, J. H. (1991). Families and delinquency: A meta-analysis of the impact of broken homes. *Social Problems, 38*, 71–93.

Wells, R. A. (1994). *Planned short-term treatment*. New York: Free Press.

Wexler, H. K. (1995). The success of therapeutic communities for substance abusers in American prisons. *Journal of Psychoactive Drugs, 27*, 37–66.

Wexler, H. K., Blackmore, J., & Lipton, D. S. (1991). Project REFORM: Developing a drug abuse treatment strategy for correction. *Journal of Drug Issues, 21,* 469–491.

Wexler, H. K., De Leon, G., Thomas, G., Kressel, D., & Peters, J. (1999). The Amity prison TC evaluation: Reincarceration outcomes. *Criminal Justice and Behavior, 26,* 147–167.

Wexler, H. K., Falkin, G. P., Lipton, D. S., Rosenblum, A. B., & Goodloe, L. P. (1988). *A model prison rehabilitation program: An evaluation of the "Stay'n Out" therapeutic community.* New York: Narcotic and Drug Research.

Wexler, H. K., & Williams, R. (1986). The Stay'N Out therapeutic community: Prison treatment for substance abusers. *Journal of Psychoactive Drugs, 28,* 221–230.

White, W. (1998). *Slaying the dragon: The history of addiction treatment and recovery in America.* Bloomington, IL: Chestnut Health Systems.

Whitehead, J. T., & Lab, S. P. (1989). A meta-analysis of juvenile correctional treatment. *Journal of Research in Crime and Delinquency, 26,* 276–295.

Wilczak, G. L., & Markstrom, C. A. (1999). The effects of parent education on parental locus of control and satisfaction of incarcerated fathers. *International Journal of Offender Therapy and Comparative Criminology, 43(1),* 90–102.

William, R. J., & Chang, S. Y. (2000). A comprehensive and comparative review of adolescent substance abuse treatment outcome. *Clinical Psychology—Science and Practice, 7,* 138–166.

Winett, D. L., Mullen, R., Lowe, L. L., & Missakian, E. A. (1992). Amity righturn: A demonstration drug abuse treatment program for inmates and parolees. In C. G. Leukefeld & F. M. Tims (Eds.), *Drug abuse treatment in prisons and jails* (pp. 84–98). Rockville, MD: U.S. Department of Health and Human Services.

Winger, G. (1988). Pharmacological modifications of cocaine and opioid self-administration. In D. Clouet, K. Asghar, & R. Brown (Eds.), *Mechanisms of cocaine abuse and toxicity* (pp. 125–136). Rockville, MD: National Institute on Drug Abuse.

Wish, E. D., Toborg, M., & Bellassai, J. (1988). *Identifying drug users and monitoring them during conditional release* (National Institute of Justice Briefing Paper). Washington, DC: U.S. Department of Justice, National Institute of Justice.

Witters, W., & Venturelli, P. (1988). *Drugs and society* (2nd ed.). Boston, MA: Jones & Bartlett.

Woititz, J. (1983). *Adult children of alcoholics.* Deerfield Beach, FL: Health Communications Press.

Wolff, N., Helminiak, T. W., Morse, G. A., Calsyn, R. J., Klinkenberg, W. D., & Trusty, M. L. (1997). Cost-effectiveness evaluation of three approaches to case management for homeless mentally ill clients. *American Journal of Psychiatry, 154,* 343–348.

Wolin, S., Bennett, L., & Jacobs, T. (1988). Assessing family rituals in alcoholic families. In E. Imber-Black, J. Roberts, & R. Whiting (Eds.), *Rituals in families and family therapy* (pp. 230–256). New York: Norton.

Women for Sobriety. (1989). *Overview.* Quakertown, PA: Author.

Wooten, H. B., & Hoelter, H. J. (1998). Operation spotlight: The community probation–community police team process. *Federal Probation, 62,* 30–35.

Worner, T. M., Zeller, B., Schwartz, H., Zwas, F., & Lyon, D. (1992). Acupuncture fails to improve treatment outcome in alcoholics. *Drug and Alcohol Dependence, 30,* 169–173.

Wren, C. (1999, June 8). In battle against heroin, scientists enlist heroin. *The New York Times,* pp. D1, D6.

Yalom, I. D. (1995). *The theory and practice of group psychotherapy* (4th ed.). New York: Basic Books.

Young, D., Dynia, P., & Belenko, S. (1996, November). *How compelling is coerced treatment? A study of different mandated treatment approaches.* Paper presented at the annual meeting of the American Society of Criminology, Chicago.

Zhang, S. (1998). In search of hopeful glimpses: A critique of research strategies in current boot camp evaluations. *Crime and Delinquency, 44,* 314–344.

Zimmer, L., & Morgan, J. (1997). *Marijuana myths: Marijuana facts.* New York: Lindesmith Center.

Zung, B. J. (1982). Evaluation of the Michigan Alcoholism Screening Test (MAST) in assessing lifetime and recent problems. *Journal of Clinical Psychology, 38,* 425–439.

INDEX

Cognitive-behavioral therapy. *See also* Behavioral therapy
    effective treatment and, 9
    with juvenile offenders, 11
    reduction of recidivism and, 52
    regulation of cognitive statements in, 51–52
Coleman, M., *103*
Community providers, linkages with, 56
Community residential programs, effectiveness of, 11
Comorbidity. *See also* Dual diagnosis
    diagnosis of, 38–39
Compton, M., *61*
Conduct disorder
    aggression replacement training and, 102–103
    behaviors associated with, 38
    in DSM–IV–TR, 37–38
    family as risk factor for, 70
    juvenile deliquency *versus*, 38
    in juvenile offenders, 145, 146
    substance use disorders and, 145
Contemplation stage, questions in, 48
Cornerstone, 121
Cost, of foster care and welfare, treatment *versus*, 54, 55
Cost-benefit research, on drug treatment, 181
Cost effectiveness
    of case management, 68
    of juvenile boot camps, 128, 129
    of multisystemic therapy, 81
    of solution-focused therapy, *50*
    of treatment, 5
        for women, 54–55
Court(s)
    drug, 131–135
    mental health, 135
Criminal activity and behavior
    drug use and, 146
    treatment reduction of, 13
Cruise, K. R., *32, 38*
Cultural competence
    Afrocentric world view and approach, 57–58
    research need for, 180
    in treatment, 56, 57–58, 178
Cyclazocine, 60

Dana, R., *17*
Daytop Village, 119–120
Delinquency. *See also* Juvenile delinquents

family as risk factor for, 70
    multisystemic therapy for, *81*
Dependence, definition of, *37*
Desipramine, for cocaine dependence, 63
Diagnosis, 36–39
    of antisocial and psychopathic personalities, 37–38
    of comorbidity, 38–39
    of conduct disorder, 37–38
    definition of, *18*
    DSM–IV–TR in, 36, 37, 38
    of substance-related disorders, 37
Diagnostic and Statistical Manual of Mental Disorders, 4th ed., text rev. (DSM–IV–TR)
    Axis II, 148, 149, 155
Diagnostic and Statistical Manual of Mental Disorders, 4th ed., text rev. (DSM–IV–TR), 36
    Axis I, inpatient treatment and, 114
    conduct disorder in, 37, 38
DiNitto, D. M., *18, 104*
Disulfiram (Antabuse)
    in dual diagnosis, 150
Dole, V., *61*
Dopamine antagonists, adverse reactions to, 62
Dopamine system, mesolimbic, in addiction, 59
Dowden, C., *12*
Drake, R. E., *145*
Drug abuse, causes of, 182–183
Drug courts, 131–135
    acupuncture component of, 136, 137
    acupuncture in, 136, 137
    advantages to offenders, 132
    communication among team members and, 134–135
    essential elements of, 132–134
    exclusions from, 134
    history of, 131–132
    as interface between criminal justice and substance abuse systems, 132
    referral to, 134
    sanction delivery in, 145
    success of, *133–134*
    treatment services provided by, 135
    types of, 131
    urine drug testing and, 135
    use of therapeutic communities by, 120
Drug Courts Program Office, *132*
Drug law

ABOUT THE AUTHORS

David W. Springer, PhD, LMSW-ACP, is the associate dean and an associate professor in the School of Social Work at the University of Texas at Austin, where he is also a senior faculty research associate of the interdisciplinary Center for Criminology and Criminal Justice Research. Previously, he worked in various clinical settings as a social worker with at-risk adolescents and their families. His scholarship and research coalesces around adolescent substance abuse, interventions for at-risk youths and juvenile delinquents, and scale development. His work has been funded by the National Institute of Mental Health, the National Institute on Drug Abuse, and the William C. Hogg Foundation.

C. Aaron McNeece, PhD, is the Walter W. Hudson Professor of Social Work at Florida State University. He has worked in both juvenile probation and adult corrections, and he has 30 years of experience in higher education. From 1992 to 2000 he served as director of the Institute for Health and Human Services Research at Florida State University, where he conducted research on approximately 130 intervention programs for substance-abusing criminal and juvenile offenders. His latest publications have focused on the connections among drugs, crime, and public policy.

Elizabeth Mayfield Arnold, PhD, LCSW, is an assistant professor in the Department of Psychiatry and Behavioral Medicine at Wake Forest University School of Medicine. Prior to her current position, Dr. Arnold worked in a variety of clinical settings and was an assistant professor in the School of Social Work at the University of North Carolina at Chapel Hill from 1999 to 2001. Dr. Arnold is the clinical director and cofounder of the ADE Project: Alternatives to Drugs via Empowerment, an outreach and case management program for women with histories of prostitution and substance abuse, in Charlotte, North Carolina. Dr. Arnold's research and publications focus on high-risk behavior, including substance abuse, suicidal behavior, and prostitution among adults and juveniles. Dr. Arnold is a member of the National Association of Social Workers and the Society for Social Work and Research.